THOR
FOR ASGARD

WRITERS: ROBERT RODI
ARTIST: SIMONE BIANCHI

COLOUR ARTIST
ISSUES #1-2: SIMONE PERUZZI
INK & INKWASH
ISSUES #3-4: SIMONE BIANCHI & ANDREA SILVESTRI
LETTERS: VC'S CORY PETIT
ASSISTANT EDITOR: SEBASTIAN GIRNER
EDITOR: AXEL ALONSO
EDITOR IN CHIEF: JOE QUESADA
PUBLISHER: DAN BUCKLEY
EXECUTIVE PRODUCER: ALAN FINE

COVER ARTIST: SIMONE BIANCHI
COVER COLOURS: SIMONE PERUZZI

THOR: FOR ASGARD. Contains material originally published in magazine form as THOR: FOR ASGARD #1-6. First printing 2010-2011. Published by Panini Publishing, a division of Panini UK Limited. Mike Riddell, Managing Director. Alan O'Keefe, Managing Editor. Mark Irvine, Production Manager. Marco M. Lupoi, Publishing Director Europe. Brady Webb, Reprint Editor. Neil Porter, Designer. Office of publication: Brockbourne House, 77 Mount Ephraim, Tunbridge Wells, Kent TN4 8BS. MARVEL, TITLE all related characters: TM & © 2010 & 2011 Marvel Entertainment, LLC and its subsidiaries. Licensed by Marvel Characters B.V. www.marvel.com. No similarity between any of the names, characters,

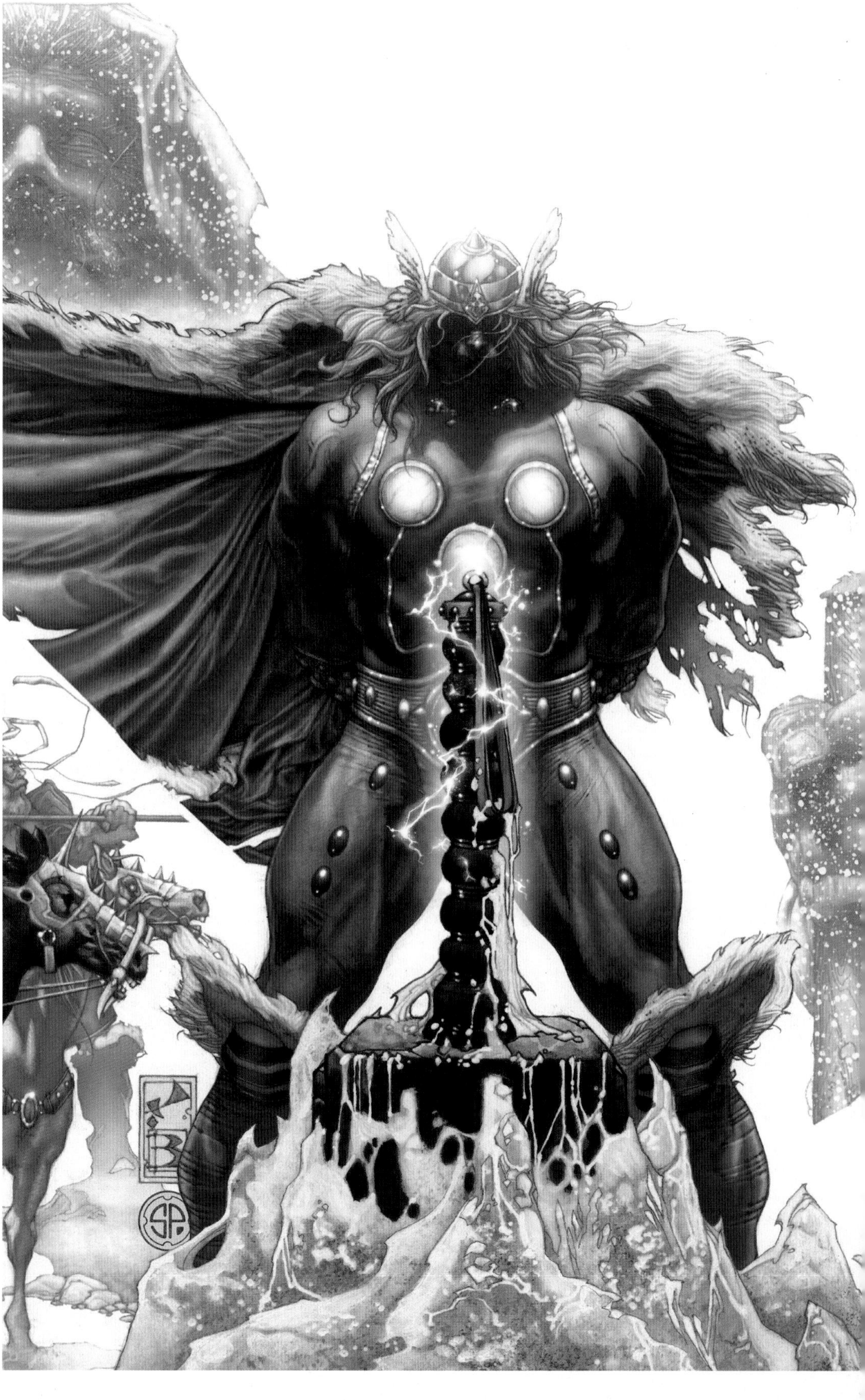

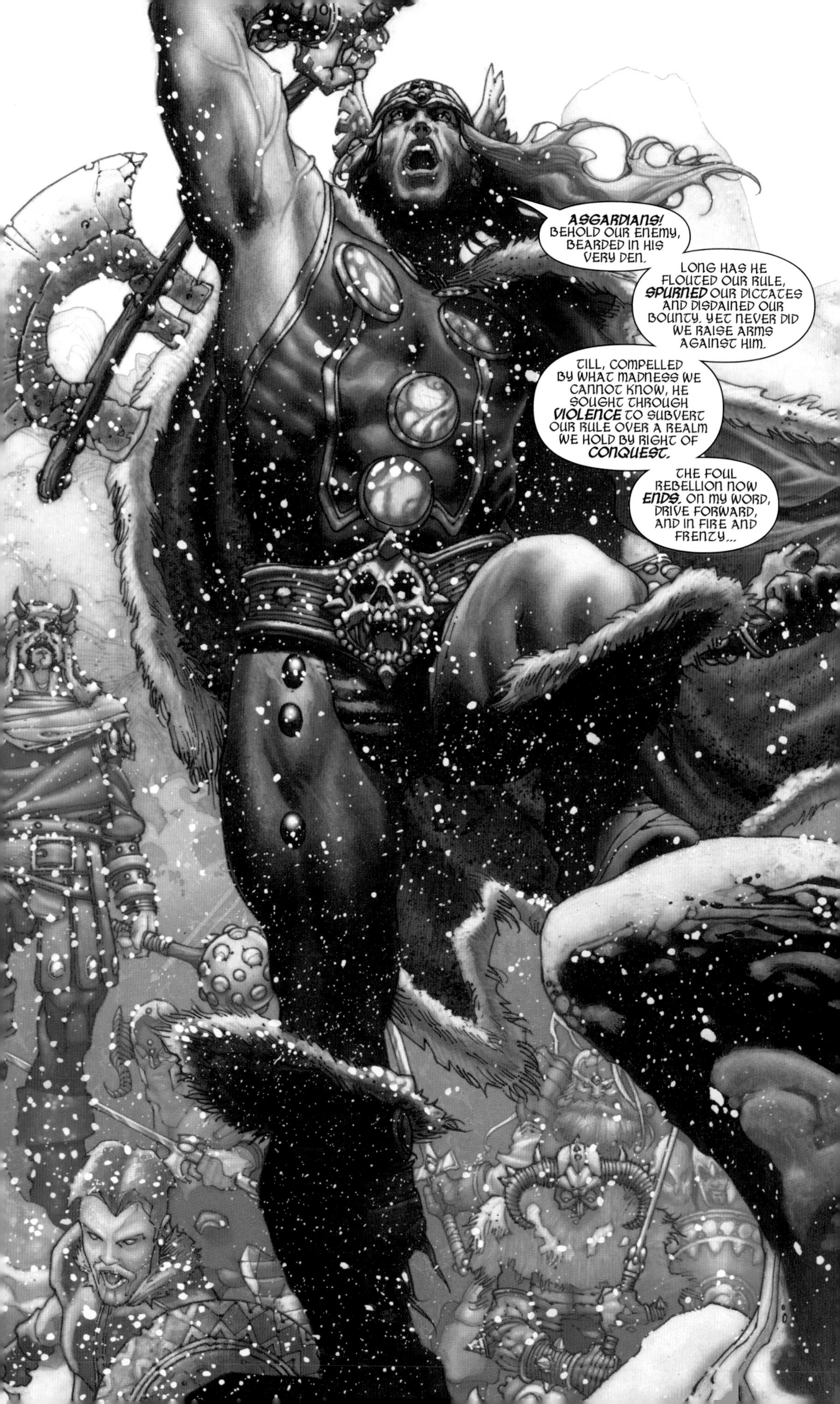
ASGARDIANS! BEHOLD OUR ENEMY, BEARDED IN HIS VERY DEN.
LONG HAS HE FLOUTED OUR RULE, SPURNED OUR DICTATES AND DISDAINED OUR BOUNTY. YET NEVER DID WE RAISE ARMS AGAINST HIM.
TILL, COMPELLED BY WHAT MADNESS WE CANNOT KNOW, HE SOUGHT THROUGH VIOLENCE TO SUBVERT OUR RULE OVER A REALM WE HOLD BY RIGHT OF CONQUEST.
THE FOUL REBELLION NOW ENDS. ON MY WORD, DRIVE FORWARD, AND IN FIRE AND FRENZY...

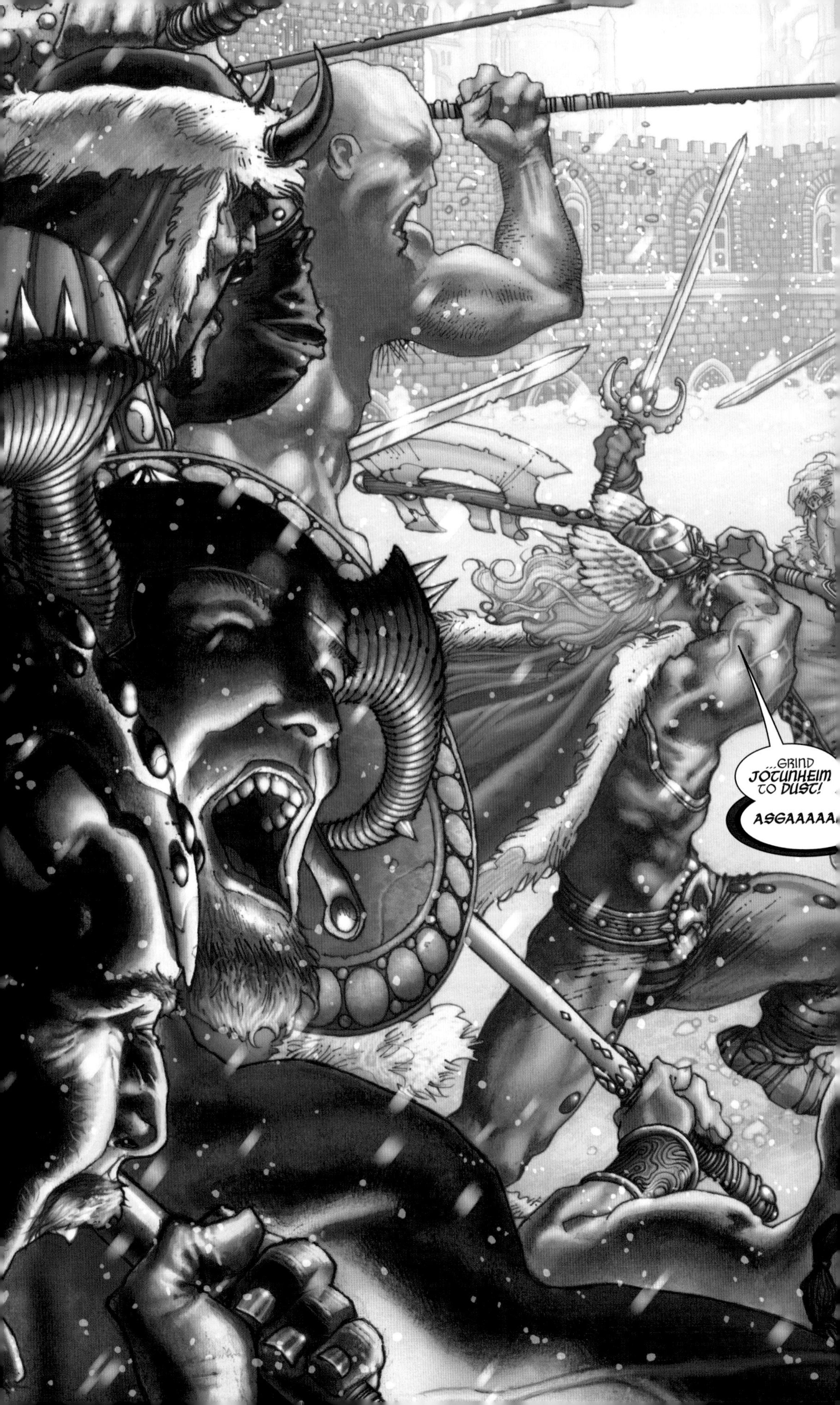
...GRIND JÖTUNHEIM TO DUST!
ASGAAAAA

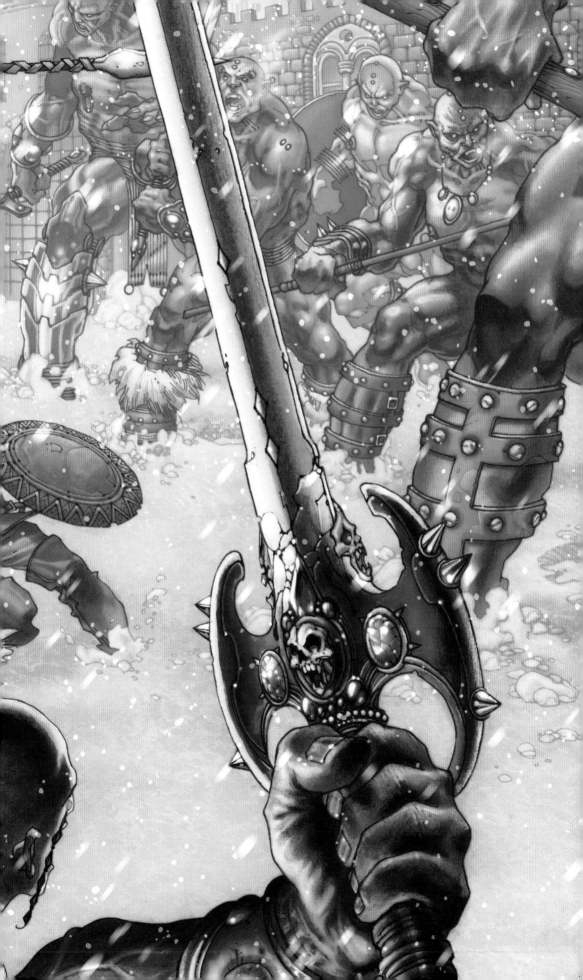

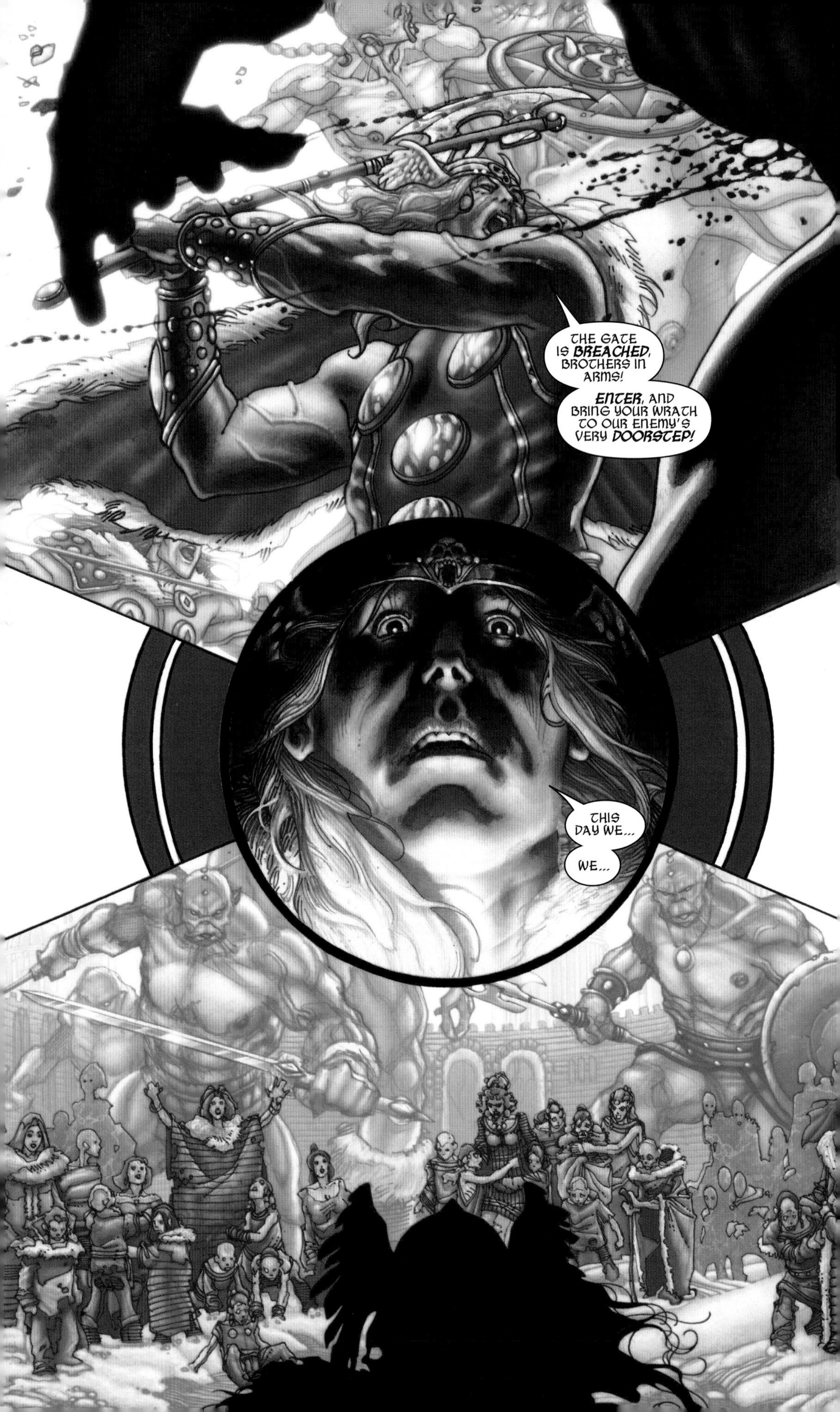
THE GATE IS **BREACHED**, BROTHERS IN ARMS!
ENTER, AND BRING YOUR WRATH TO OUR ENEMY'S VERY **DOORSTEP!**
THIS DAY WE...
WE...

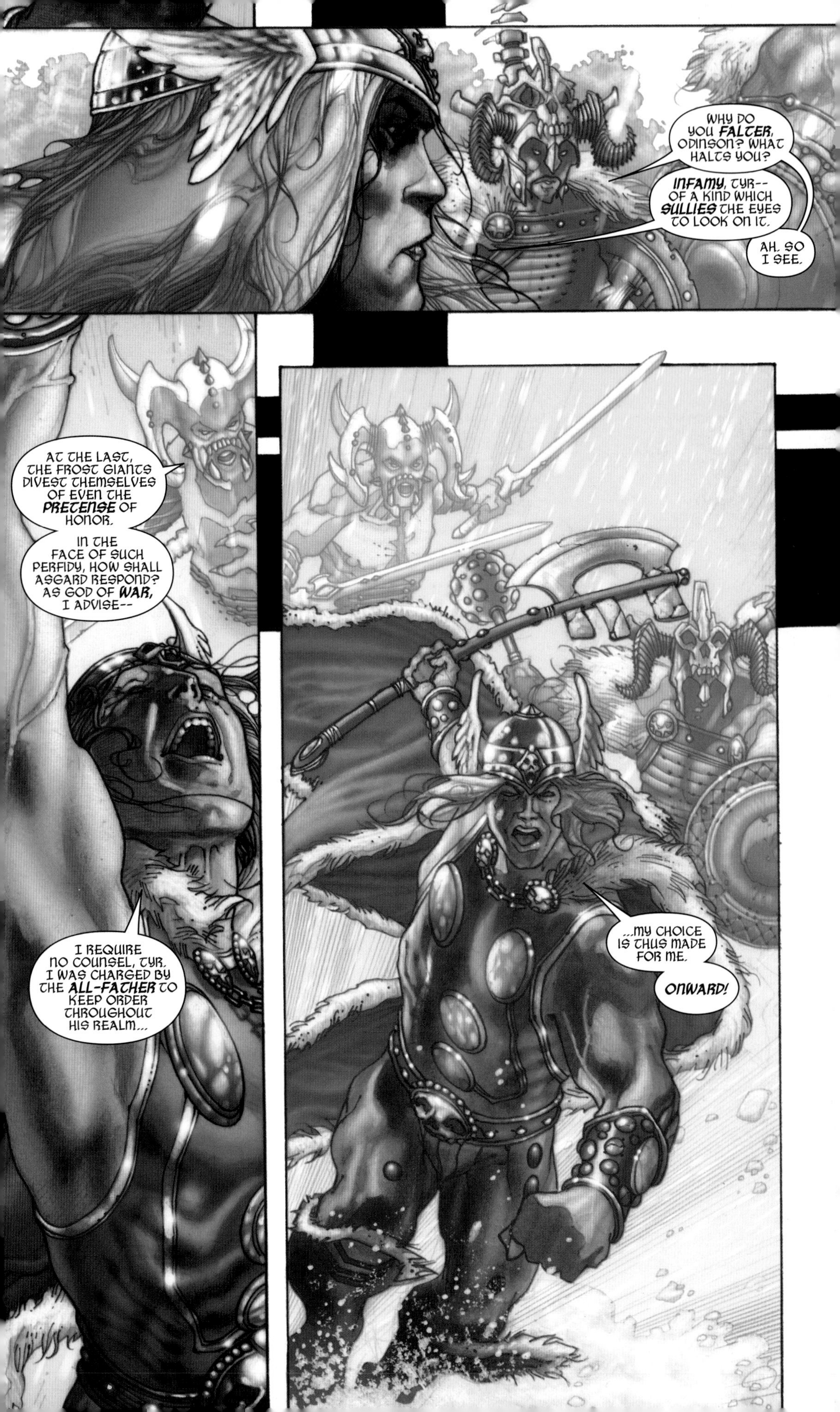
WHY DO YOU FALTER, ODINSON? WHAT HALTS YOU?
INFAMY, TYR-- OF A KIND WHICH SULLIES THE EYES TO LOOK ON IT.
AH. SO I SEE.
AT THE LAST, THE FROST GIANTS DIVEST THEMSELVES OF EVEN THE PRETENSE OF HONOR.
IN THE FACE OF SUCH PERFIDY, HOW SHALL ASGARD RESPOND? AS GOD OF WAR, I ADVISE--
I REQUIRE NO COUNSEL, TYR. I WAS CHARGED BY THE ALL-FATHER TO KEEP ORDER THROUGHOUT HIS REALM...
...MY CHOICE IS THUS MADE FOR ME.
ONWARD!

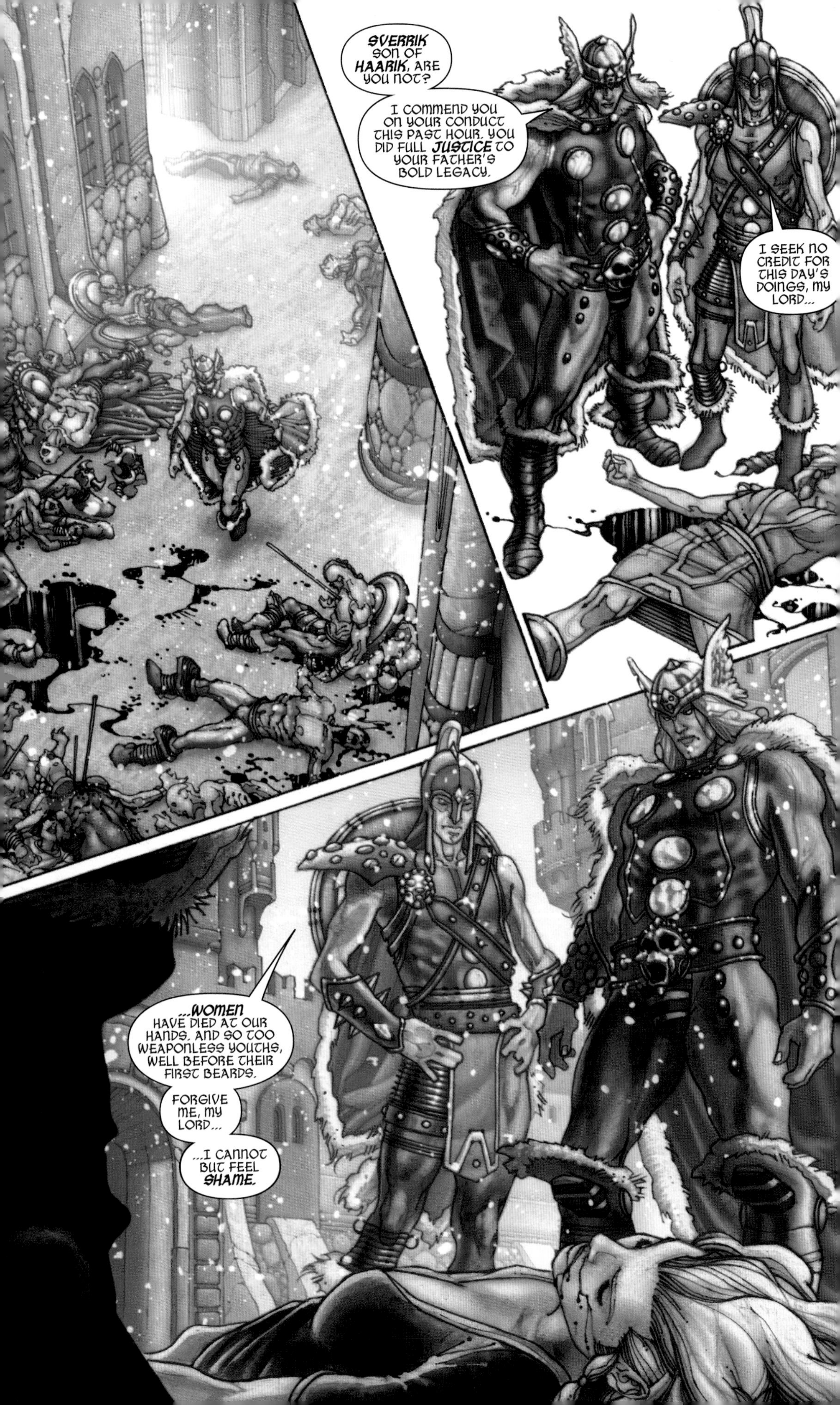
SVERRIK SON OF HAARIK, ARE YOU NOT?
I COMMEND YOU ON YOUR CONDUCT THIS PAST HOUR. YOU DID FULL JUSTICE TO YOUR FATHER'S BOLD LEGACY.
I SEEK NO CREDIT FOR THIS DAY'S DOINGS, MY LORD...
...WOMEN HAVE DIED AT OUR HANDS, AND SO TOO WEAPONLESS YOUTHS, WELL BEFORE THEIR FIRST BEARDS.
FORGIVE ME, MY LORD...
...I CANNOT BUT FEEL SHAME.

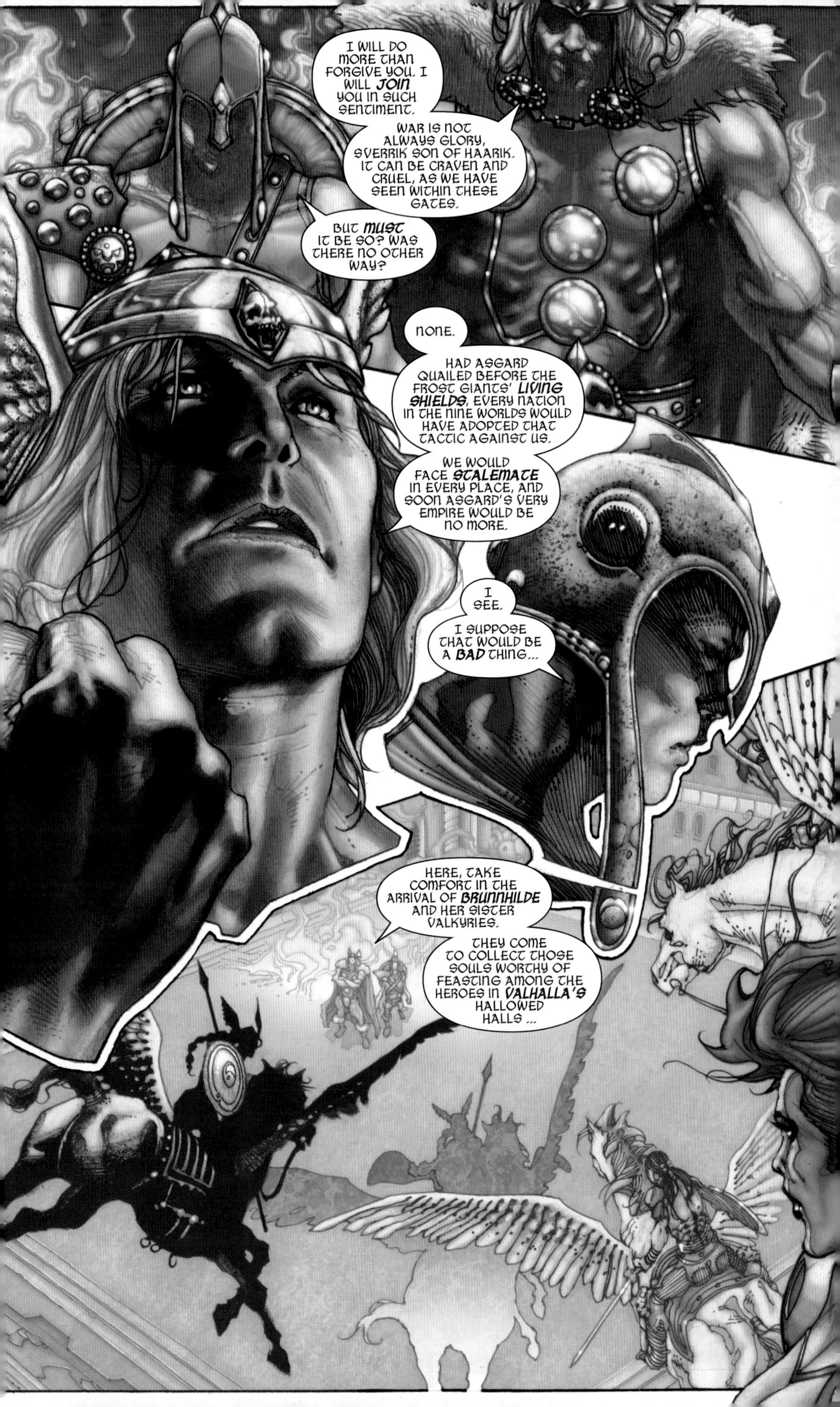

I WILL DO MORE THAN FORGIVE YOU. I WILL JOIN YOU IN SUCH SENTIMENT.
WAR IS NOT ALWAYS GLORY, SVERRIK SON OF HAARIK. IT CAN BE CRAVEN AND CRUEL, AS WE HAVE SEEN WITHIN THESE GATES.
BUT MUST IT BE SO? WAS THERE NO OTHER WAY?
NONE.
HAD ASGARD QUAILED BEFORE THE FROST GIANTS' LIVING SHIELDS, EVERY NATION IN THE NINE WORLDS WOULD HAVE ADOPTED THAT TACTIC AGAINST US.
WE WOULD FACE STALEMATE IN EVERY PLACE, AND SOON ASGARD'S VERY EMPIRE WOULD BE NO MORE.
I SEE.
I SUPPOSE THAT WOULD BE A BAD THING...
HERE, TAKE COMFORT IN THE ARRIVAL OF BRUNNHILDE AND HER SISTER VALKYRIES.
THEY COME TO COLLECT THOSE SOULS WORTHY OF FEASTING AMONG THE HEROES IN VALHALLA'S HALLOWED HALLS ...

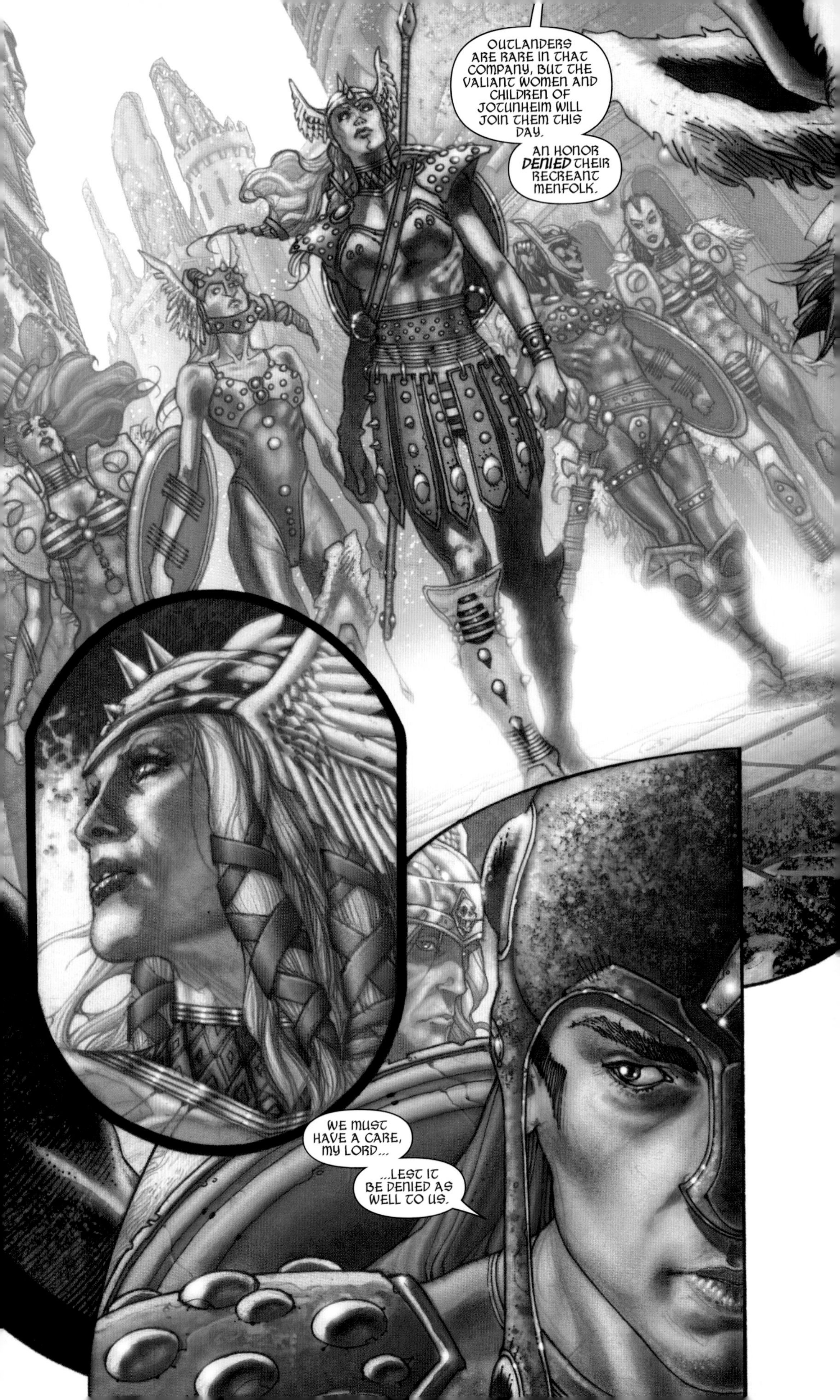

OUTLANDERS ARE RARE IN THAT COMPANY, BUT THE VALIANT WOMEN AND CHILDREN OF JOTUNHEIM WILL JOIN THEM THIS DAY.
AN HONOR **DENIED** THEIR RECREANT MENFOLK.
WE MUST HAVE A CARE, MY LORD...
...LEST IT BE DENIED AS WELL TO US.

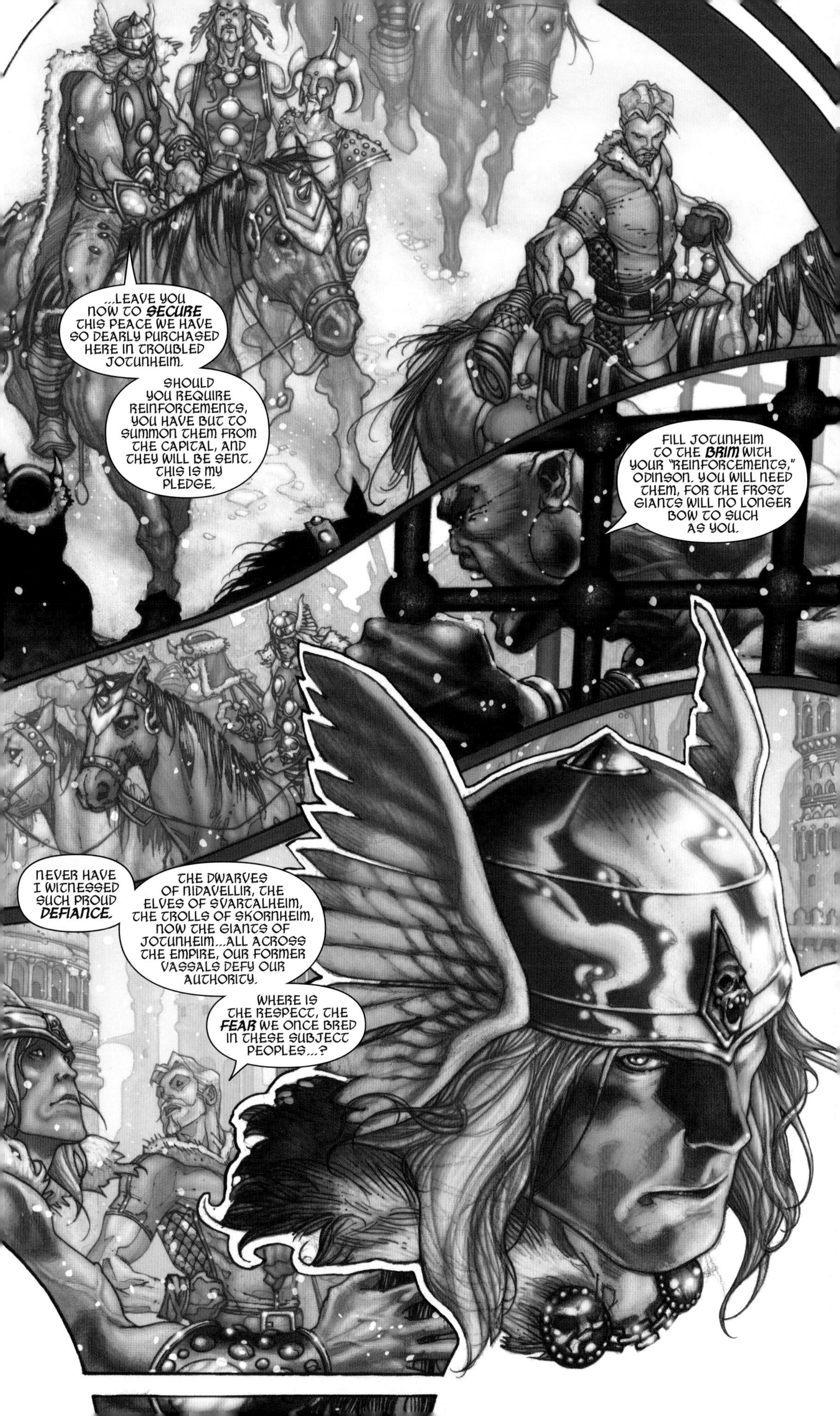
...LEAVE YOU NOW TO SECURE THIS PEACE WE HAVE SO DEARLY PURCHASED HERE IN TROUBLED JOTUNHEIM.
SHOULD YOU REQUIRE REINFORCEMENTS, YOU HAVE BUT TO SUMMON THEM FROM THE CAPITAL, AND THEY WILL BE SENT. THIS IS MY PLEDGE.
FILL JOTUNHEIM TO THE BRIM WITH YOUR "REINFORCEMENTS," ODINSON. YOU WILL NEED THEM, FOR THE FROST GIANTS WILL NO LONGER BOW TO SUCH AS YOU.
NEVER HAVE I WITNESSED SUCH PROUD DEFIANCE.
THE DWARVES OF NIDAVELLIR, THE ELVES OF SVARTALHEIM, THE TROLLS OF SKORNHEIM, NOW THE GIANTS OF JOTUNHEIM...ALL ACROSS THE EMPIRE, OUR FORMER VASSALS DEFY OUR AUTHORITY.
WHERE IS THE RESPECT, THE FEAR WE ONCE BRED IN THESE SUBJECT PEOPLES...?

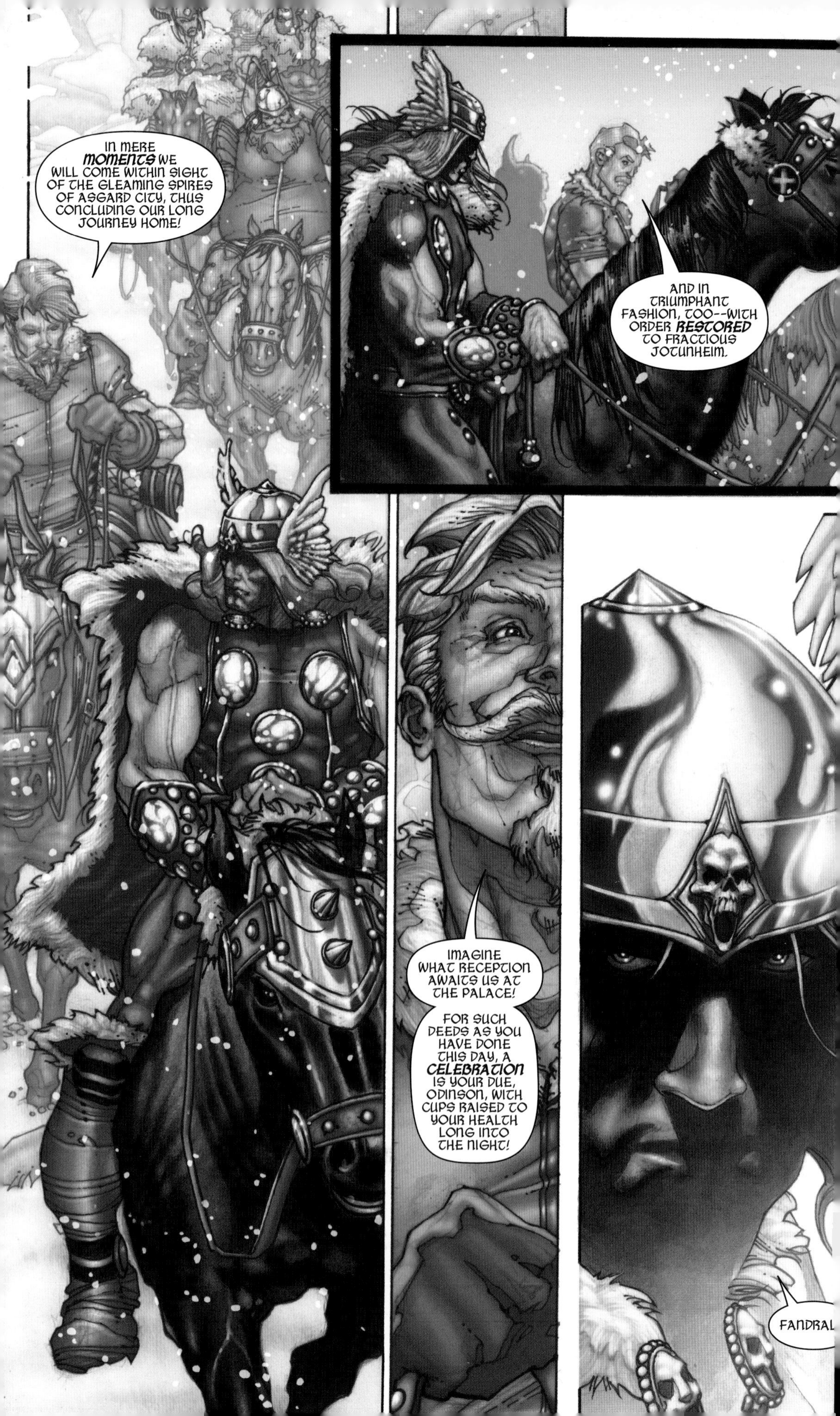
IN MERE MOMENTS WE WILL COME WITHIN SIGHT OF THE GLEAMING SPIRES OF ASGARD CITY, THUS CONCLUDING OUR LONG JOURNEY HOME!
AND IN TRIUMPHANT FASHION, TOO--WITH ORDER RESTORED TO FRACTIOUS JOTUNHEIM.
IMAGINE WHAT RECEPTION AWAITS US AT THE PALACE!
FOR SUCH DEEDS AS YOU HAVE DONE THIS DAY, A CELEBRATION IS YOUR DUE, ODINSON, WITH CUPS RAISED TO YOUR HEALTH LONG INTO THE NIGHT!
FANDRAL

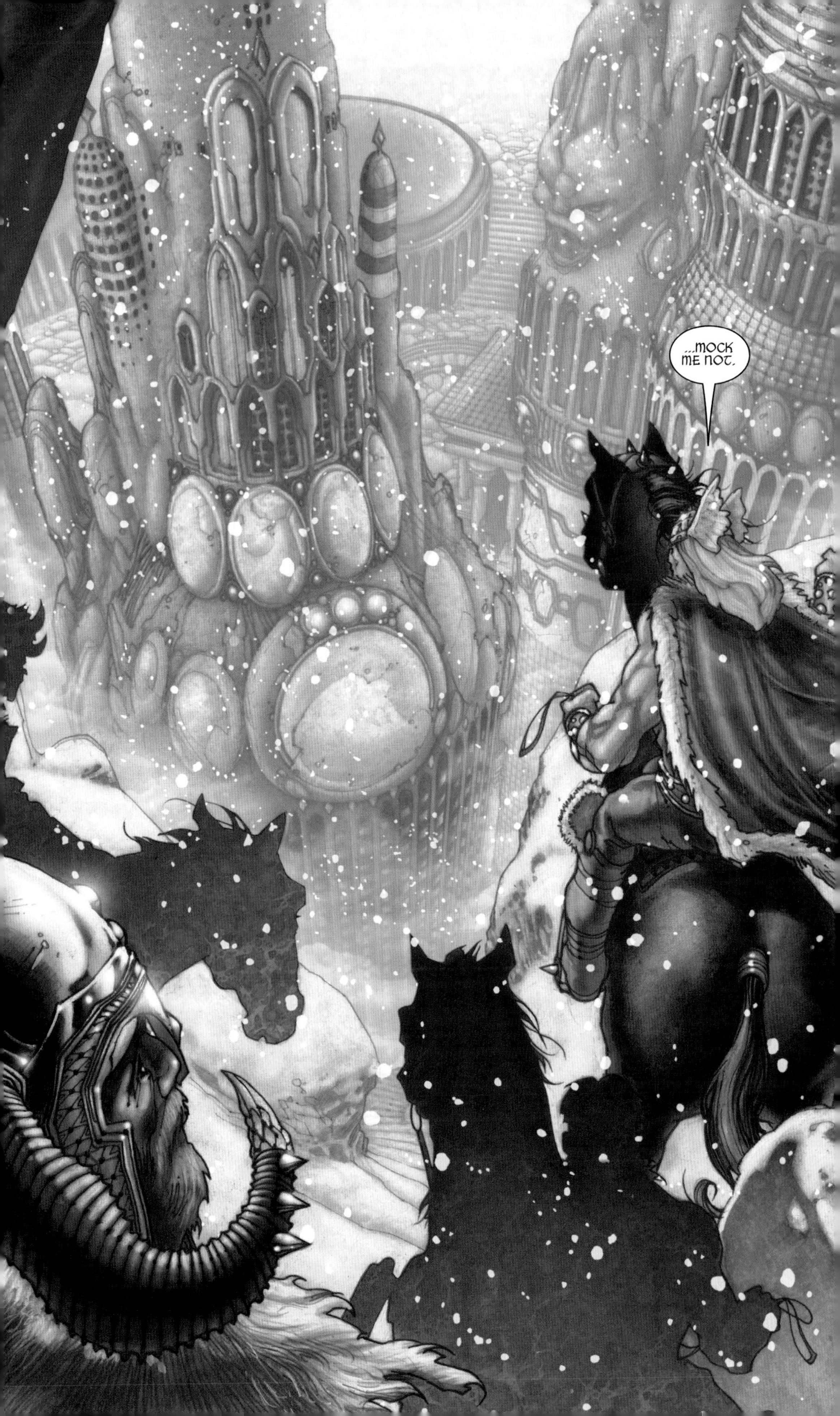
...MOCK ME NOT.

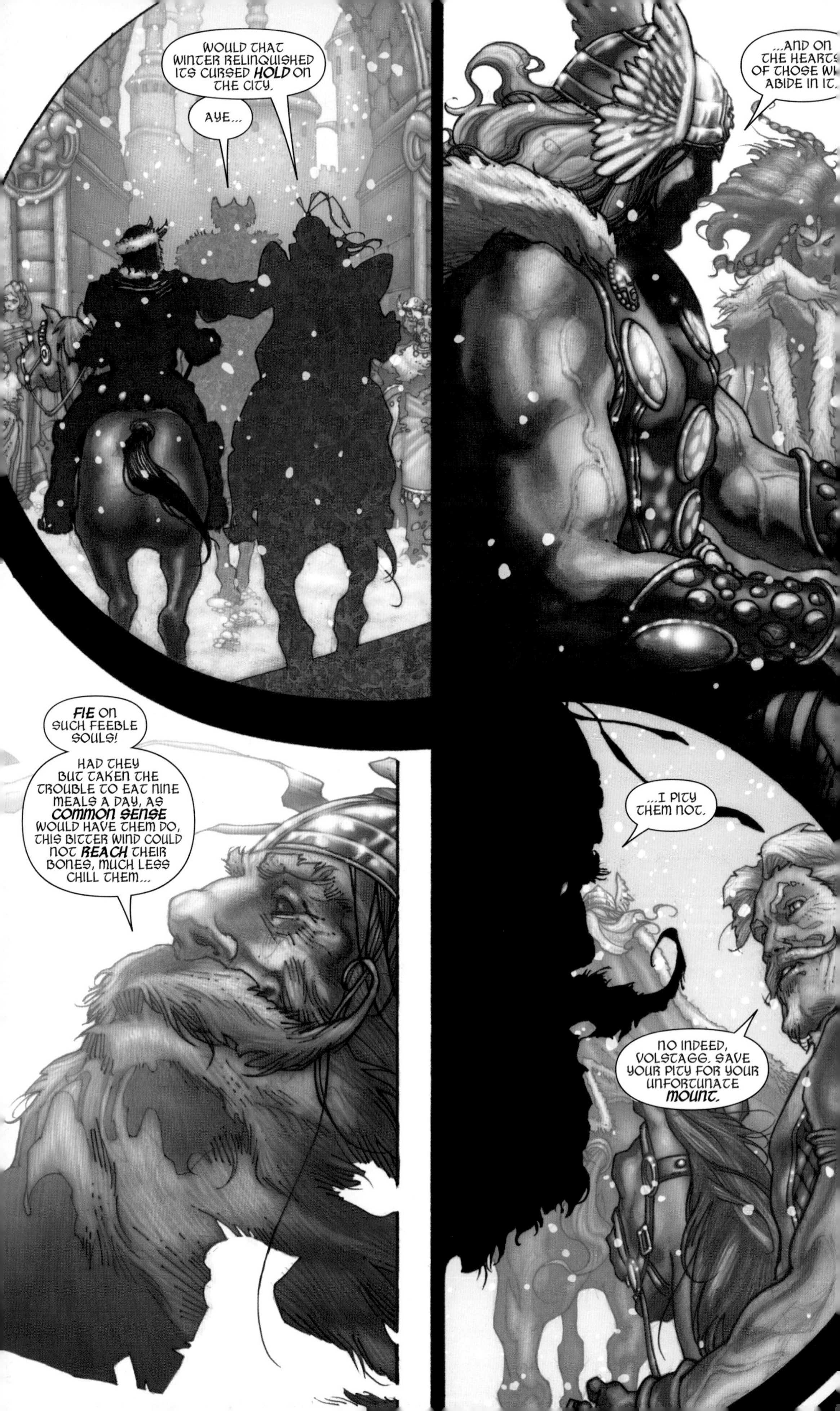
WOULD THAT WINTER RELINQUISHED ITS CURSED HOLD ON THE CITY.
AYE...
...AND ON THE HEARTS OF THOSE WH ABIDE IN IT.
FIE ON SUCH FEEBLE SOULS!
HAD THEY BUT TAKEN THE TROUBLE TO EAT NINE MEALS A DAY, AS COMMON SENSE WOULD HAVE THEM DO, THIS BITTER WIND COULD NOT REACH THEIR BONES, MUCH LESS CHILL THEM...
...I PITY THEM NOT.
NO INDEED, VOLSTAGG. SAVE YOUR PITY FOR YOUR UNFORTUNATE MOUNT.

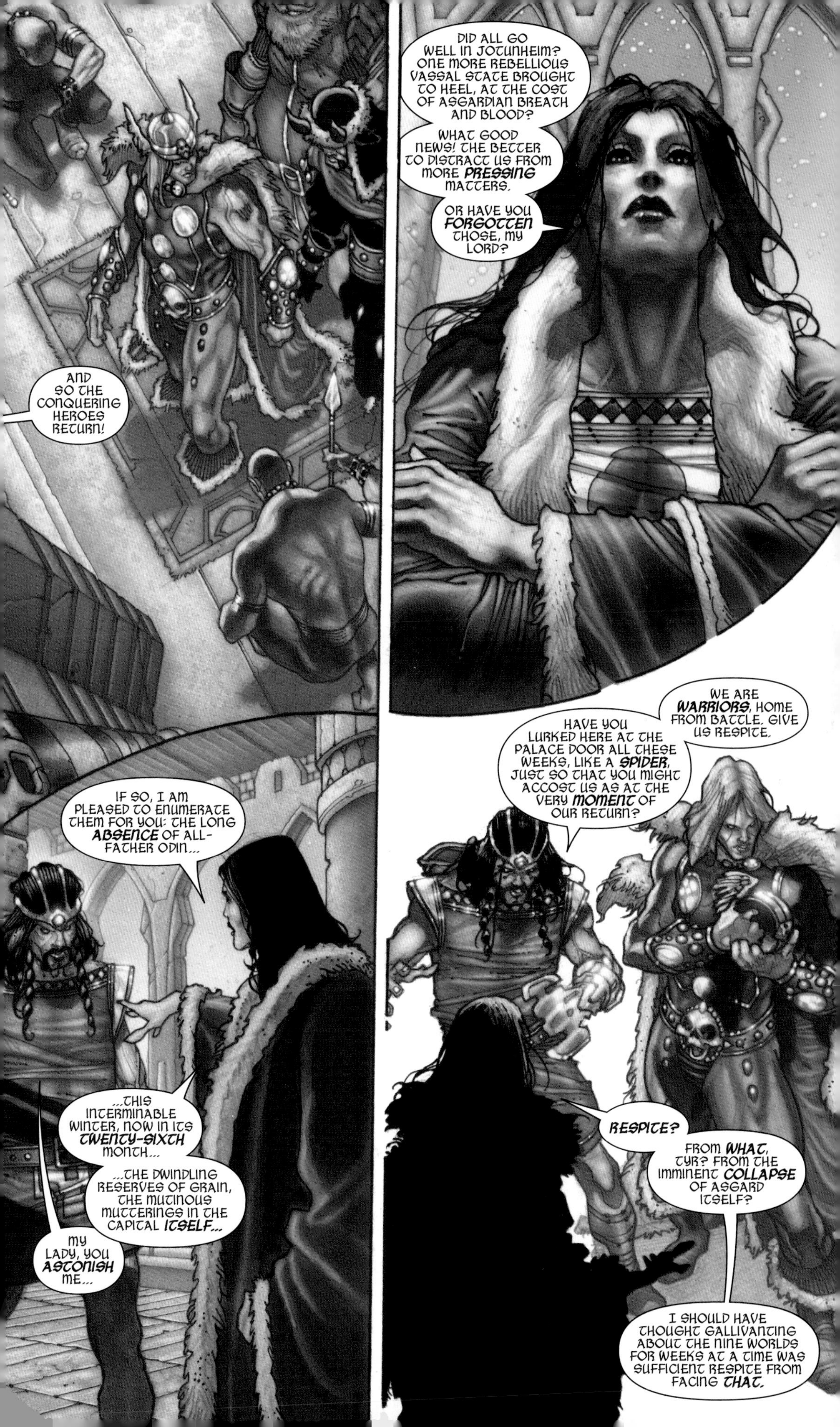
AND SO THE CONQUERING HEROES RETURN!
DID ALL GO WELL IN JOTUNHEIM? ONE MORE REBELLIOUS VASSAL STATE BROUGHT TO HEEL, AT THE COST OF ASGARDIAN BREATH AND BLOOD?
WHAT GOOD NEWS! THE BETTER TO DISTRACT US FROM MORE PRESSING MATTERS.
OR HAVE YOU FORGOTTEN THOSE, MY LORD?
IF SO, I AM PLEASED TO ENUMERATE THEM FOR YOU: THE LONG ABSENCE OF ALL-FATHER ODIN...
...THIS INTERMINABLE WINTER, NOW IN ITS TWENTY-SIXTH MONTH...
...THE DWINDLING RESERVES OF GRAIN, THE MUTINOUS MUTTERINGS IN THE CAPITAL ITSELF...
MY LADY, YOU ASTONISH ME...
HAVE YOU LURKED HERE AT THE PALACE DOOR ALL THESE WEEKS, LIKE A SPIDER, JUST SO THAT YOU MIGHT ACCOST US AS AT THE VERY MOMENT OF OUR RETURN?
WE ARE WARRIORS, HOME FROM BATTLE. GIVE US RESPITE.
RESPITE?
FROM WHAT, TYR? FROM THE IMMINENT COLLAPSE OF ASGARD ITSELF?
I SHOULD HAVE THOUGHT GALLIVANTING ABOUT THE NINE WORLDS FOR WEEKS AT A TIME WAS SUFFICIENT RESPITE FROM FACING THAT.

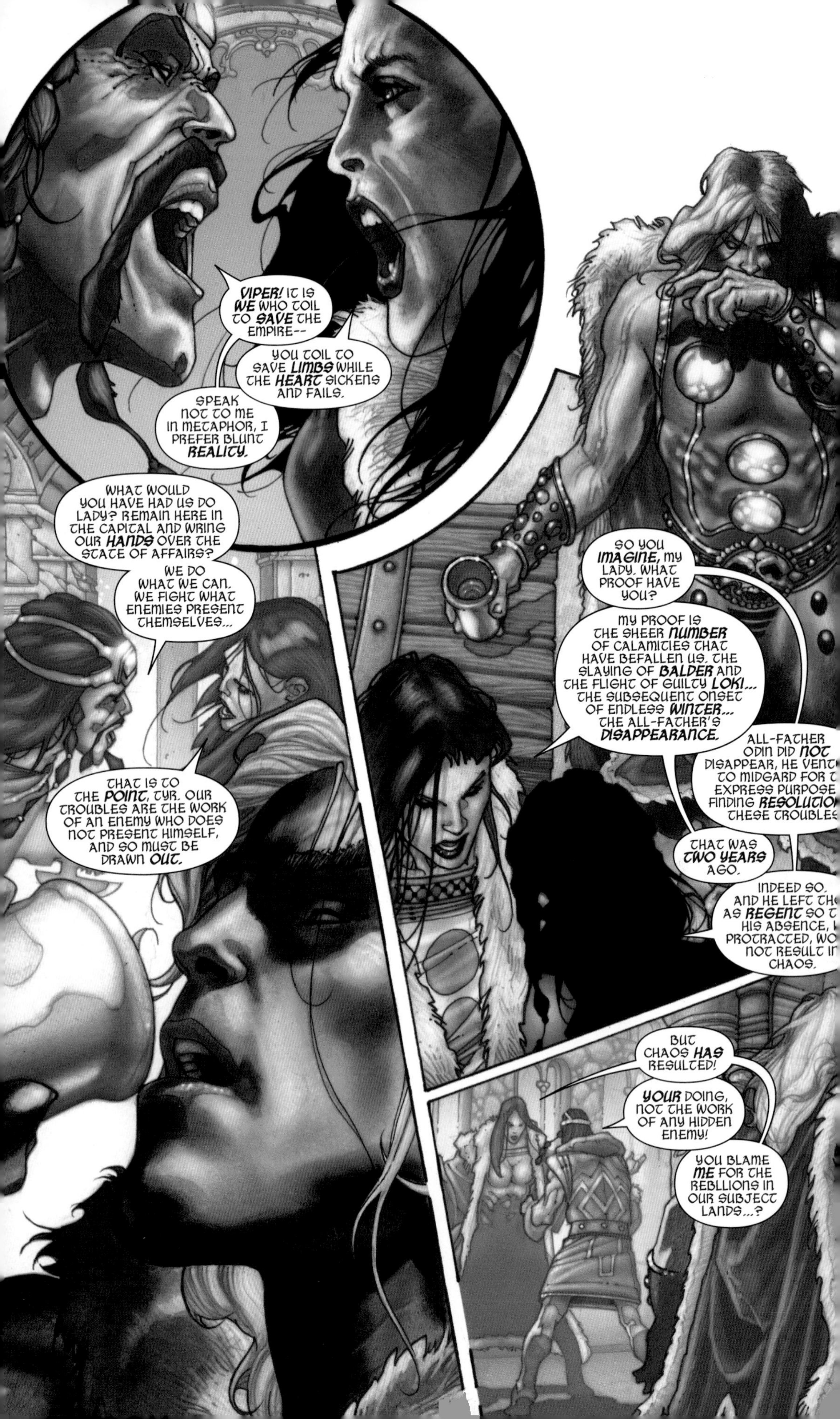
VIPER! IT IS WE WHO TOIL TO SAVE THE EMPIRE--
YOU TOIL TO SAVE LIMBS WHILE THE HEART SICKENS AND FAILS.
SPEAK NOT TO ME IN METAPHOR, I PREFER BLUNT REALITY.
WHAT WOULD YOU HAVE HAD US DO LADY? REMAIN HERE IN THE CAPITAL AND WRING OUR HANDS OVER THE STATE OF AFFAIRS?
WE DO WHAT WE CAN. WE FIGHT WHAT ENEMIES PRESENT THEMSELVES...
THAT IS TO THE POINT, TYR. OUR TROUBLES ARE THE WORK OF AN ENEMY WHO DOES NOT PRESENT HIMSELF, AND SO MUST BE DRAWN OUT.
SO YOU IMAGINE, MY LADY. WHAT PROOF HAVE YOU?
MY PROOF IS THE SHEER NUMBER OF CALAMITIES THAT HAVE BEFALLEN US. THE SLAYING OF BALDER AND THE FLIGHT OF GUILTY LOKI... THE SUBSEQUENT ONSET OF ENDLESS WINTER... THE ALL-FATHER'S DISAPPEARANCE.
THAT WAS TWO YEARS AGO.
BUT CHAOS HAS RESULTED!
YOUR DOING, NOT THE WORK OF ANY HIDDEN ENEMY!
YOU BLAME ME FOR THE REBLLIONS IN OUR SUBJECT LANDS...?

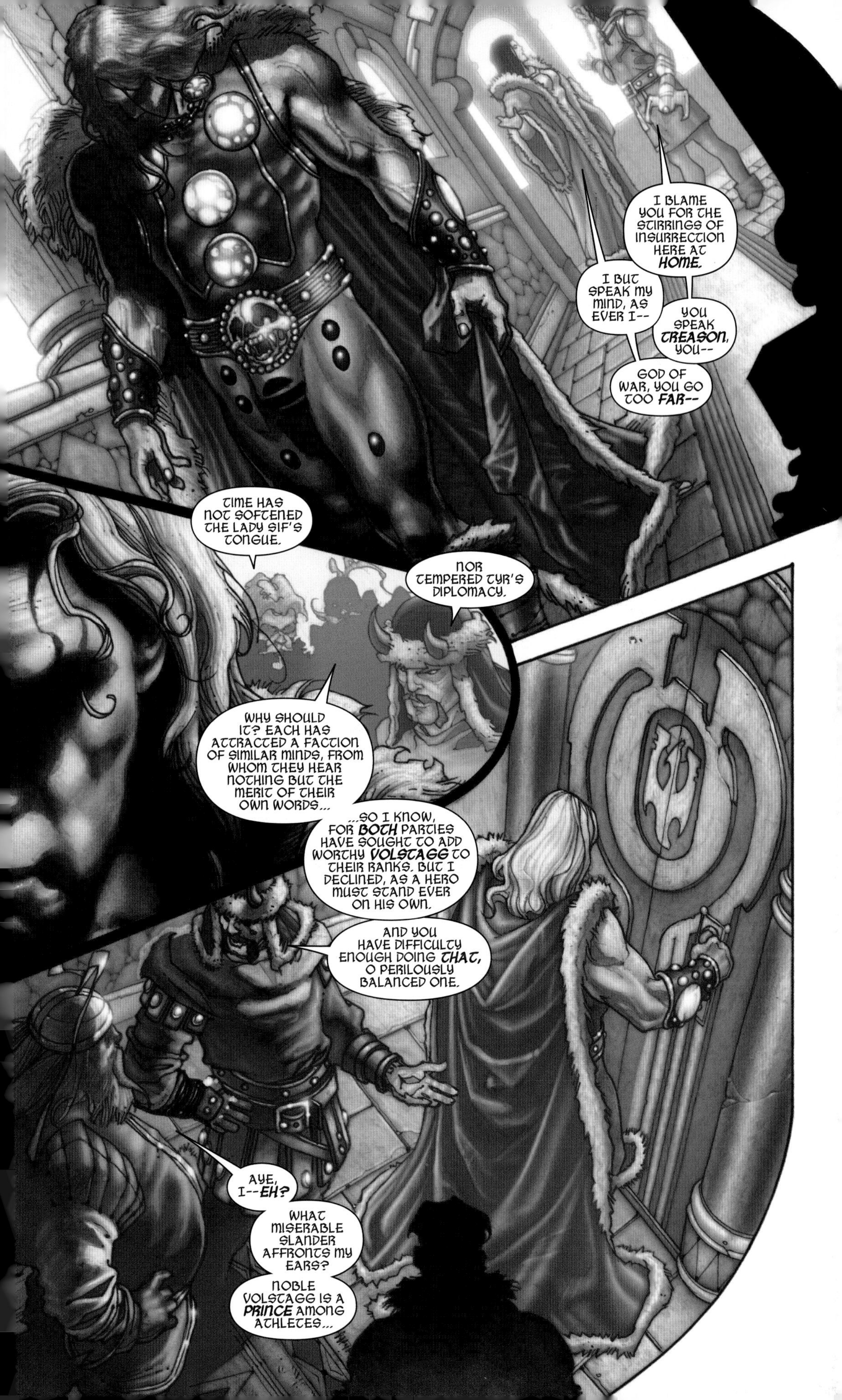

I BLAME YOU FOR THE STIRRINGS OF INSURRECTION HERE AT HOME.
I BUT SPEAK MY MIND, AS EVER I--
YOU SPEAK TREASON, YOU--
GOD OF WAR, YOU GO TOO FAR--
TIME HAS NOT SOFTENED THE LADY SIF'S TONGUE.
NOR TEMPERED TYR'S DIPLOMACY.
WHY SHOULD IT? EACH HAS ATTRACTED A FACTION OF SIMILAR MINDS, FROM WHOM THEY HEAR NOTHING BUT THE MERIT OF THEIR OWN WORDS...
...SO I KNOW, FOR BOTH PARTIES HAVE SOUGHT TO ADD WORTHY VOLSTAGG TO THEIR RANKS. BUT I DECLINED, AS A HERO MUST STAND EVER ON HIS OWN.
AND YOU HAVE DIFFICULTY ENOUGH DOING THAT, O PERILOUSLY BALANCED ONE.
AYE, I--EH?
WHAT MISERABLE SLANDER AFFRONTS MY EARS?
NOBLE VOLSTAGG IS A PRINCE AMONG ATHLETES...

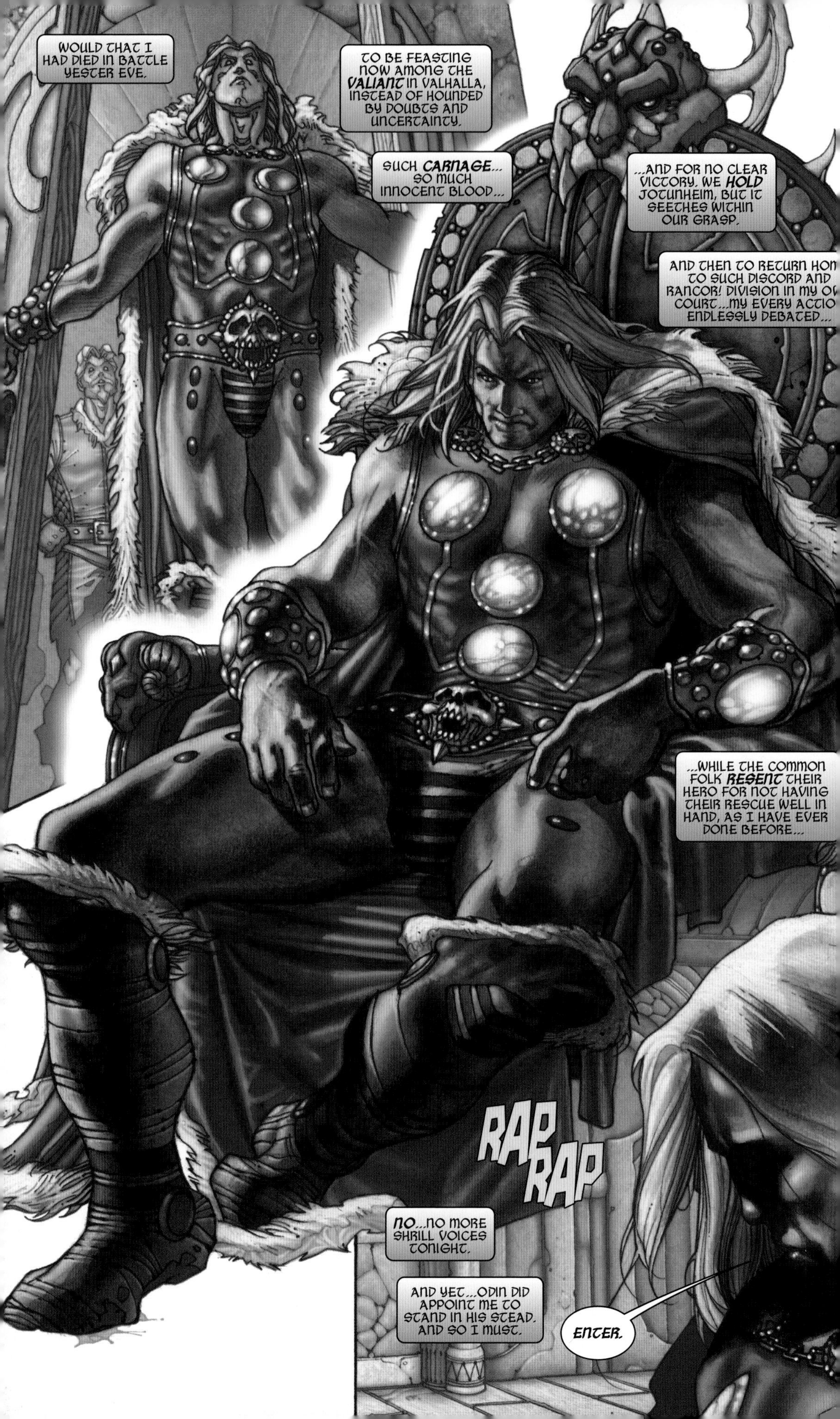
WOULD THAT I HAD DIED IN BATTLE YESTER EVE.
TO BE FEASTING NOW AMONG THE VALIANT IN VALHALLA, INSTEAD OF HOUNDED BY DOUBTS AND UNCERTAINTY.
SUCH CARNAGE... SO MUCH INNOCENT BLOOD...
...AND FOR NO CLEAR VICTORY. WE HOLD JOTUNHEIM, BUT IT SEETHES WITHIN OUR GRASP.
AND THEN TO RETURN HO TO SUCH DISCORD AND RANCOR! DIVISION IN MY O COURT...MY EVERY ACTIO ENDLESSLY DEBATED...
...WHILE THE COMMON FOLK RESENT THEIR HERO FOR NOT HAVING THEIR RESCUE WELL IN HAND, AS I HAVE EVER DONE BEFORE...
RAP RAP
NO...NO MORE SHRILL VOICES TONIGHT.
AND YET...ODIN DID APPOINT ME TO STAND IN HIS STEAD. AND SO I MUST.
ENTER.

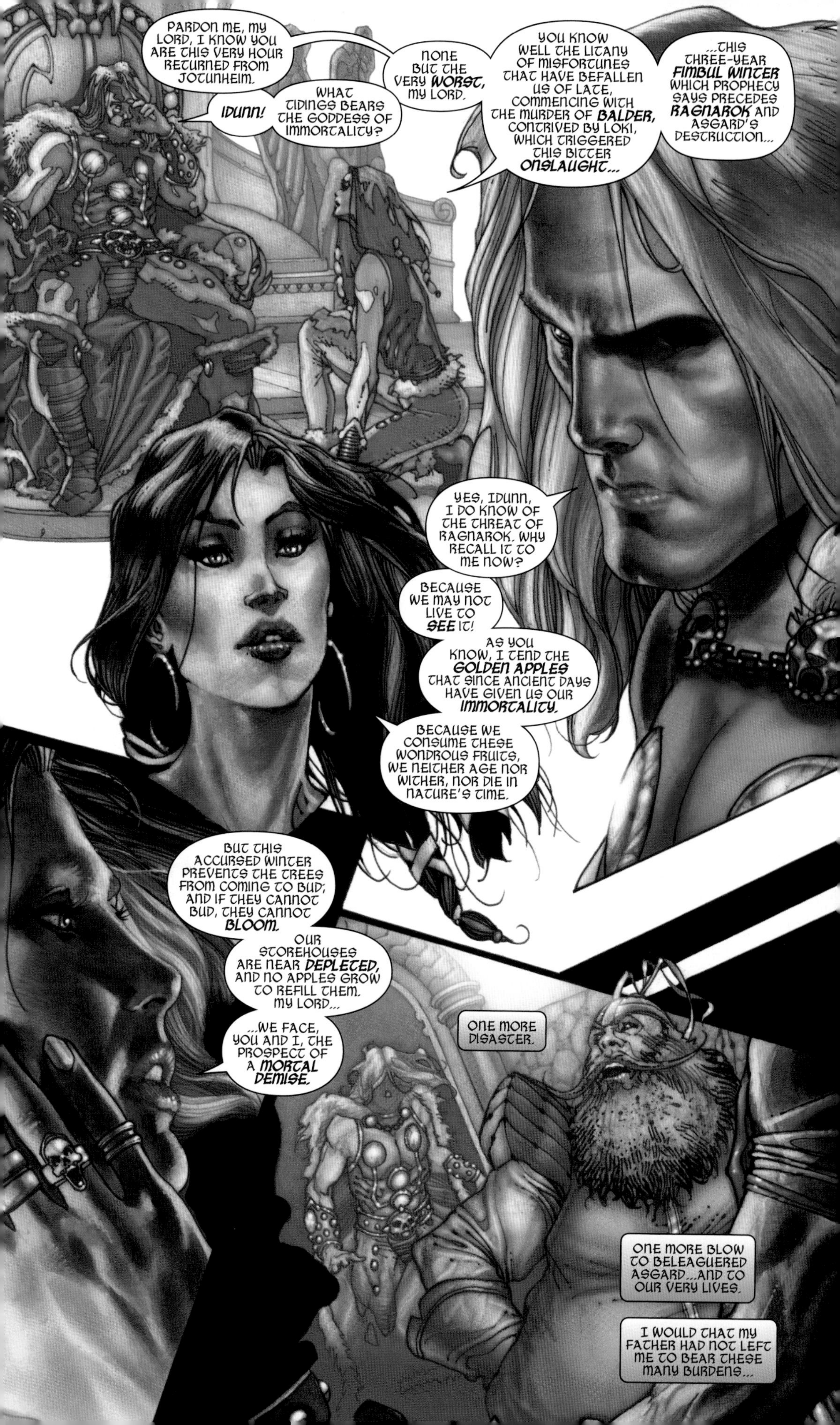
PARDON ME, MY LORD, I KNOW YOU ARE THIS VERY HOUR RETURNED FROM JOTUNHEIM.
IDUNN!
WHAT TIDINGS BEARS THE GODDESS OF IMMORTALITY?
NONE BUT THE VERY WORST, MY LORD.
YOU KNOW WELL THE LITANY OF MISFORTUNES THAT HAVE BEFALLEN US OF LATE, COMMENCING WITH THE MURDER OF BALDER, CONTRIVED BY LOKI, WHICH TRIGGERED THIS BITTER ONSLAUGHT...
...THIS THREE-YEAR FIMBUL WINTER WHICH PROPHECY SAYS PRECEDES RAGNAROK AND ASGARD'S DESTRUCTION...
YES, IDUNN, I DO KNOW OF THE THREAT OF RAGNAROK. WHY RECALL IT TO ME NOW?
BECAUSE WE MAY NOT LIVE TO SEE IT!
AS YOU KNOW, I TEND THE GOLDEN APPLES THAT SINCE ANCIENT DAYS HAVE GIVEN US OUR IMMORTALITY.
BECAUSE WE CONSUME THESE WONDROUS FRUITS, WE NEITHER AGE NOR WITHER, NOR DIE IN NATURE'S TIME.
BUT THIS ACCURSED WINTER PREVENTS THE TREES FROM COMING TO BUD; AND IF THEY CANNOT BUD, THEY CANNOT BLOOM.
OUR STOREHOUSES ARE NEAR DEPLETED, AND NO APPLES GROW TO REFILL THEM. MY LORD...
...WE FACE, YOU AND I, THE PROSPECT OF A MORTAL DEMISE.
ONE MORE DISASTER.
ONE MORE BLOW TO BELEAGUERED ASGARD...AND TO OUR VERY LIVES.
I WOULD THAT MY FATHER HAD NOT LEFT ME TO BEAR THESE MANY BURDENS...

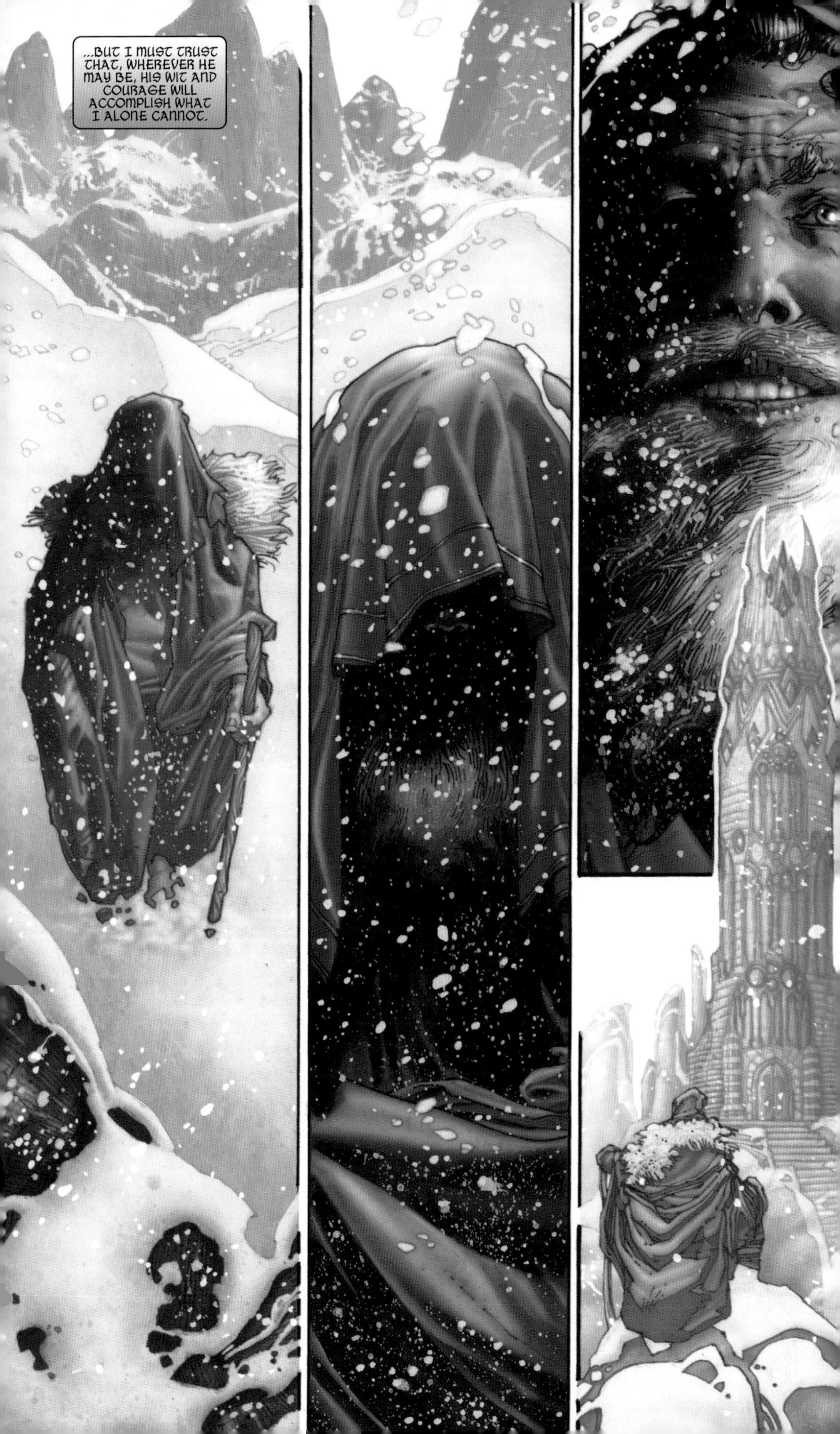
...BUT I MUST TRUST THAT, WHEREVER HE MAY BE, HIS WIT AND COURAGE WILL ACCOMPLISH WHAT I ALONE CANNOT.

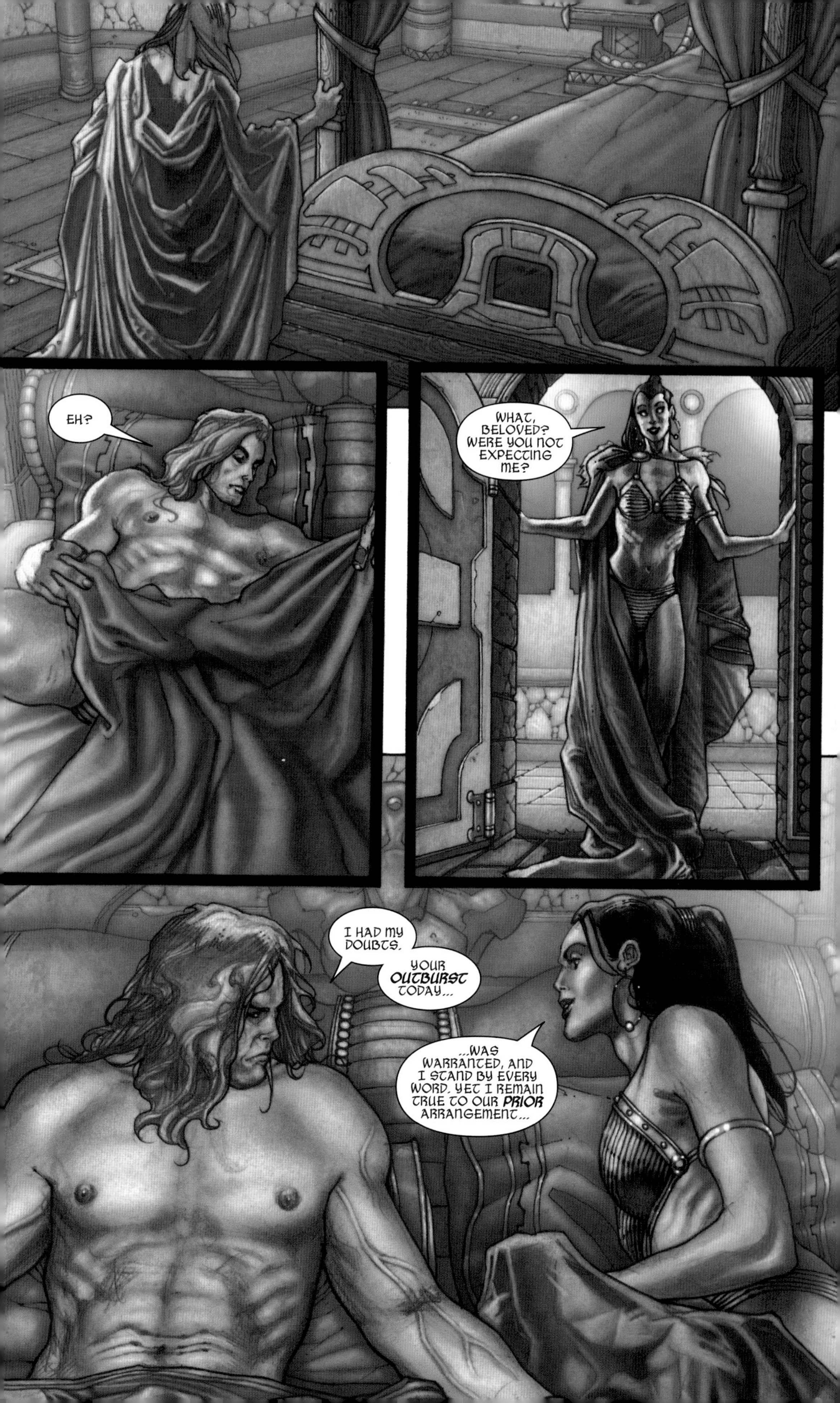
EH?
WHAT, BELOVED? WERE YOU NOT EXPECTING ME?
I HAD MY DOUBTS.
YOUR OUTBURST TODAY...
...WAS WARRANTED, AND I STAND BY EVERY WORD. YET I REMAIN TRUE TO OUR PRIOR ARRANGEMENT...

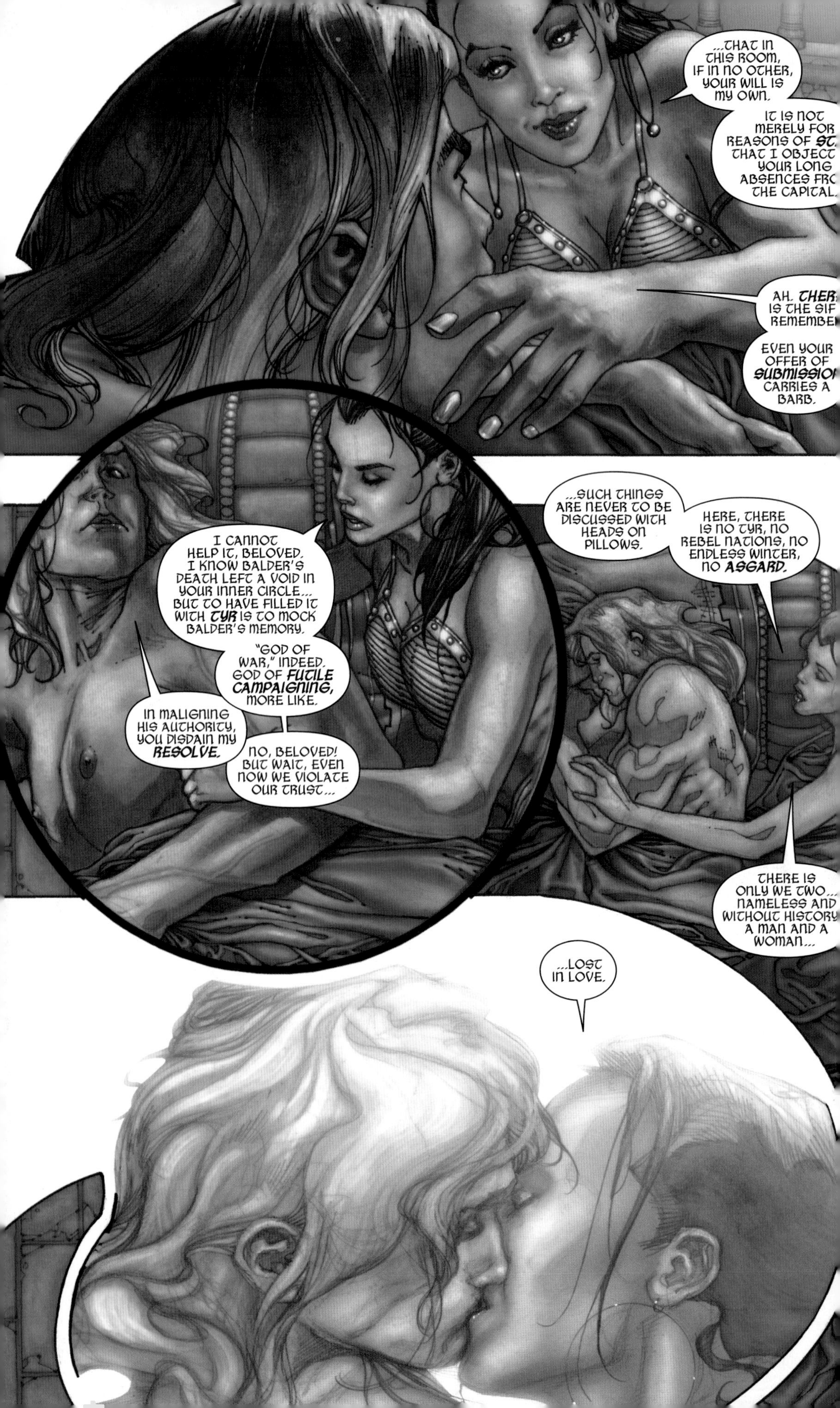

...THAT IN THIS ROOM, IF IN NO OTHER, YOUR WILL IS MY OWN.
IT IS NOT MERELY FOR REASONS OF ST THAT I OBJECT YOUR LONG ABSENCES FRO THE CAPITAL.
AH. THER IS THE SIF REMEMBE
EVEN YOUR OFFER OF SUBMISSIO CARRIES A BARB.
I CANNOT HELP IT, BELOVED. I KNOW BALDER'S DEATH LEFT A VOID IN YOUR INNER CIRCLE... BUT TO HAVE FILLED IT WITH TYR IS TO MOCK BALDER'S MEMORY.
"GOD OF WAR," INDEED. GOD OF FUTILE CAMPAIGNING, MORE LIKE.
IN MALIGNING HIS AUTHORITY, YOU DISDAIN MY RESOLVE.
NO, BELOVED! BUT WAIT, EVEN NOW WE VIOLATE OUR TRUST...
...SUCH THINGS ARE NEVER TO BE DISCUSSED WITH HEADS ON PILLOWS.
HERE, THERE IS NO TYR, NO REBEL NATIONS, NO ENDLESS WINTER, NO ASGARD.
THERE IS ONLY WE TWO... NAMELESS AND WITHOUT HISTORY A MAN AND A WOMAN...
...LOST IN LOVE.

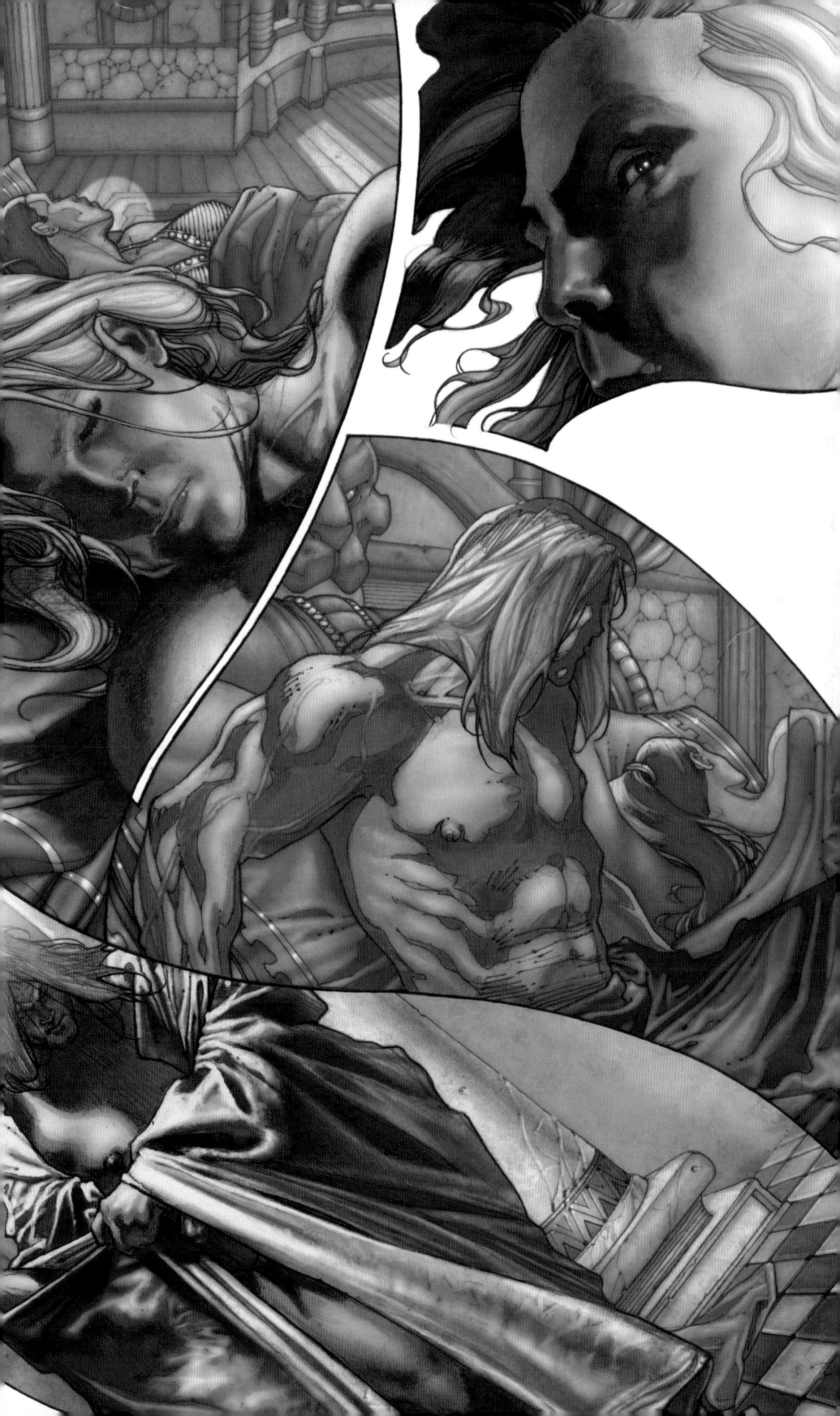

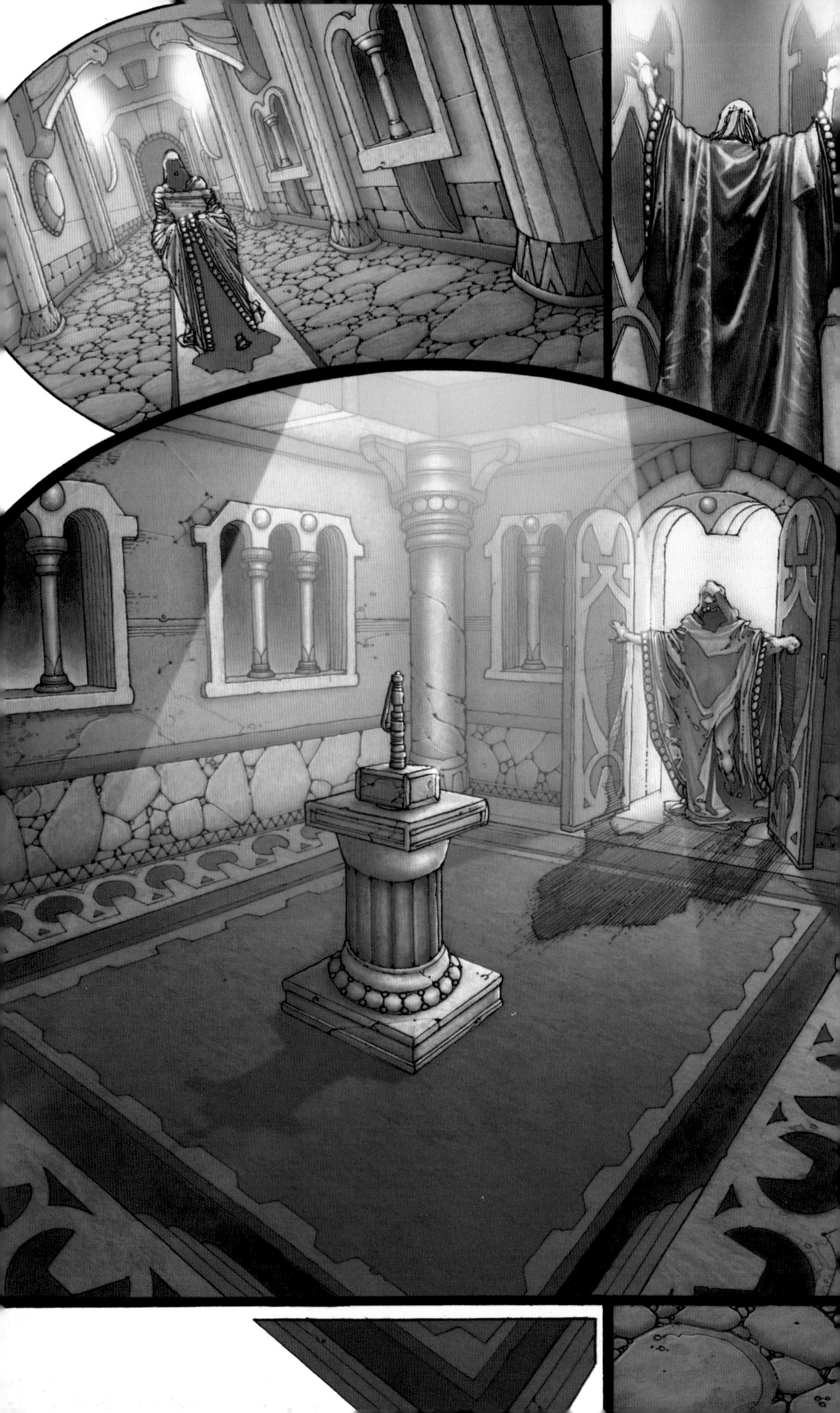

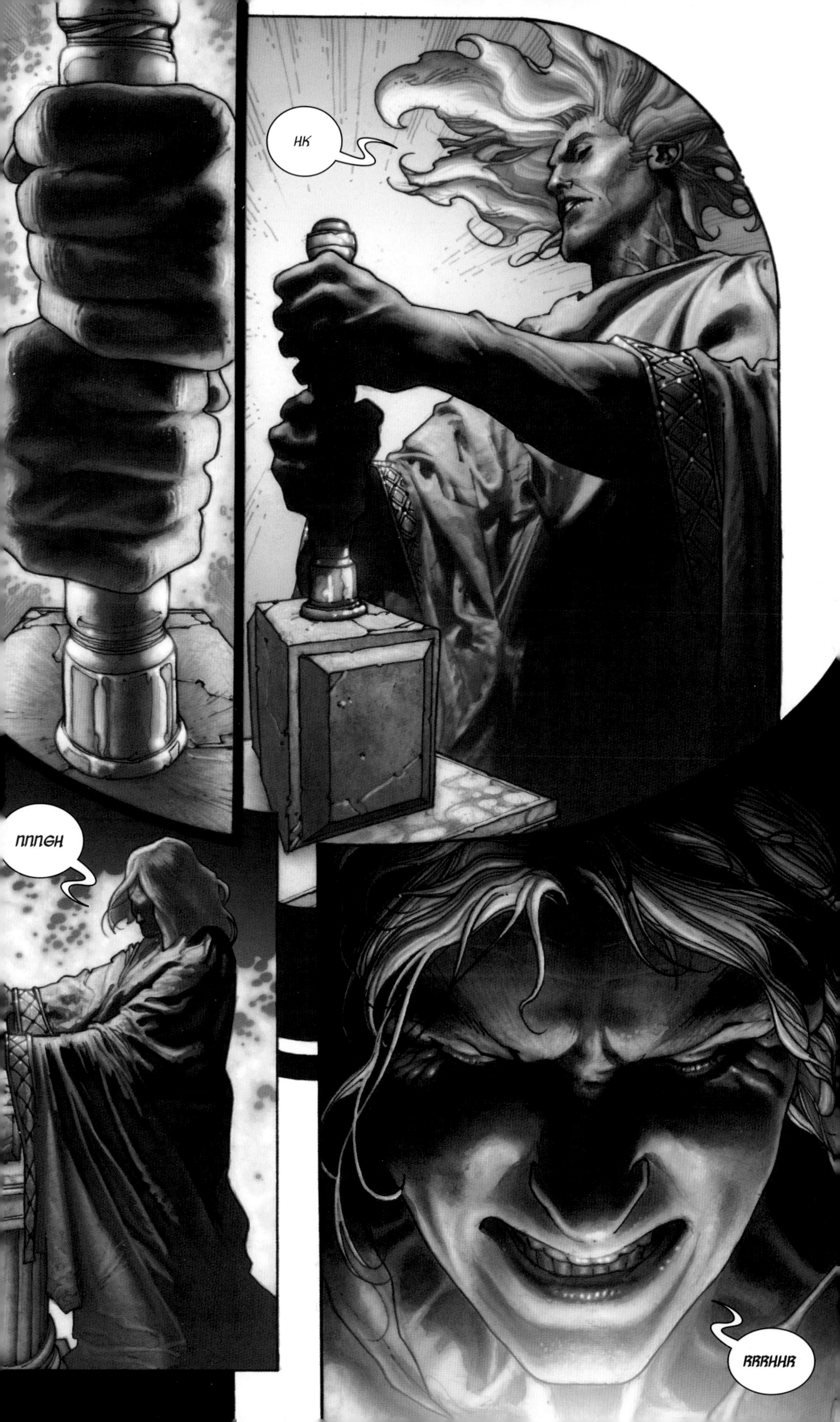
HK
NNNGH
RRRHHR

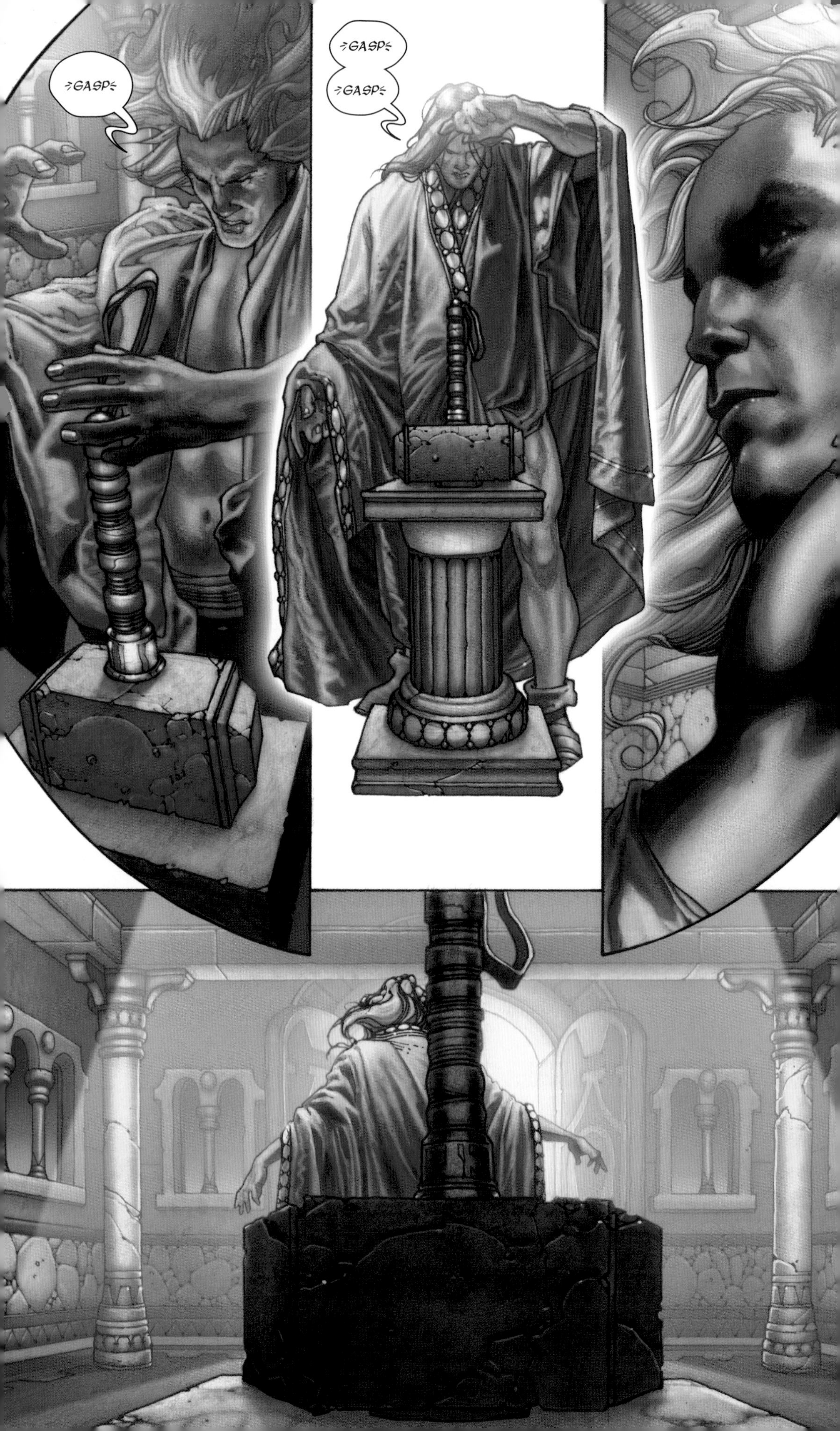

GASP
GASP
GASP

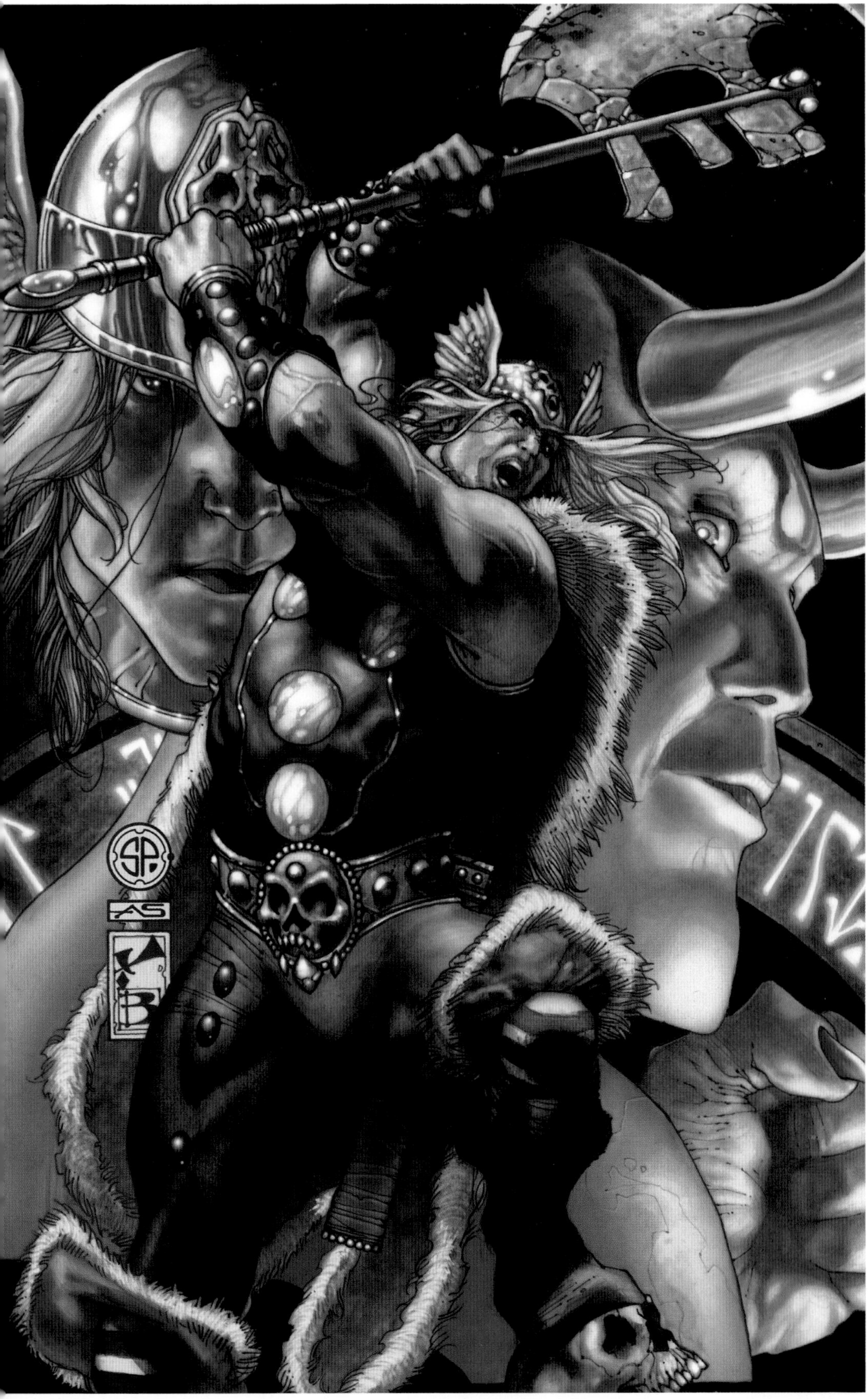

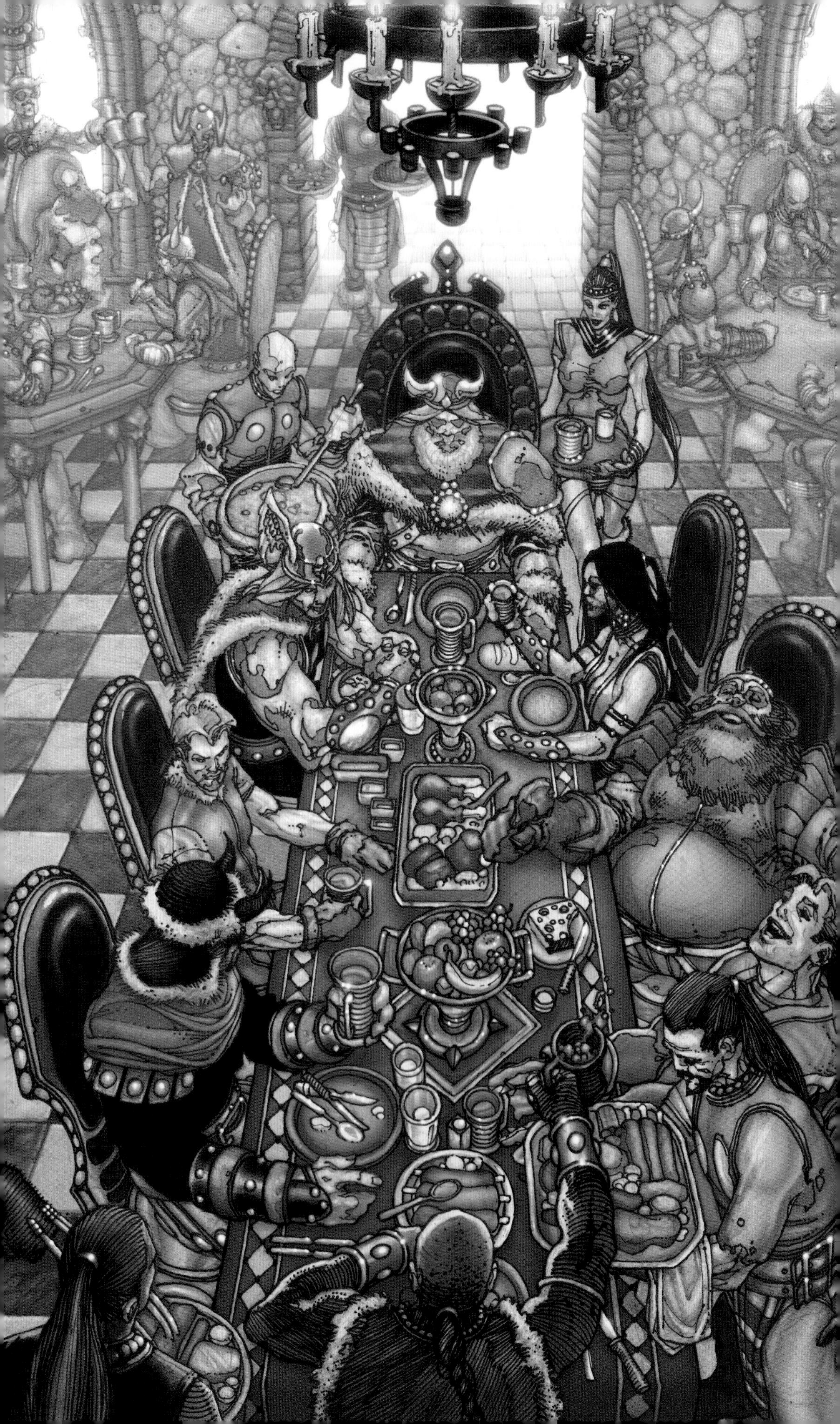

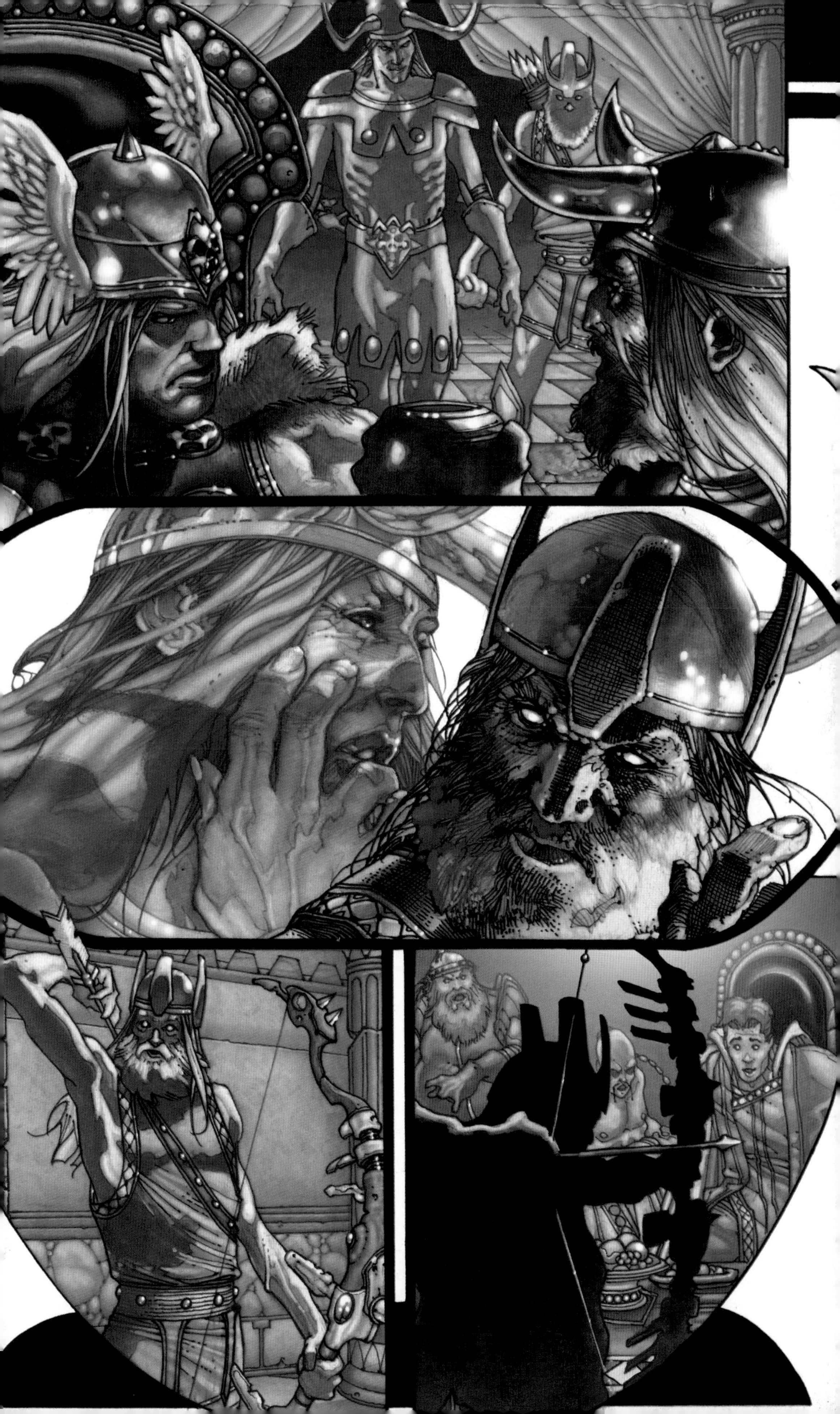

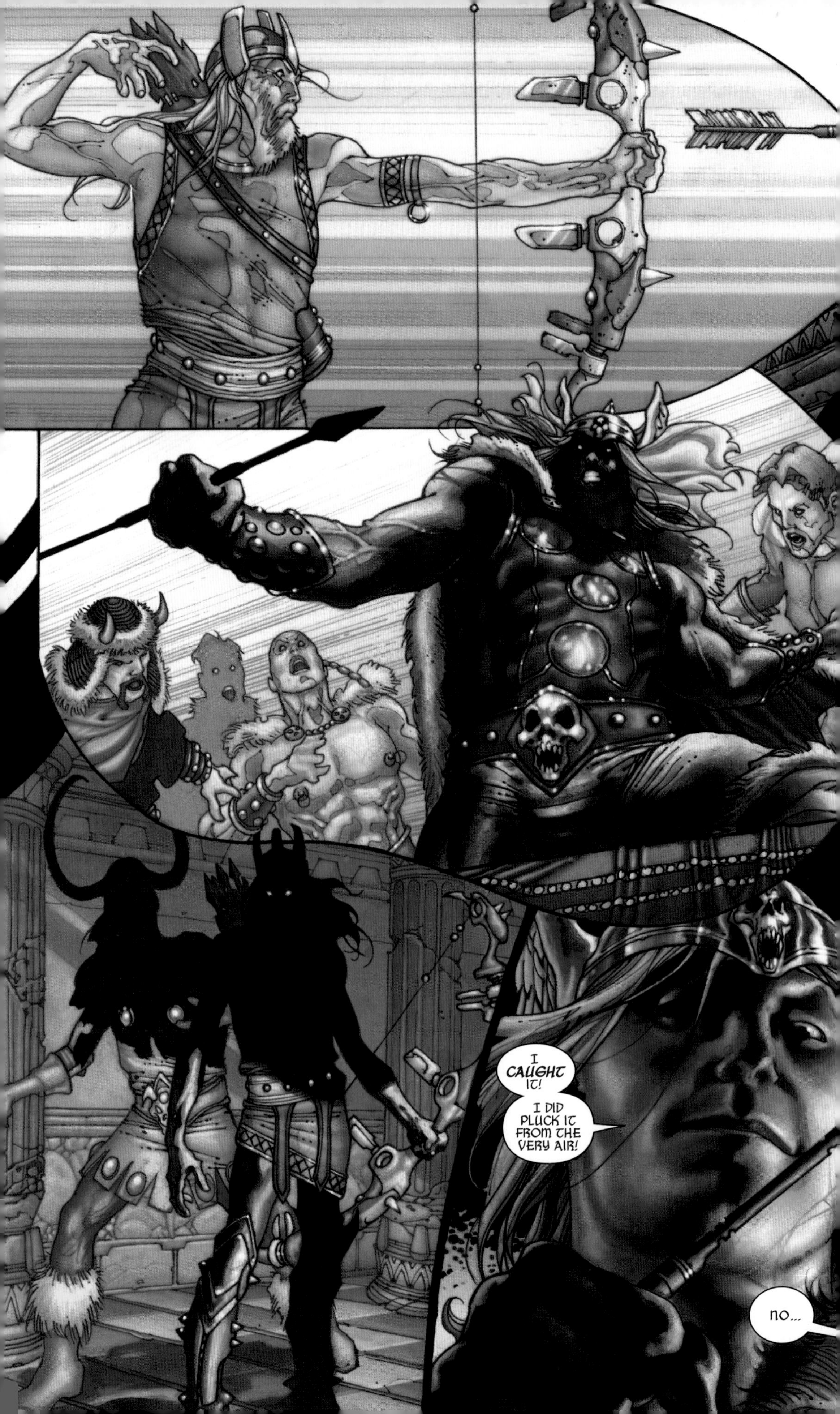
I CAUGHT IT!
I DID PLUCK IT FROM THE VERY AIR!
no...

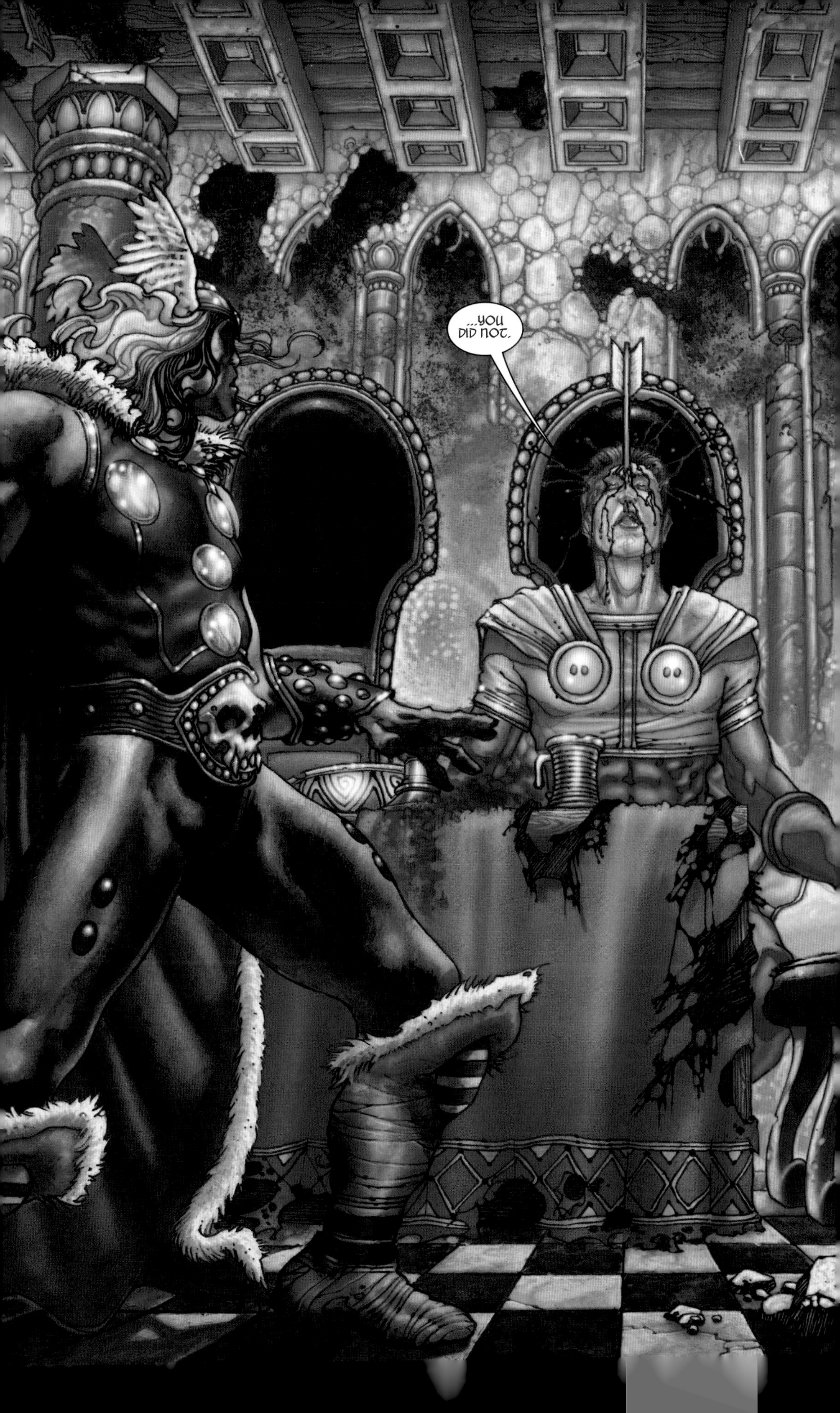
...YOU DID NOT.

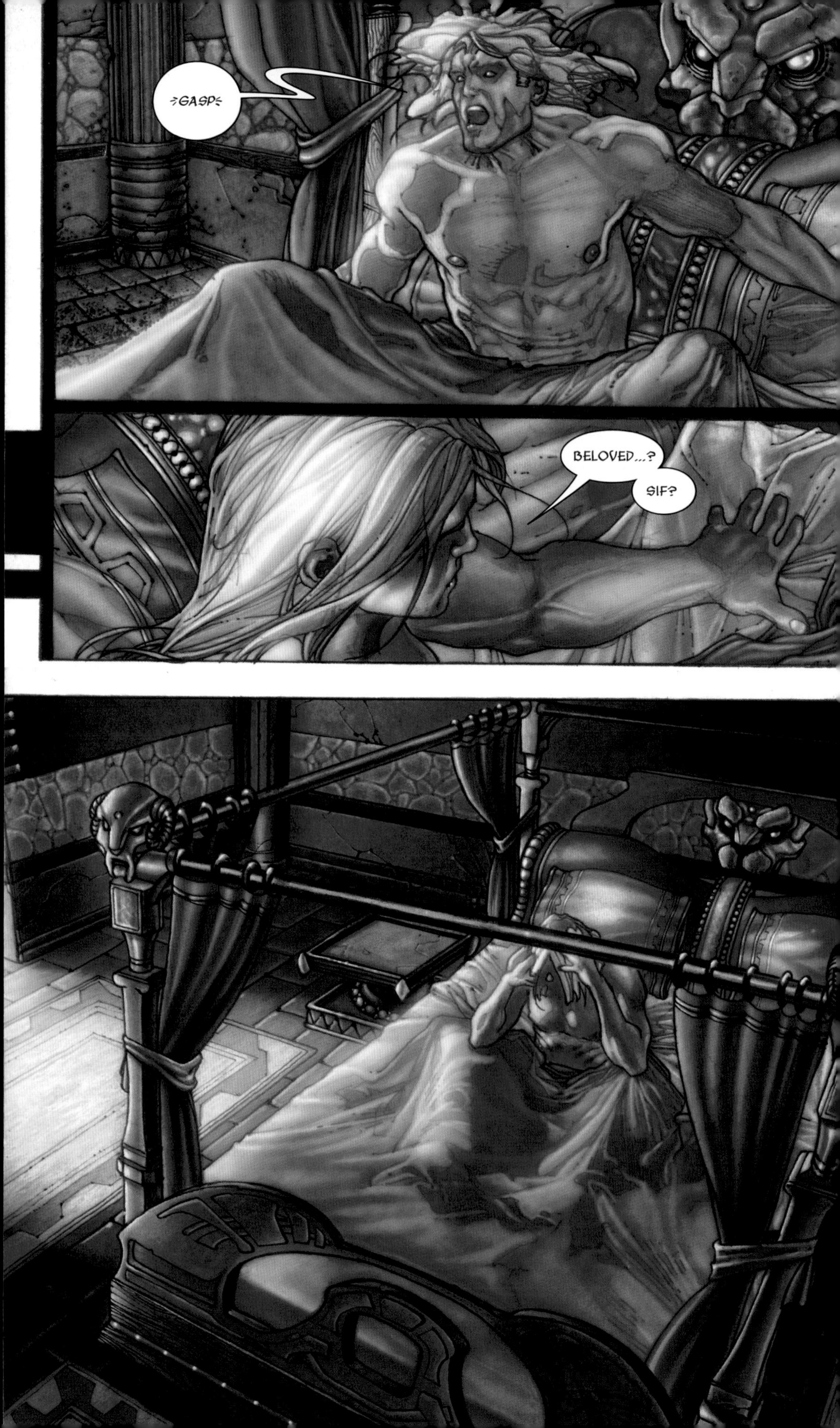
GASP
BELOVED...?
SIF?

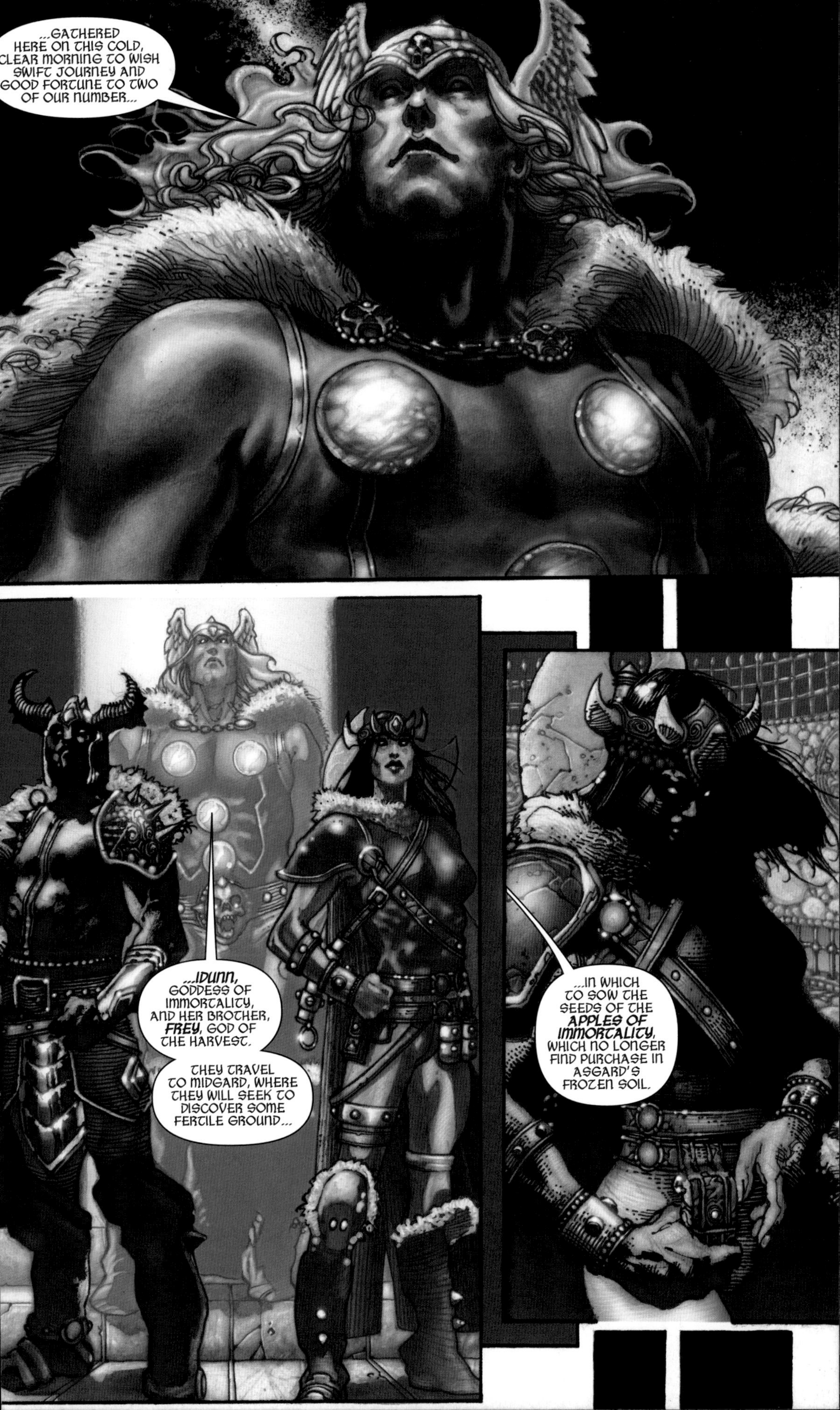
...GATHERED HERE ON THIS COLD, CLEAR MORNING TO WISH SWIFT JOURNEY AND GOOD FORTUNE TO TWO OF OUR NUMBER...
...IDUNN, GODDESS OF IMMORTALITY, AND HER BROTHER, FREY, GOD OF THE HARVEST.
THEY TRAVEL TO MIDGARD, WHERE THEY WILL SEEK TO DISCOVER SOME FERTILE GROUND...
...IN WHICH TO SOW THE SEEDS OF THE APPLES OF IMMORTALITY, WHICH NO LONGER FIND PURCHASE IN ASGARD'S FROZEN SOIL.

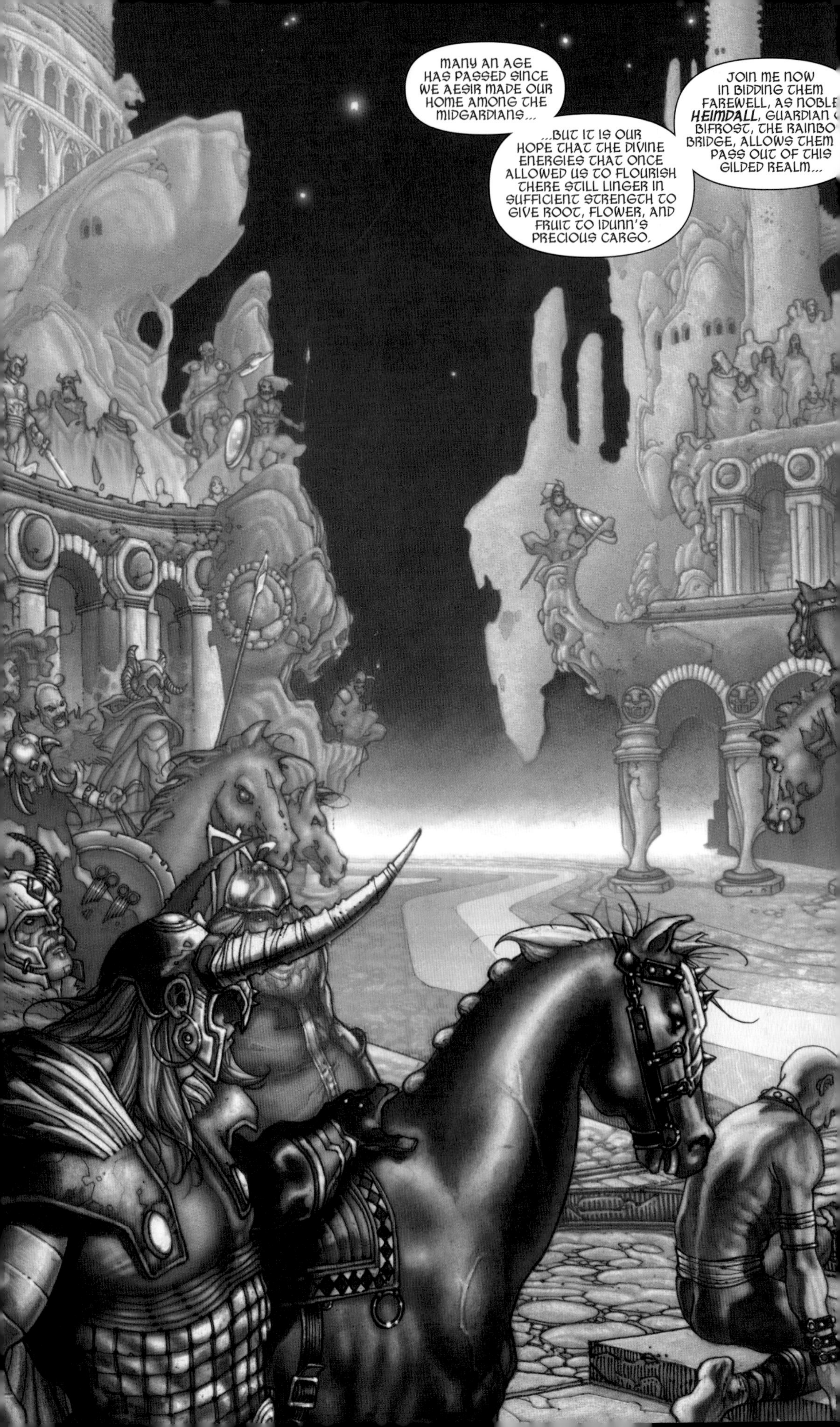
MANY AN AGE HAS PASSED SINCE WE AESIR MADE OUR HOME AMONG THE MIDGARDIANS...
...BUT IT IS OUR HOPE THAT THE DIVINE ENERGIES THAT ONCE ALLOWED US TO FLOURISH THERE STILL LINGER IN SUFFICIENT STRENGTH TO GIVE ROOT, FLOWER, AND FRUIT TO IDUNN'S PRECIOUS CARGO.
JOIN ME NOW IN BIDDING THEM FAREWELL, AS NOBLE **HEIMDALL**, GUARDIAN BIFROST, THE RAINBO BRIDGE, ALLOWS THEM PASS OUT OF THIS GILDED REALM...

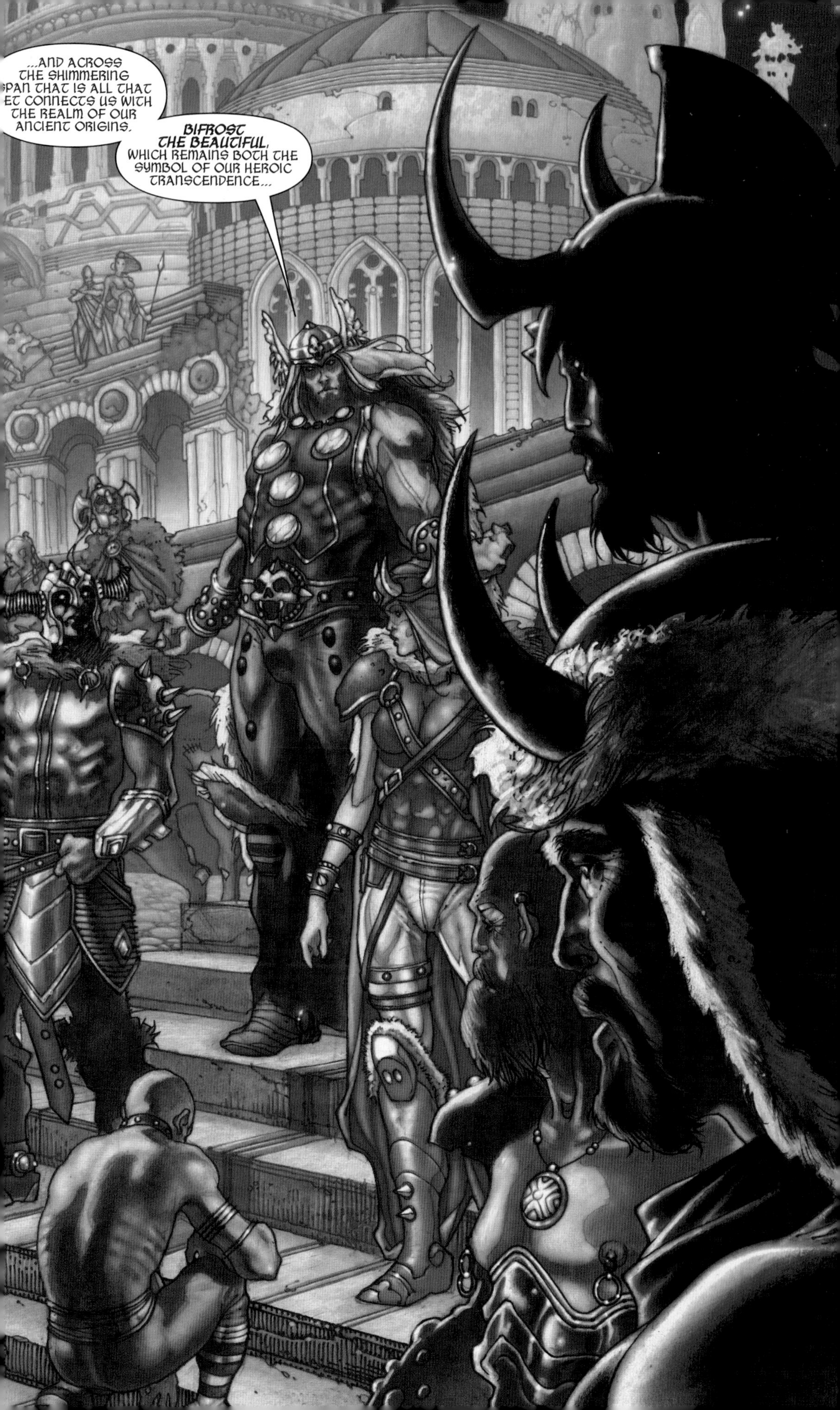
...AND ACROSS THE SHIMMERING PAN THAT IS ALL THAT ET CONNECTS US WITH THE REALM OF OUR ANCIENT ORIGINS.
BIFROST THE BEAUTIFUL, WHICH REMAINS BOTH THE SYMBOL OF OUR HEROIC TRANSCENDENCE...

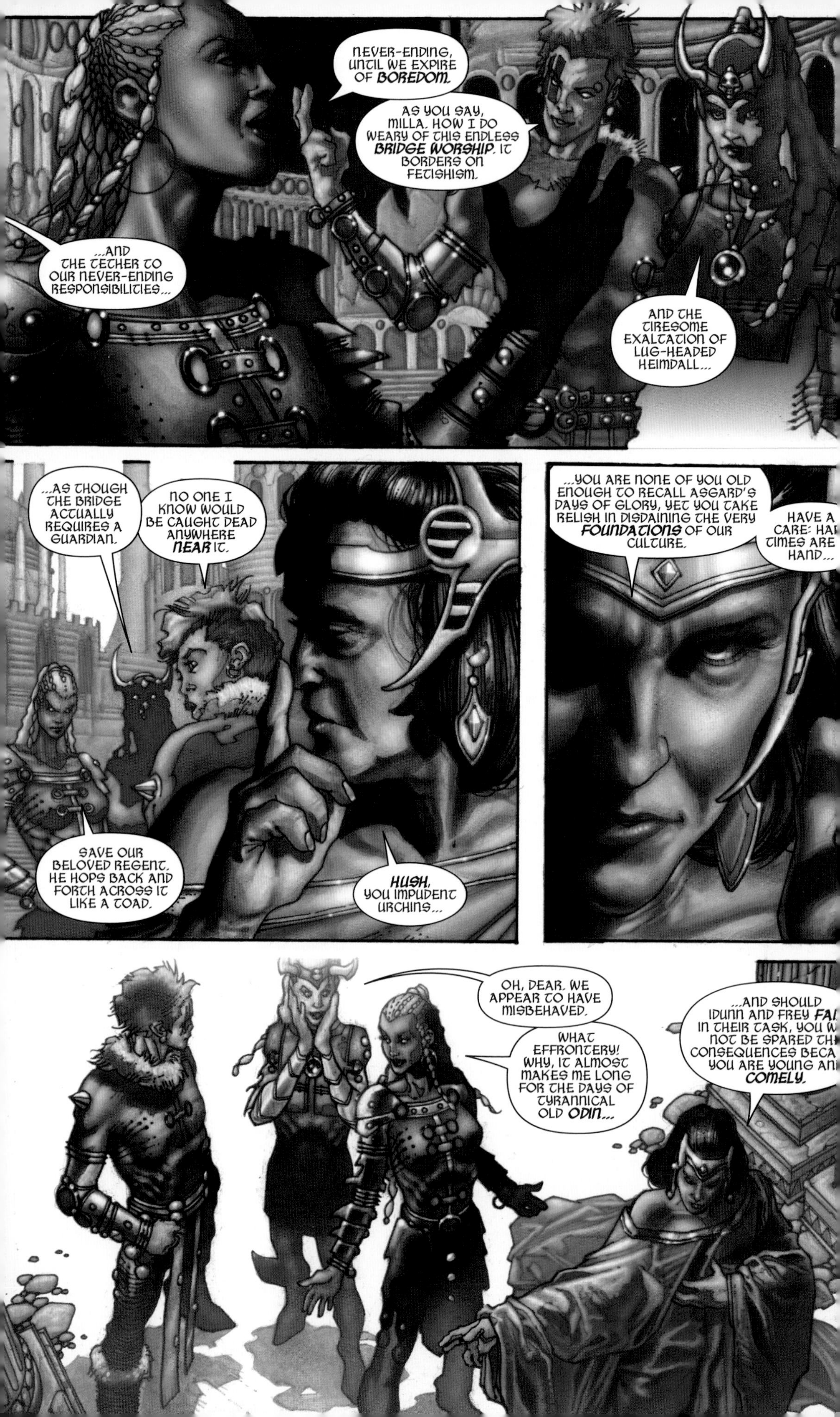

...AND THE TETHER TO OUR NEVER-ENDING RESPONSIBILITIES...
NEVER-ENDING, UNTIL WE EXPIRE OF BOREDOM.
AS YOU SAY, MILLA. HOW I DO WEARY OF THIS ENDLESS BRIDGE WORSHIP. IT BORDERS ON FETISHISM.
AND THE TIRESOME EXALTATION OF LUG-HEADED HEIMDALL...
...AS THOUGH THE BRIDGE ACTUALLY REQUIRES A GUARDIAN.
NO ONE I KNOW WOULD BE CAUGHT DEAD ANYWHERE NEAR IT.
SAVE OUR BELOVED REGENT. HE HOPS BACK AND FORTH ACROSS IT LIKE A TOAD.
HUSH, YOU IMPUDENT URCHINS...
...YOU ARE NONE OF YOU OLD ENOUGH TO RECALL ASGARD'S DAYS OF GLORY, YET YOU TAKE RELISH IN DISDAINING THE VERY FOUNDATIONS OF OUR CULTURE.
HAVE A CARE: HA
TIMES ARE
HAND...
OH, DEAR. WE APPEAR TO HAVE MISBEHAVED.
WHAT EFFRONTERY! WHY, IT ALMOST MAKES ME LONG FOR THE DAYS OF TYRANNICAL OLD ODIN...
...AND SHOULD IDUNN AND FREY FA
IN THEIR TASK, YOU W
NOT BE SPARED TH
CONSEQUENCES BECA
YOU ARE YOUNG AN
COMELY.

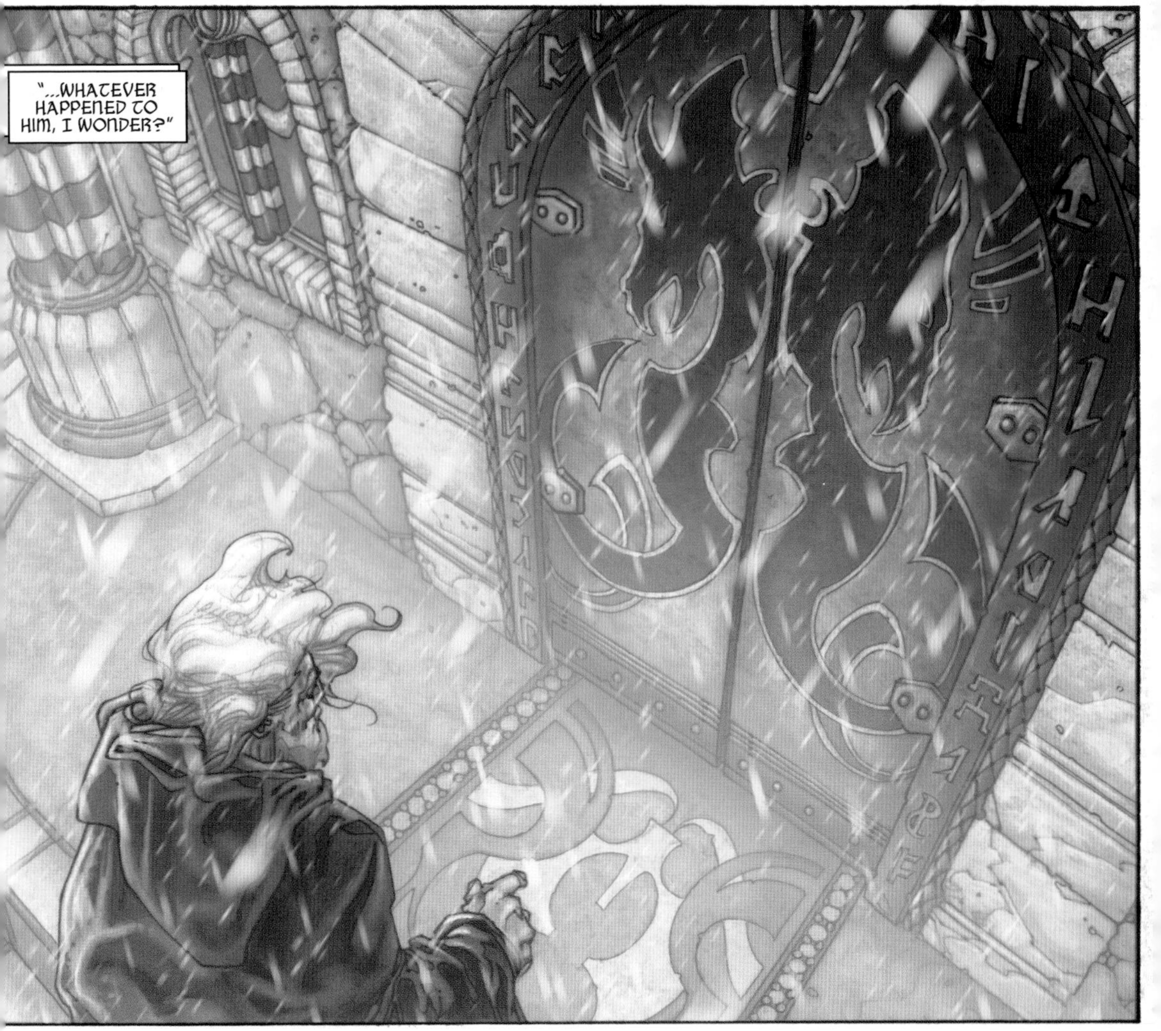
"...WHATEVER HAPPENED TO HIM, I WONDER?"

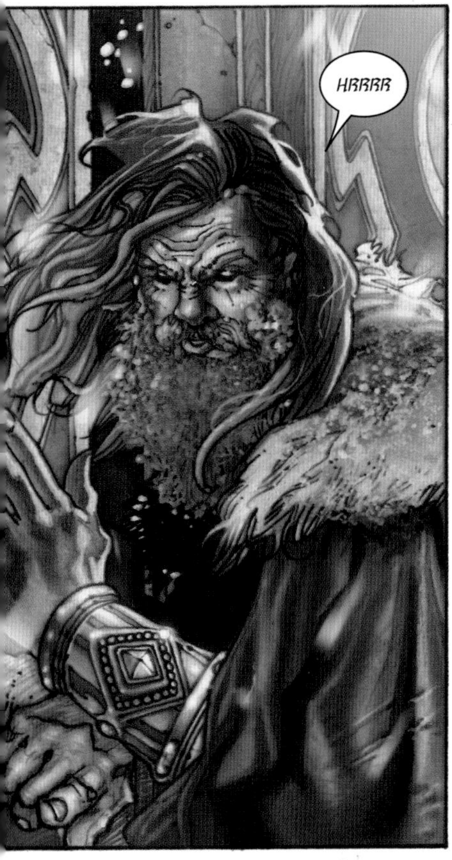
HRRRR

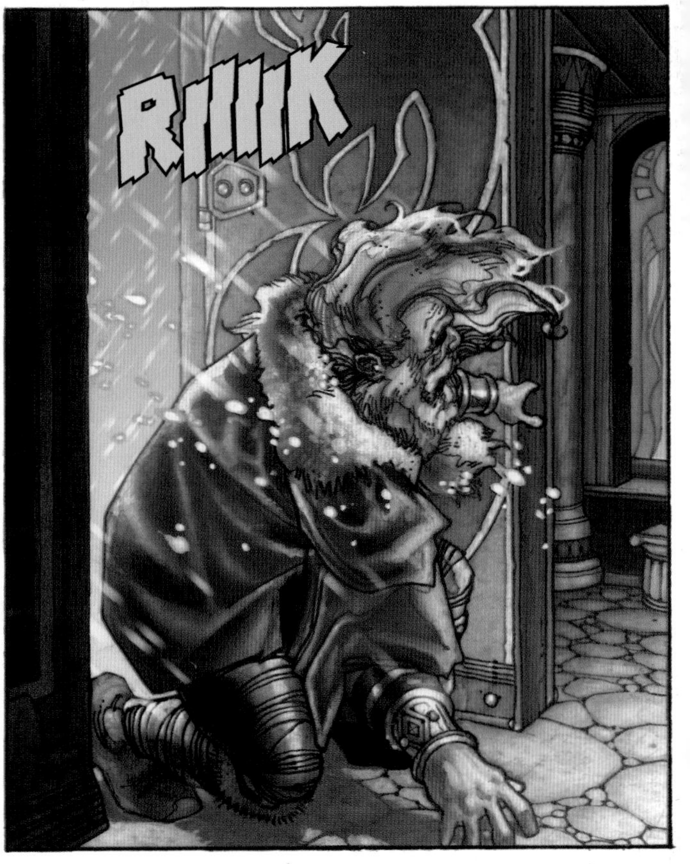
RIIIIK

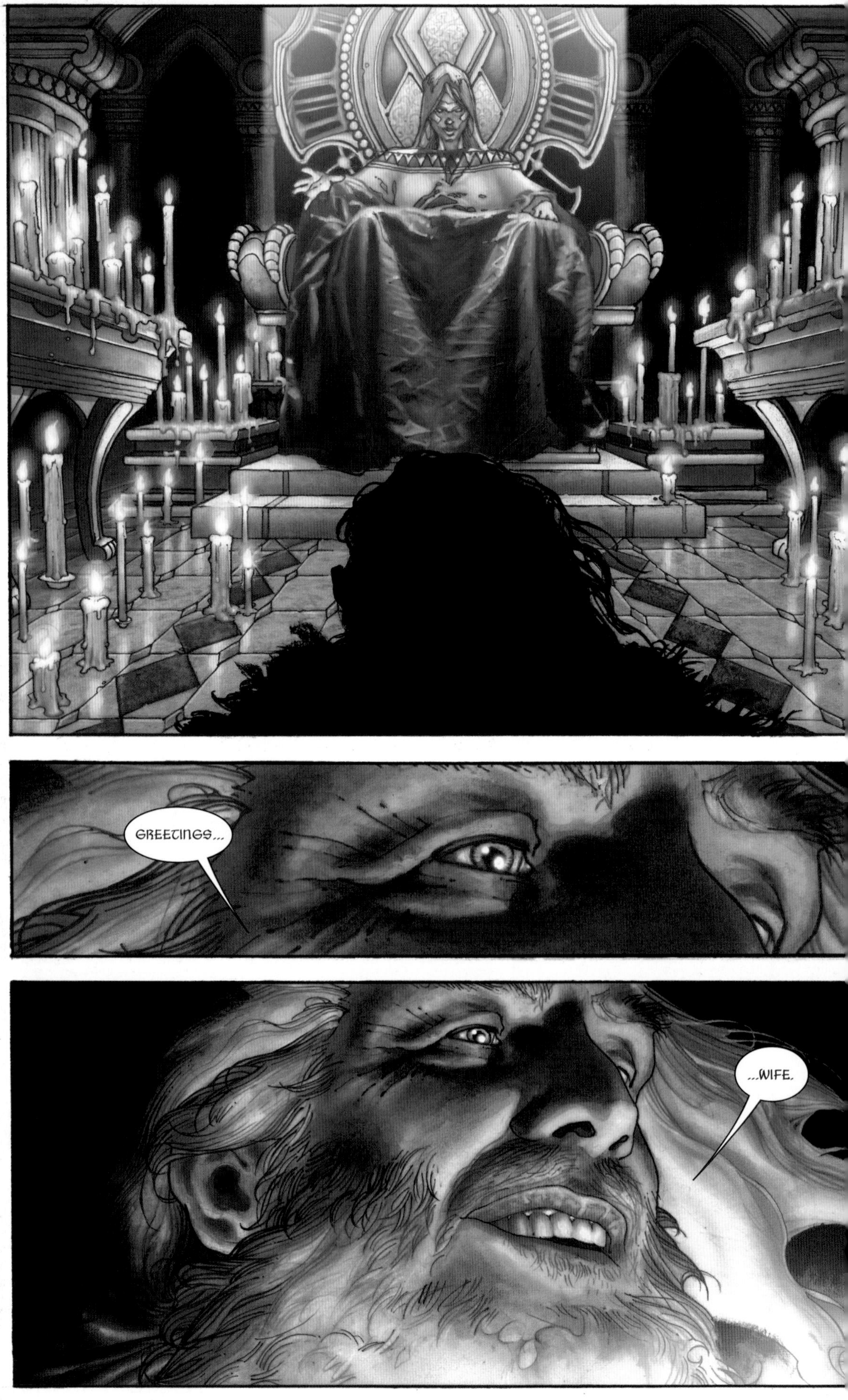
GREETINGS...
...WIFE.

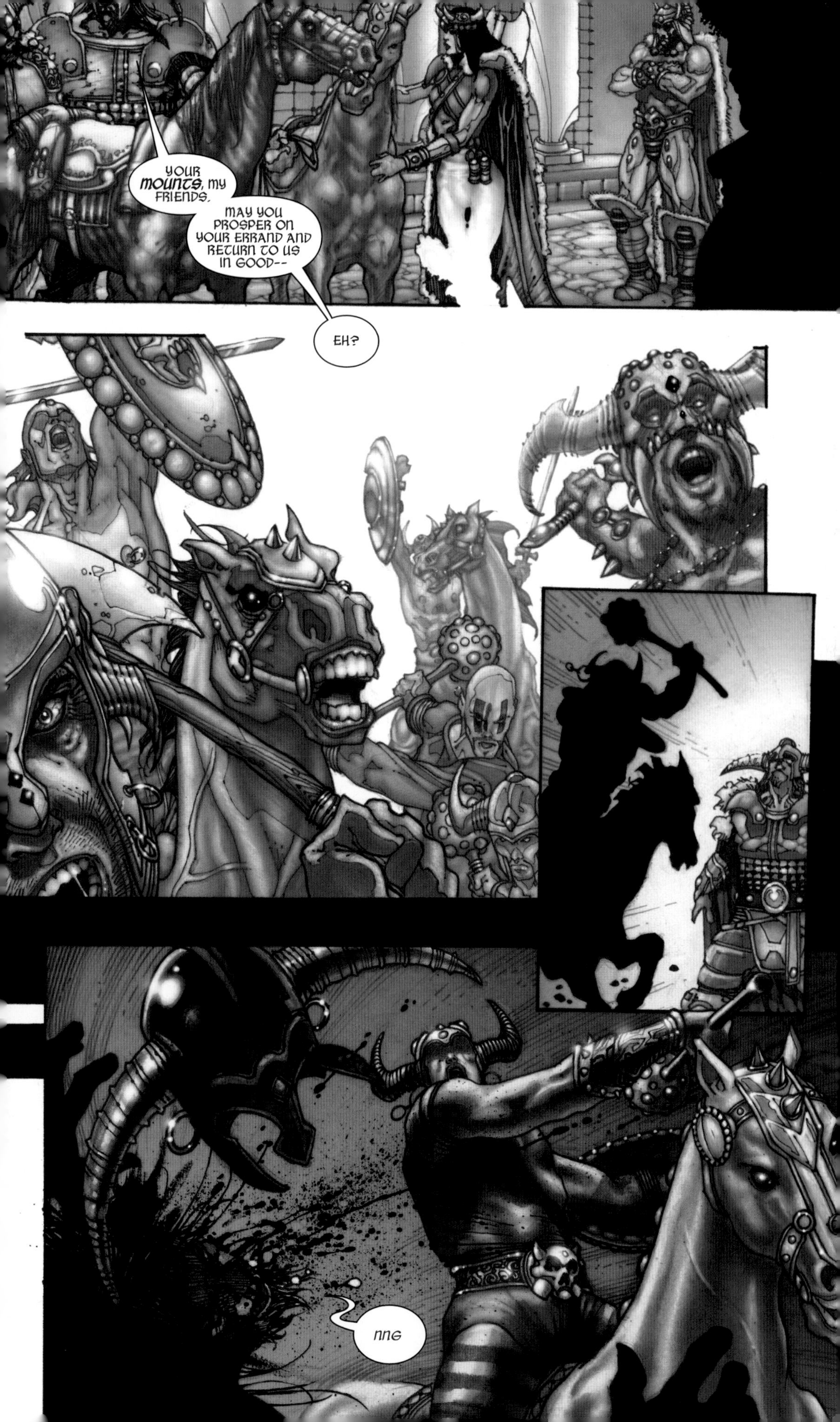
YOUR MOUNTS, MY FRIENDS.
MAY YOU PROSPER ON YOUR ERRAND AND RETURN TO US IN GOOD--
EH?
NNG

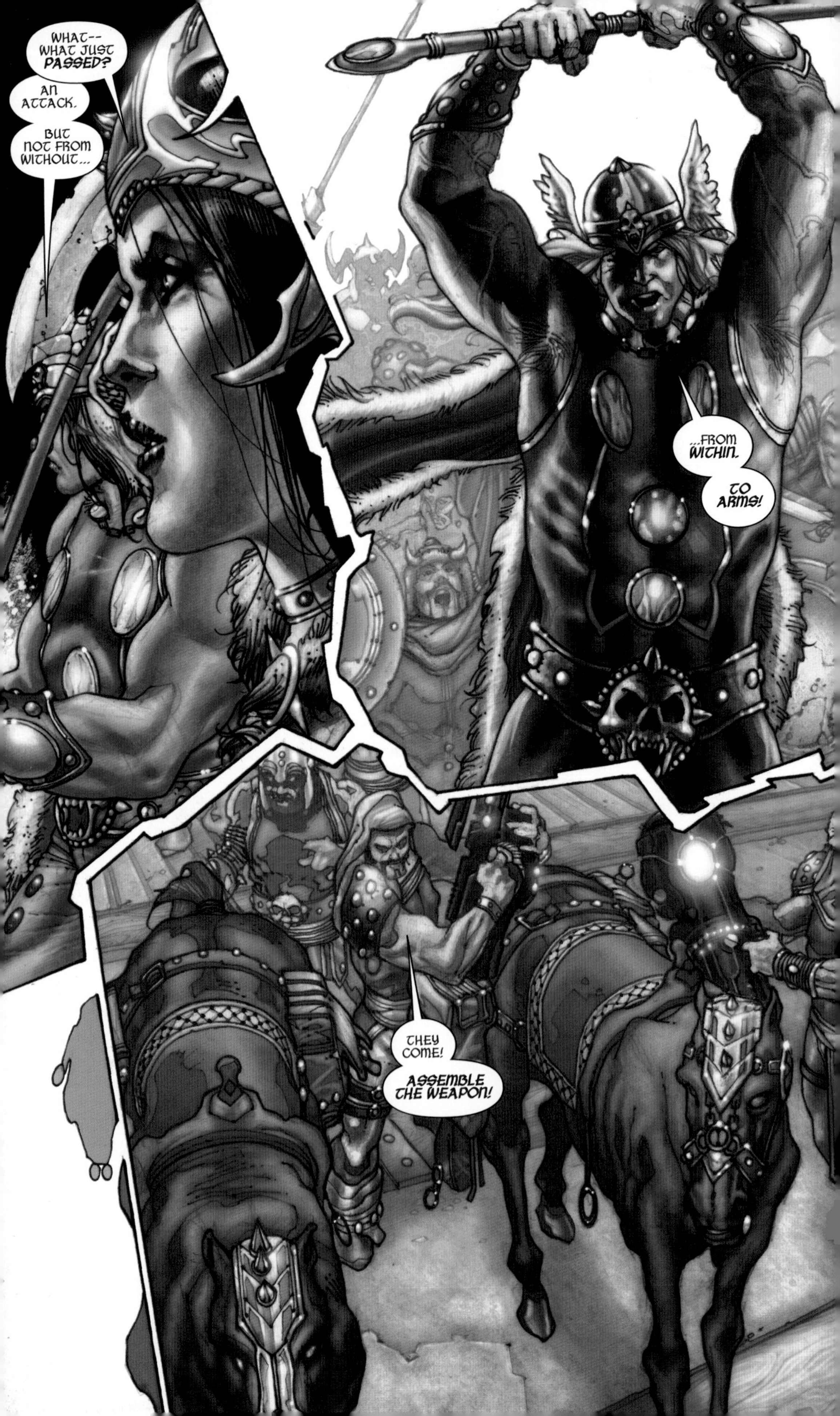
WHAT--
WHAT JUST PASSED?
AN ATTACK.
BUT NOT FROM WITHOUT...
...FROM WITHIN.
TO ARMS!
THEY COME!
ASSEMBLE THE WEAPON!

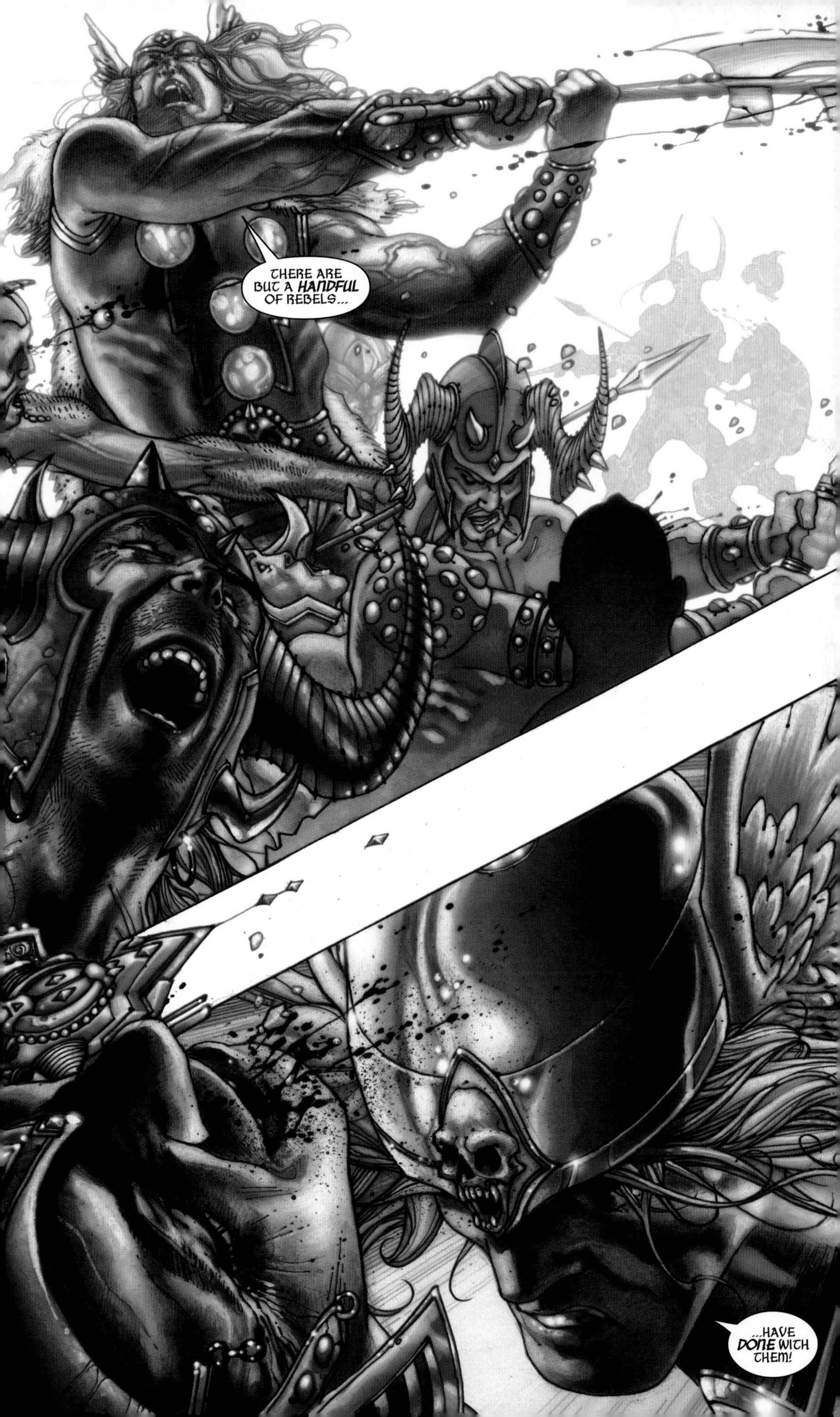
THERE ARE BUT A HANDFUL OF REBELS...
...HAVE DONE WITH THEM!

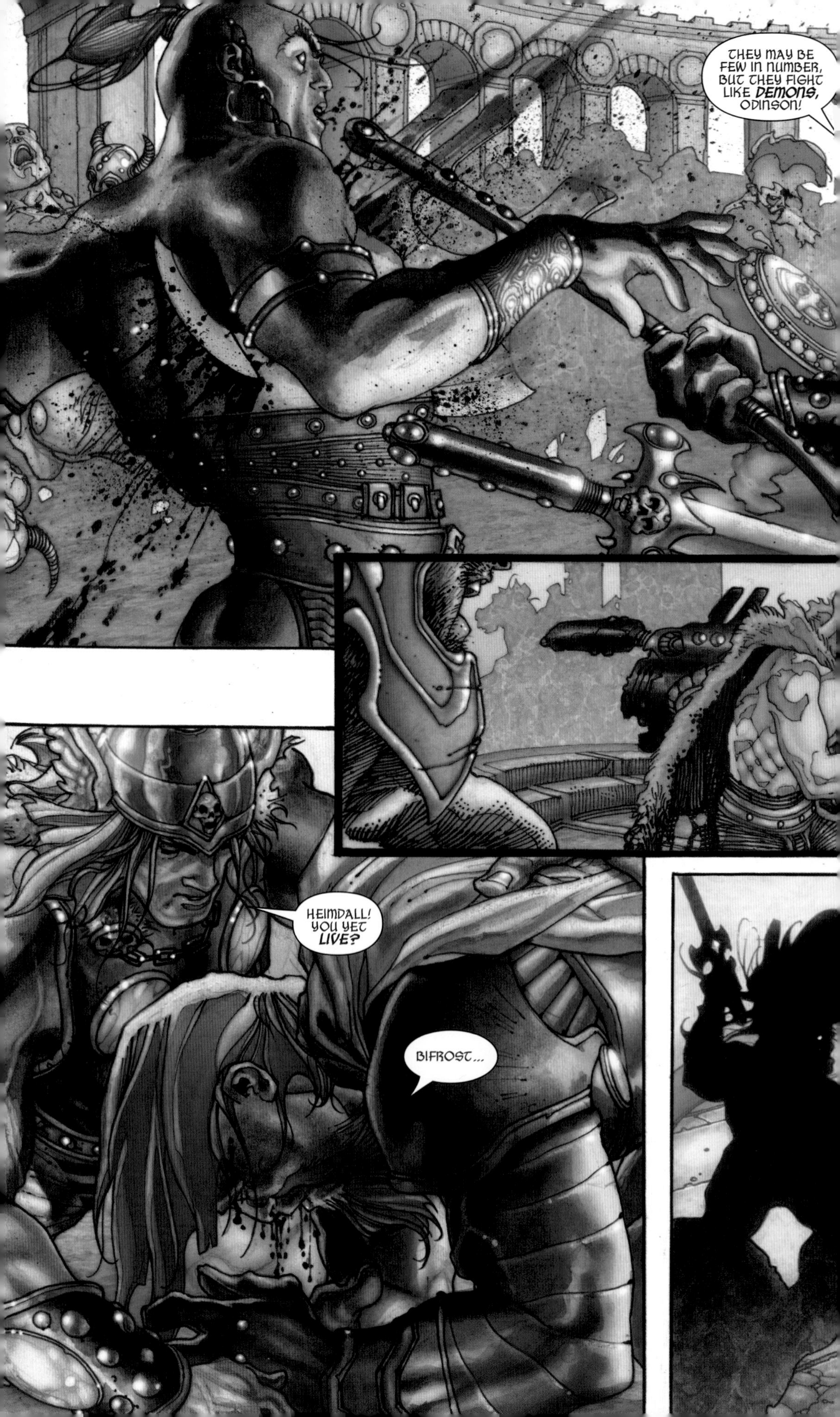
THEY MAY BE FEW IN NUMBER, BUT THEY FIGHT LIKE DEMONS, ODINSON!
HEIMDALL! YOU YET LIVE?
BIFROST...

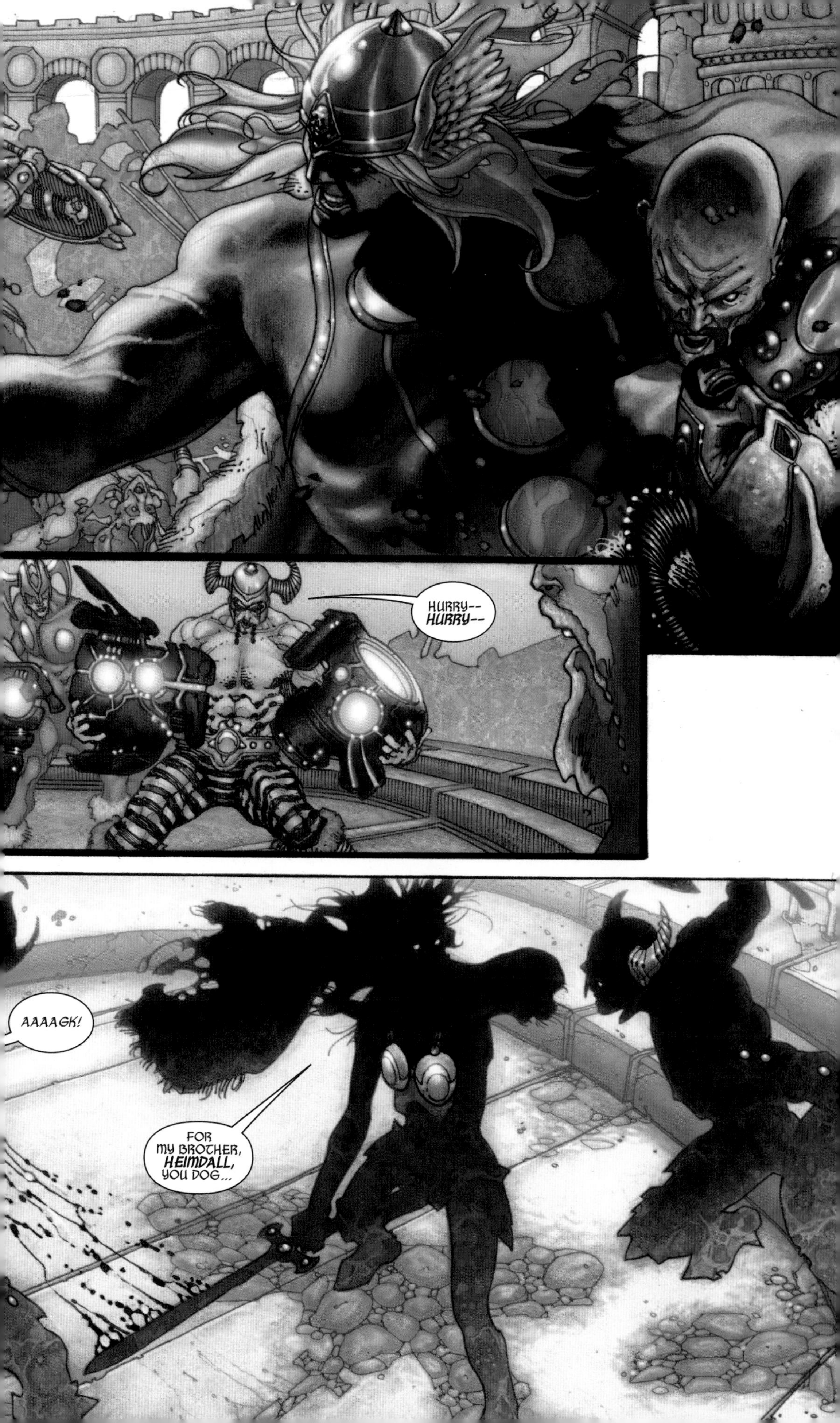
HURRY--
HURRY--
AAAAGK!
FOR MY BROTHER, HEIMDALL, YOU DOG...

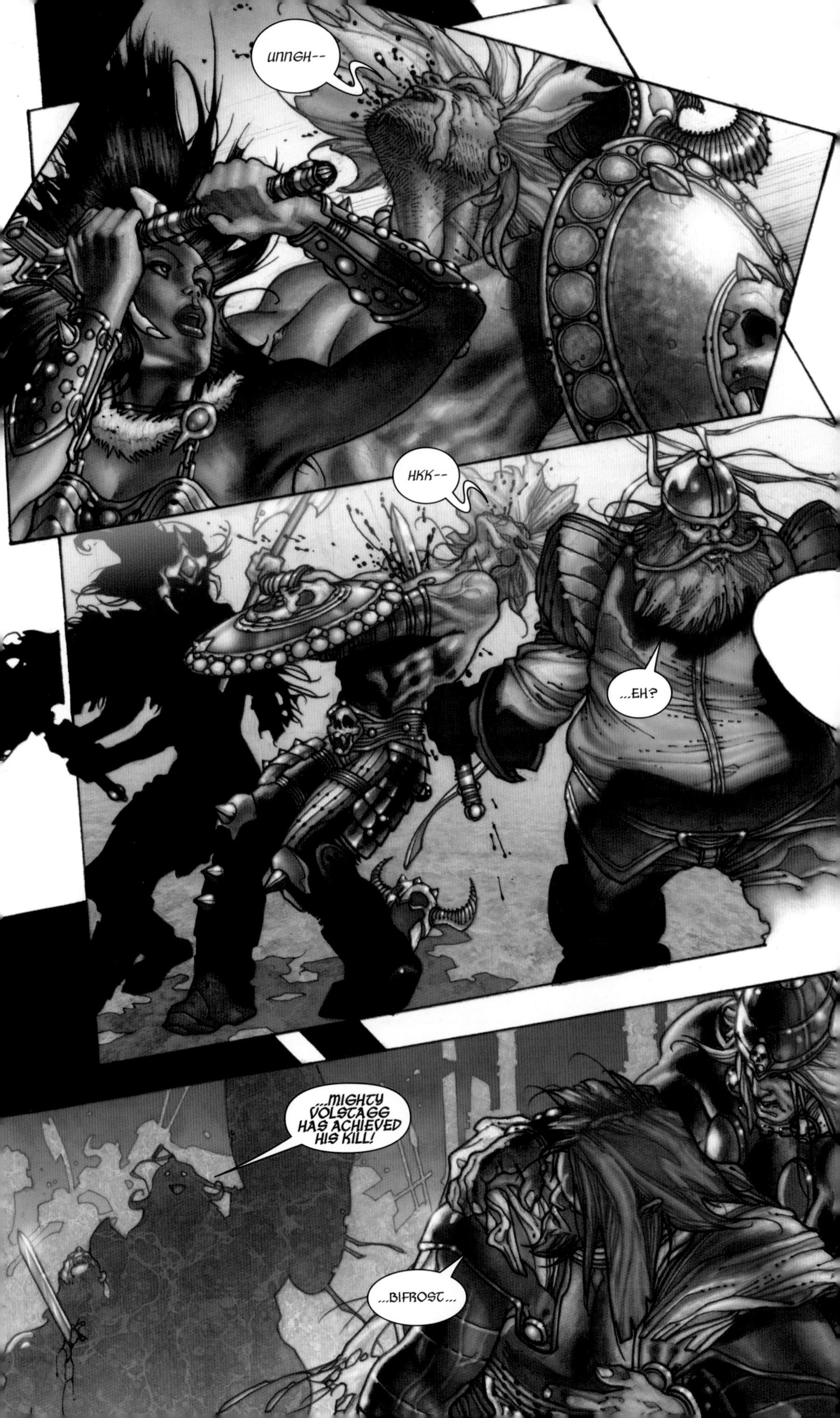
UNNGH--
HKK--
...EH?
...MIGHTY VOLSTAGG HAS ACHIEVED HIS KILL!
...BIFROST...

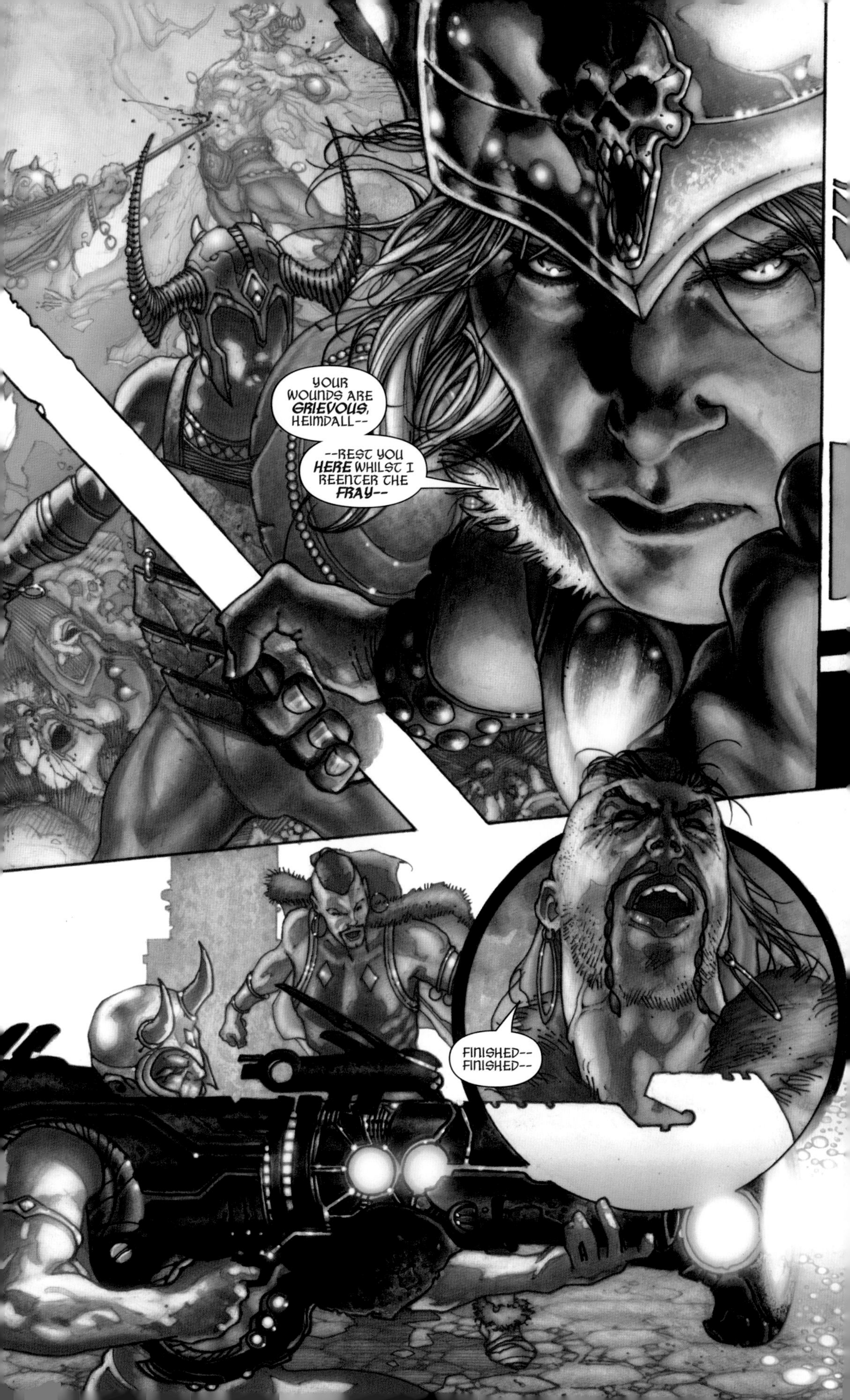
YOUR WOUNDS ARE GRIEVOUS, HEIMDALL--
--REST YOU HERE WHILST I REENTER THE FRAY--
FINISHED-- FINISHED--

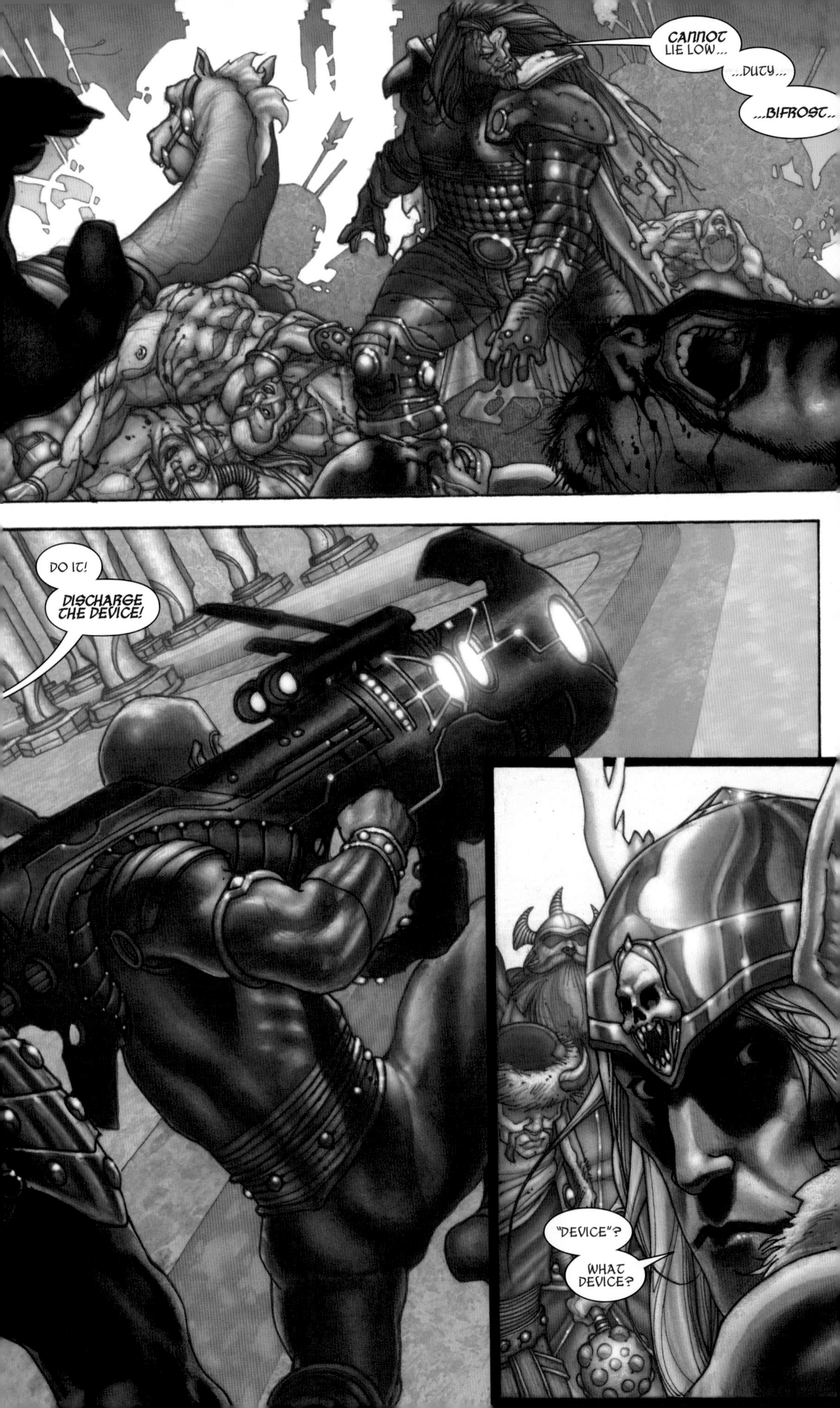
CANNOT LIE LOW...
...DUTY...
...BIFROST...
DO IT!
DISCHARGE THE DEVICE!
"DEVICE"?
WHAT DEVICE?

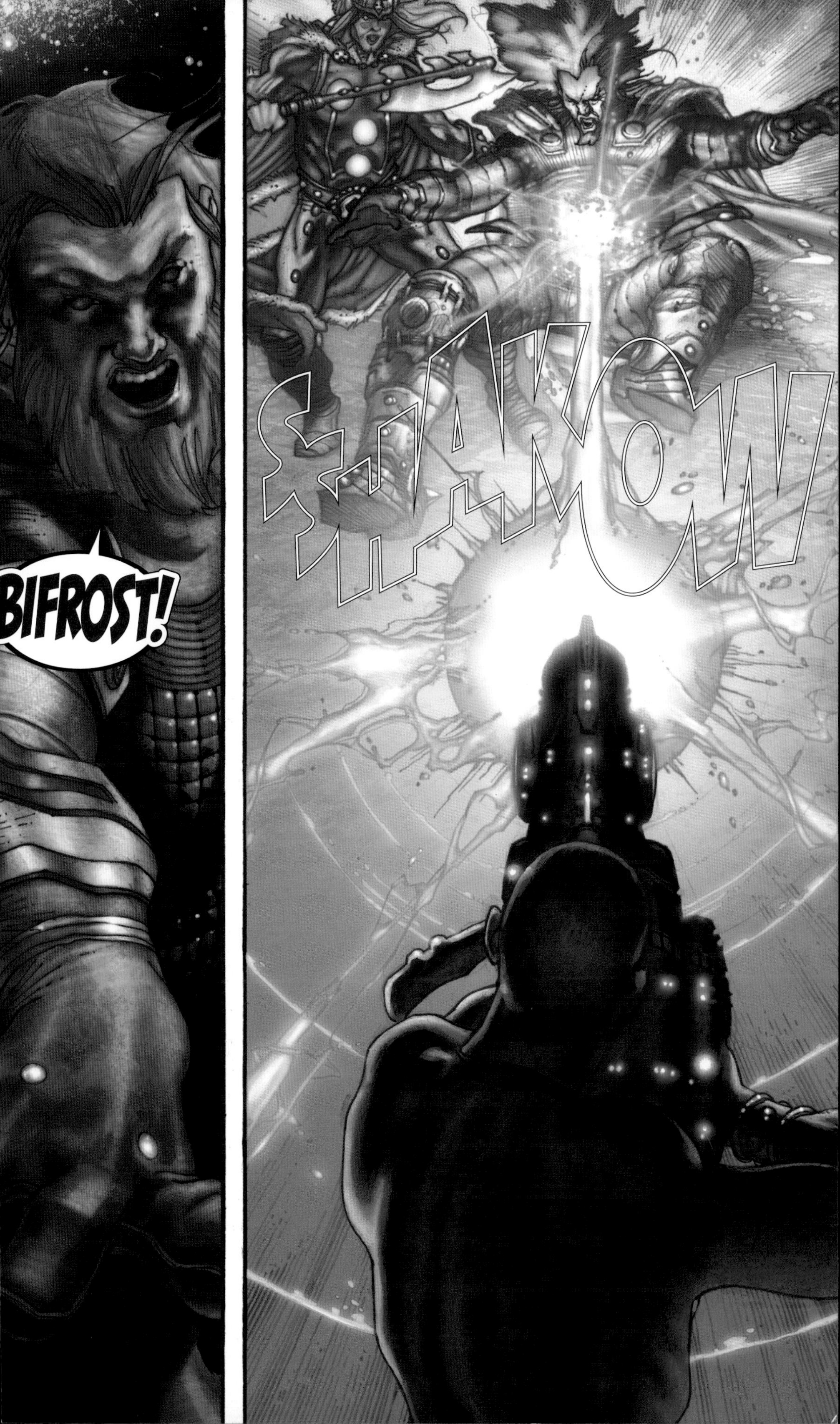
BIFROST!
SHAKOW

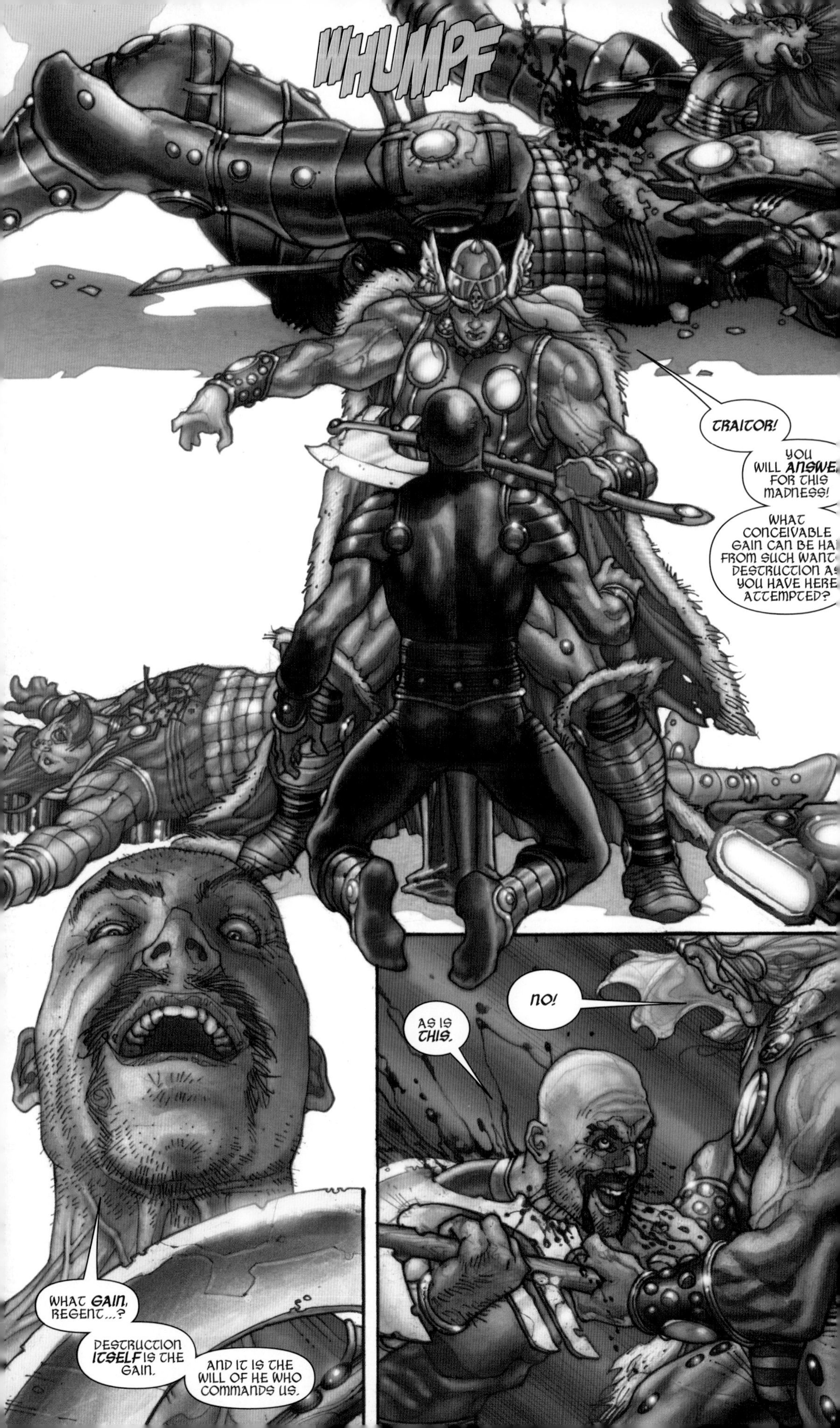
WHUMPF
TRAITOR!
YOU WILL ANSWE FOR THIS MADNESS!
WHAT CONCEIVABLE GAIN CAN BE HA FROM SUCH WANT DESTRUCTION A YOU HAVE HERE ATTEMPTED?
WHAT GAIN, REGENT...?
DESTRUCTION ITSELF IS THE GAIN.
AND IT IS THE WILL OF HE WHO COMMANDS US.
AS IS THIS.
NO!

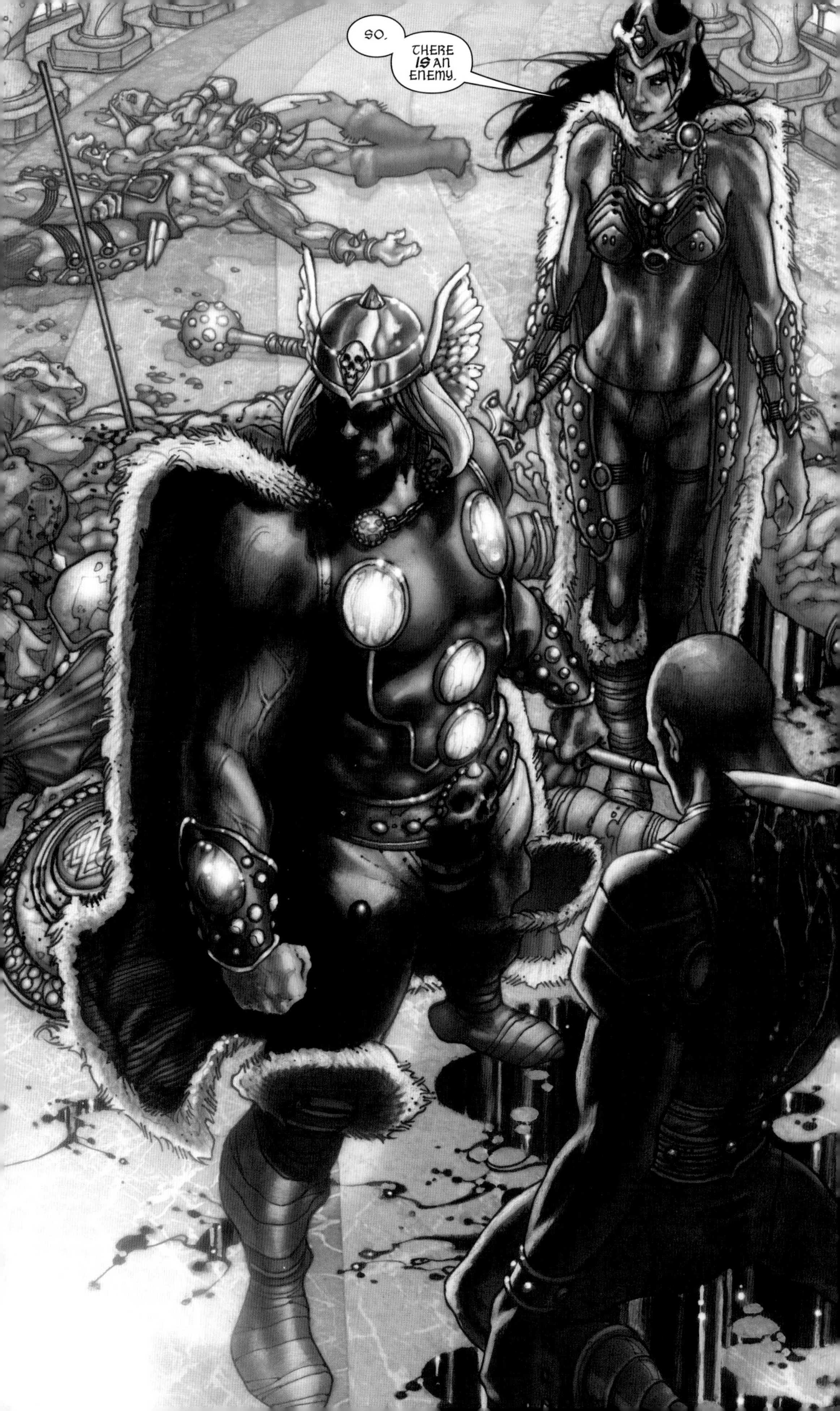
SO.
THERE IS AN ENEMY.

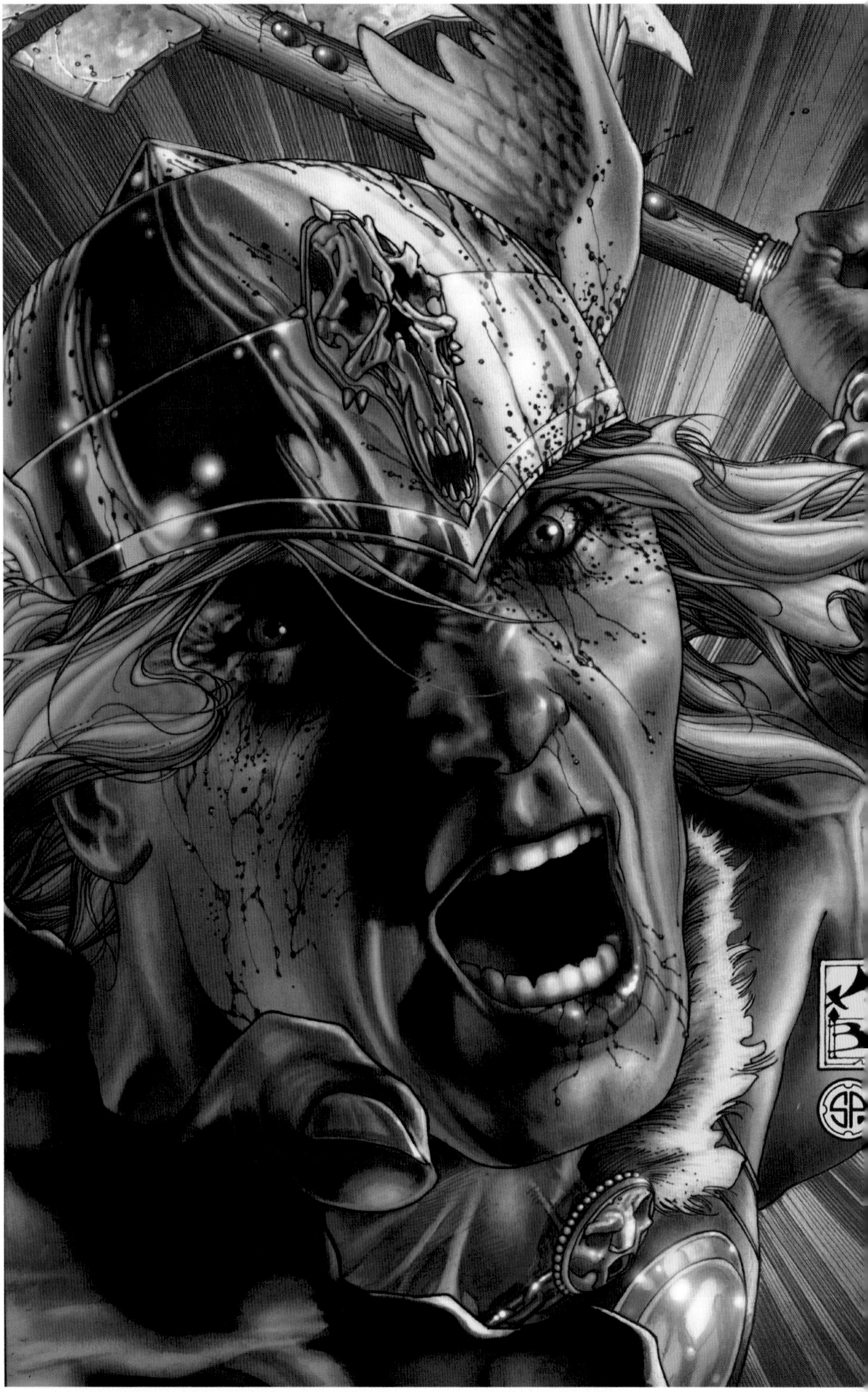

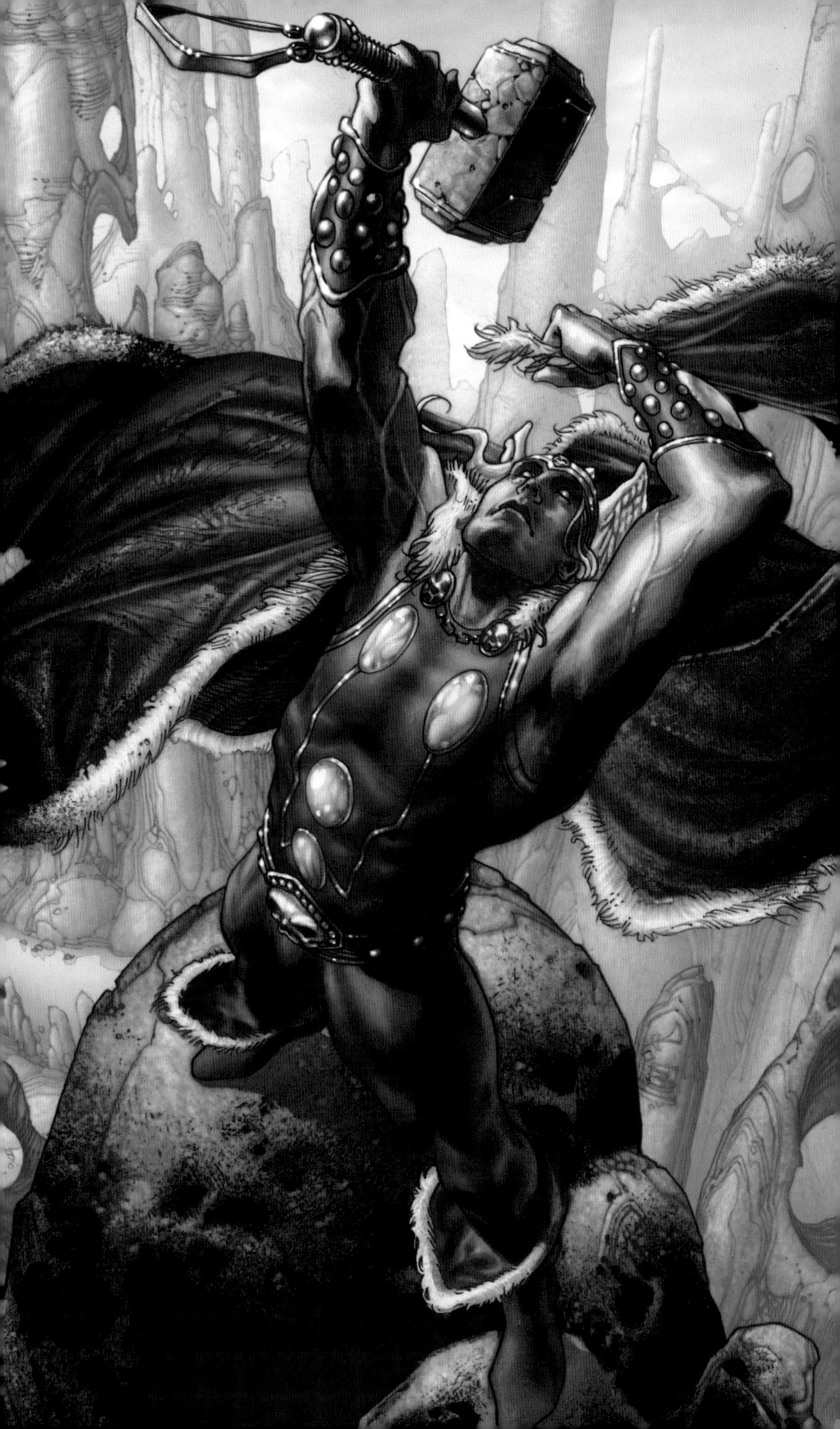

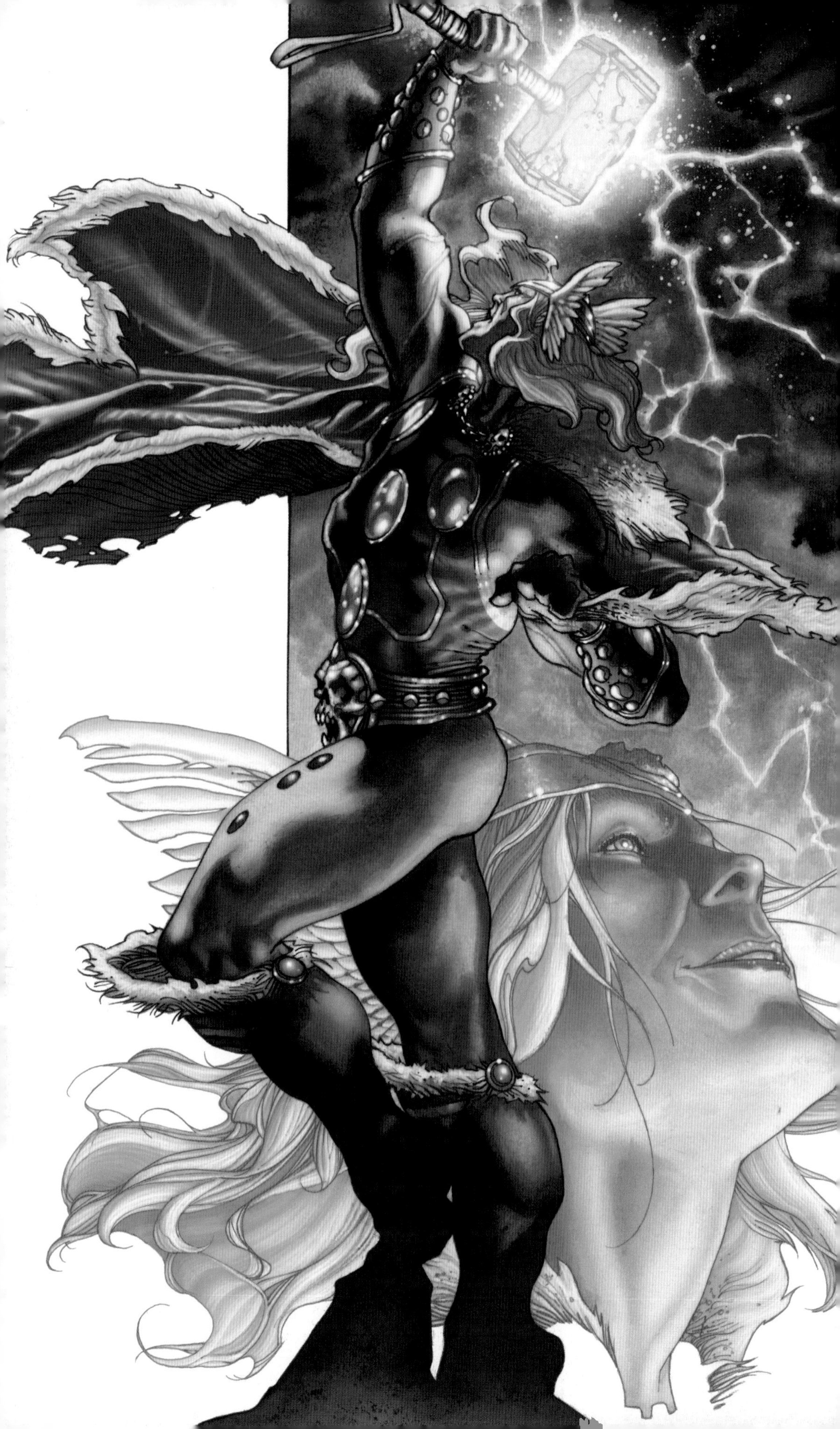

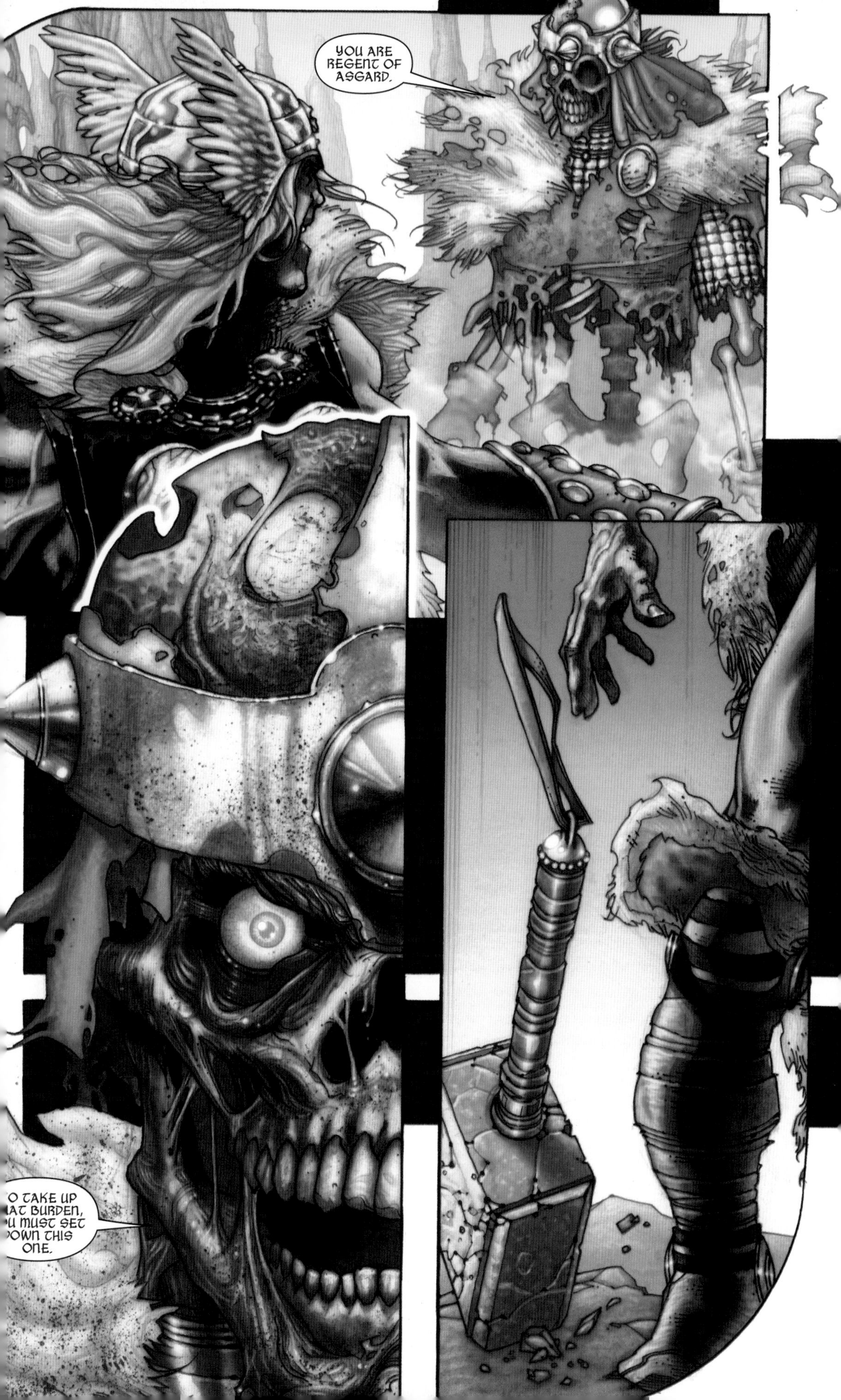
YOU ARE REGENT OF ASGARD.
O TAKE UP AT BURDEN, U MUST SET OWN THIS ONE.

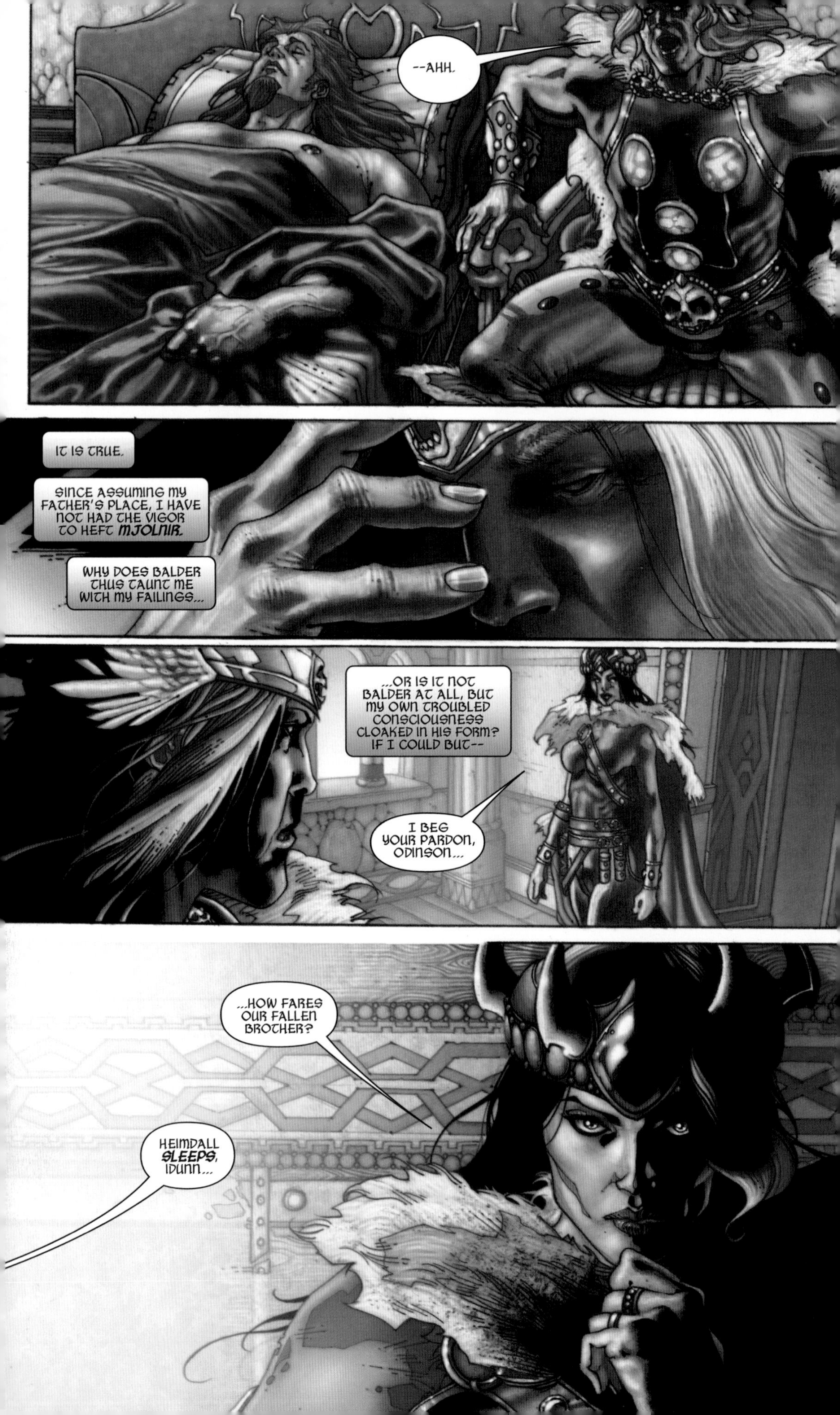
--AHH.
IT IS TRUE.
SINCE ASSUMING MY FATHER'S PLACE, I HAVE NOT HAD THE VIGOR TO HEFT MJOLNIR.
WHY DOES BALDER THUS TAUNT ME WITH MY FAILINGS...
...OR IS IT NOT BALDER AT ALL, BUT MY OWN TROUBLED CONSCIOUSNESS CLOAKED IN HIS FORM? IF I COULD BUT--
I BEG YOUR PARDON, ODINSON...
...HOW FARES OUR FALLEN BROTHER?
HEIMDALL SLEEPS, IDUNN...

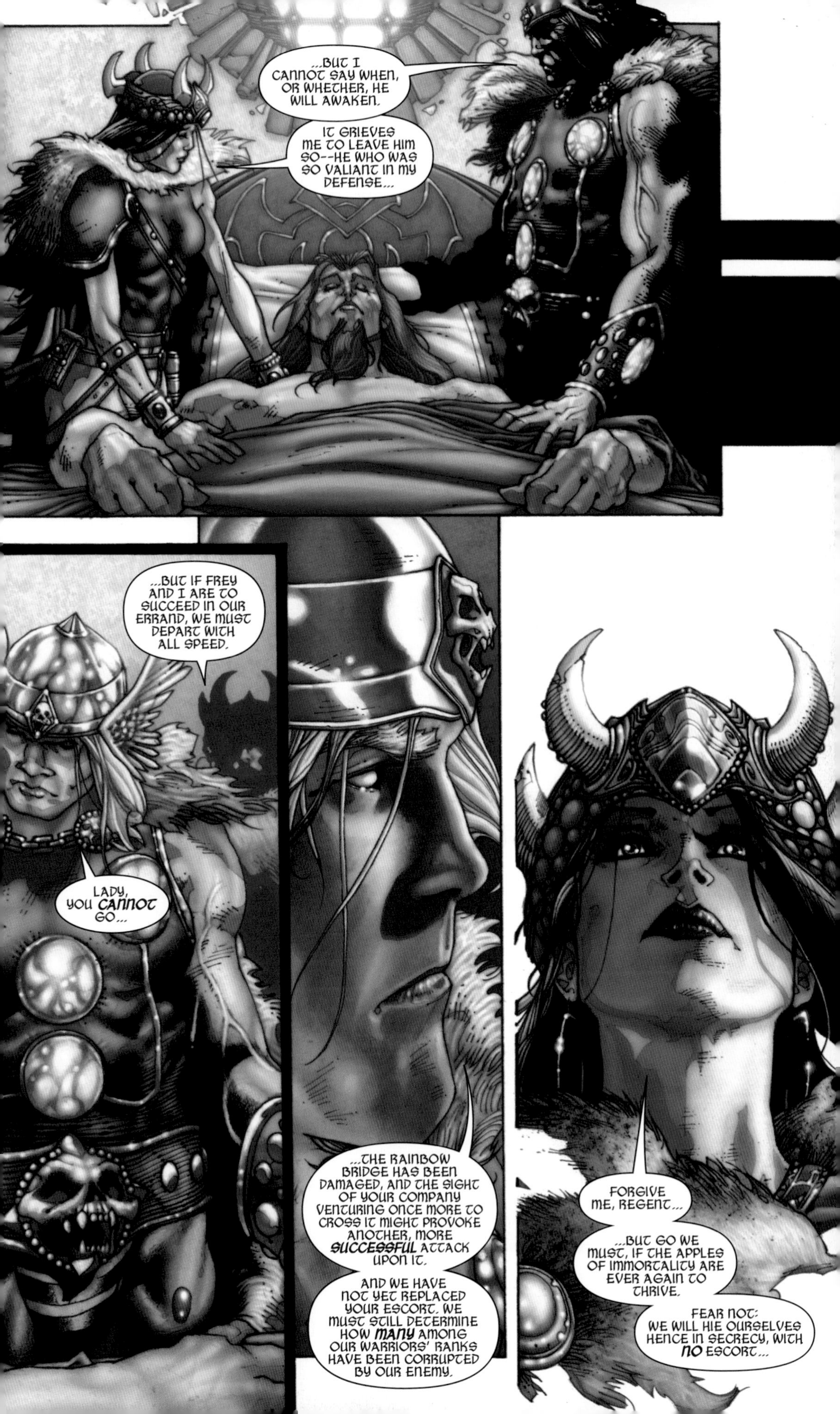

...BUT I CANNOT SAY WHEN, OR WHETHER, HE WILL AWAKEN.
IT GRIEVES ME TO LEAVE HIM SO--HE WHO WAS SO VALIANT IN MY DEFENSE...
...BUT IF FREY AND I ARE TO SUCCEED IN OUR ERRAND, WE MUST DEPART WITH ALL SPEED.
LADY, YOU **CANNOT** GO...
...THE RAINBOW BRIDGE HAS BEEN DAMAGED, AND THE SIGHT OF YOUR COMPANY VENTURING ONCE MORE TO CROSS IT MIGHT PROVOKE ANOTHER, MORE ***SUCCESSFUL*** ATTACK UPON IT.
AND WE HAVE NOT YET REPLACED YOUR ESCORT. WE MUST STILL DETERMINE HOW ***MANY*** AMONG OUR WARRIORS' RANKS HAVE BEEN CORRUPTED BY OUR ENEMY.
FORGIVE ME, REGENT...
...BUT GO WE MUST, IF THE APPLES OF IMMORTALITY ARE EVER AGAIN TO THRIVE.
FEAR NOT: WE WILL HIE OURSELVES HENCE IN SECRECY, WITH **NO** ESCORT...

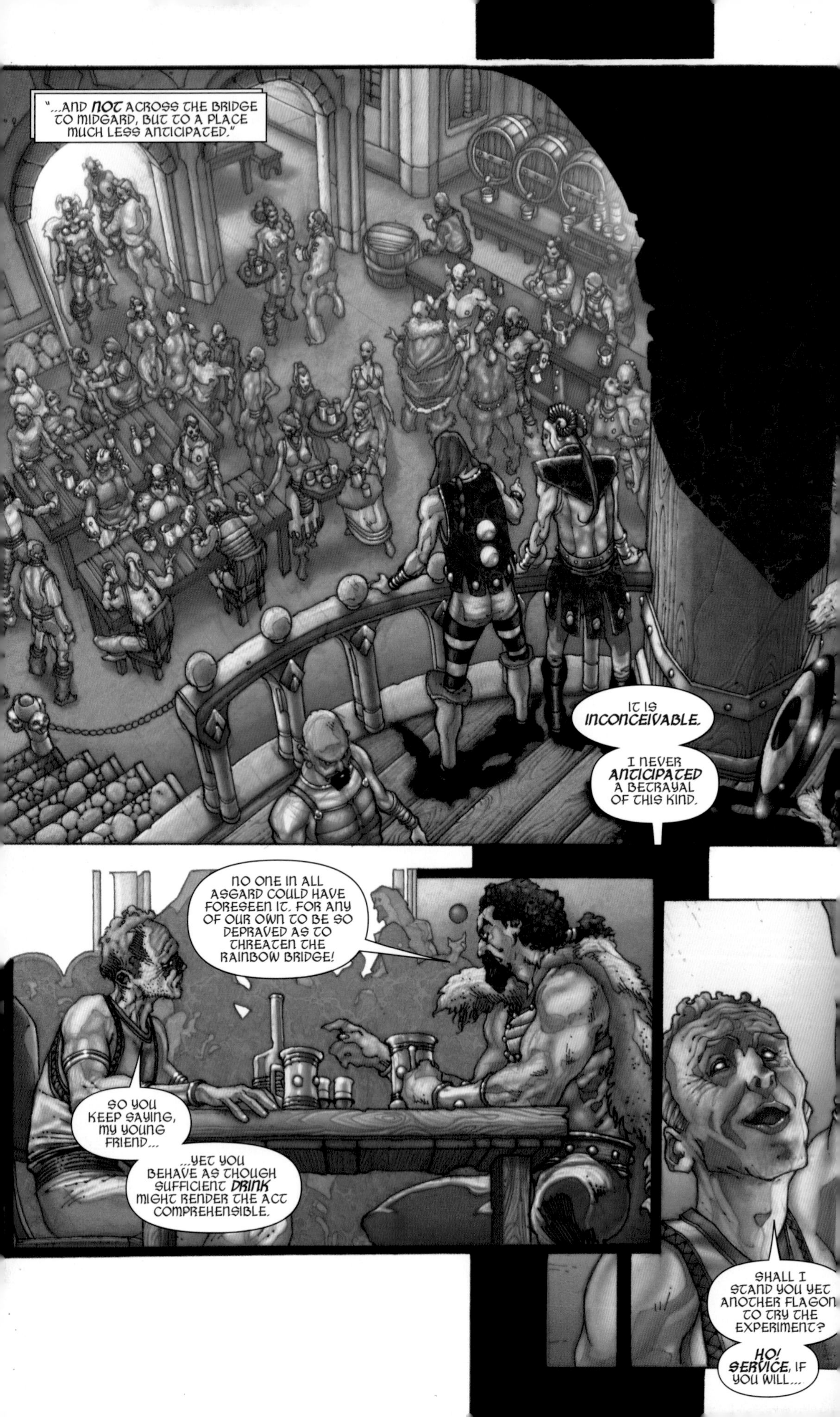
"...AND NOT ACROSS THE BRIDGE TO MIDGARD, BUT TO A PLACE MUCH LESS ANTICIPATED."
IT IS INCONCEIVABLE.
I NEVER ANTICIPATED A BETRAYAL OF THIS KIND.
NO ONE IN ALL ASGARD COULD HAVE FORESEEN IT. FOR ANY OF OUR OWN TO BE SO DEPRAVED AS TO THREATEN THE RAINBOW BRIDGE!
SO YOU KEEP SAYING, MY YOUNG FRIEND...
...YET YOU BEHAVE AS THOUGH SUFFICIENT DRINK MIGHT RENDER THE ACT COMPREHENSIBLE.
SHALL I STAND YOU YET ANOTHER FLAGON TO TRY THE EXPERIMENT?
HO! SERVICE, IF YOU WILL...

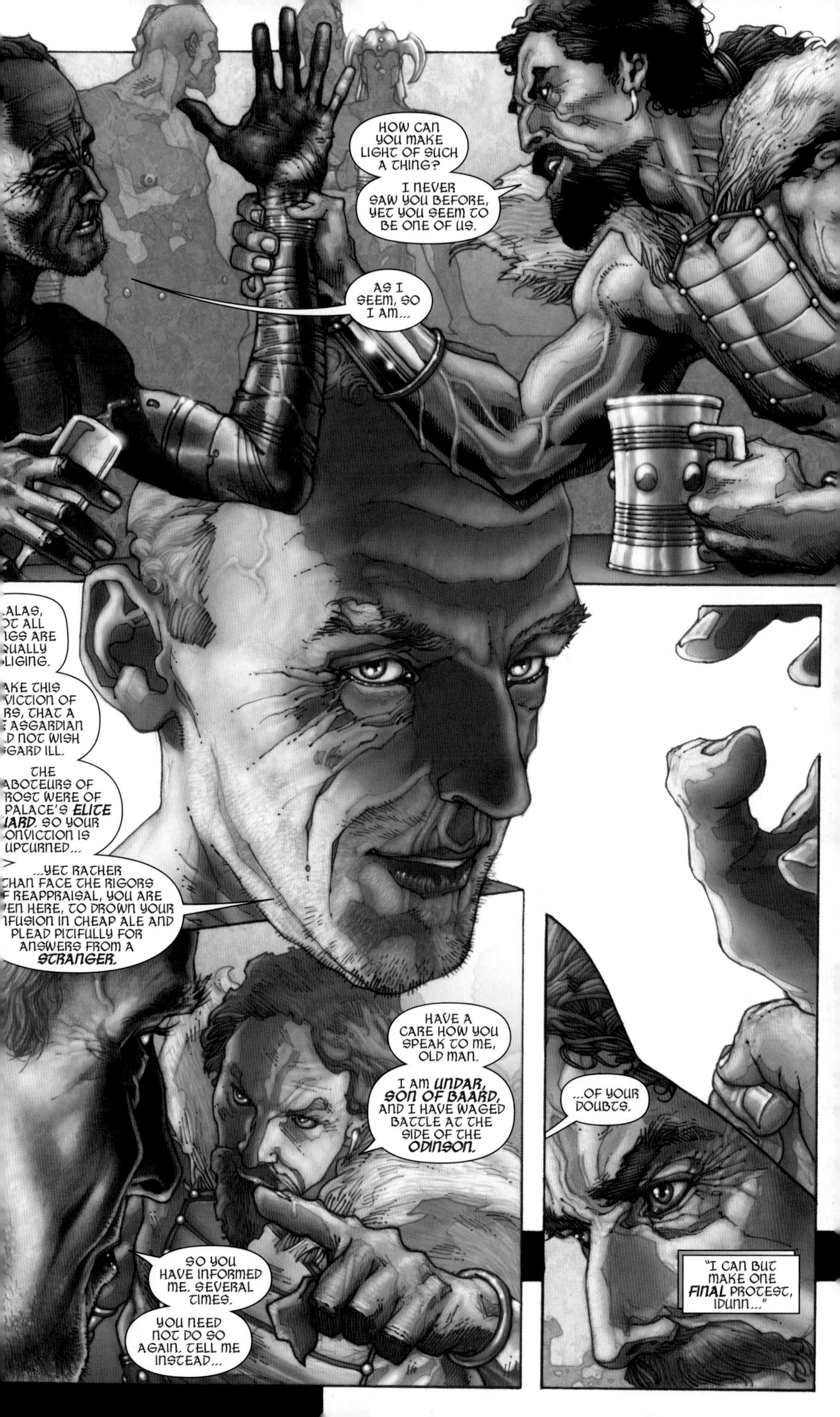

HOW CAN YOU MAKE LIGHT OF SUCH A THING?
I NEVER SAW YOU BEFORE, YET YOU SEEM TO BE ONE OF US.
AS I SEEM, SO I AM...
ALAS, OT ALL IGS ARE QUALLY LIGING.
AKE THIS VICTION OF RS, THAT A ASGARDIAN D NOT WISH SGARD ILL.
THE ABOTEURS OF ROST WERE OF PALACE'S ELITE ARD. SO YOUR ONVICTION IS UPTURNED...
...YET RATHER THAN FACE THE RIGORS F REAPPRAISAL, YOU ARE VEN HERE, TO DROWN YOUR NFUSION IN CHEAP ALE AND PLEAD PITIFULLY FOR ANSWERS FROM A STRANGER.
HAVE A CARE HOW YOU SPEAK TO ME, OLD MAN.
I AM UNDAR, SON OF BAARD, AND I HAVE WAGED BATTLE AT THE SIDE OF THE ODINSON.
SO YOU HAVE INFORMED ME. SEVERAL TIMES.
YOU NEED NOT DO SO AGAIN. TELL ME INSTEAD...
...OF YOUR DOUBTS.
"I CAN BUT MAKE ONE FINAL PROTEST, IDUNN..."

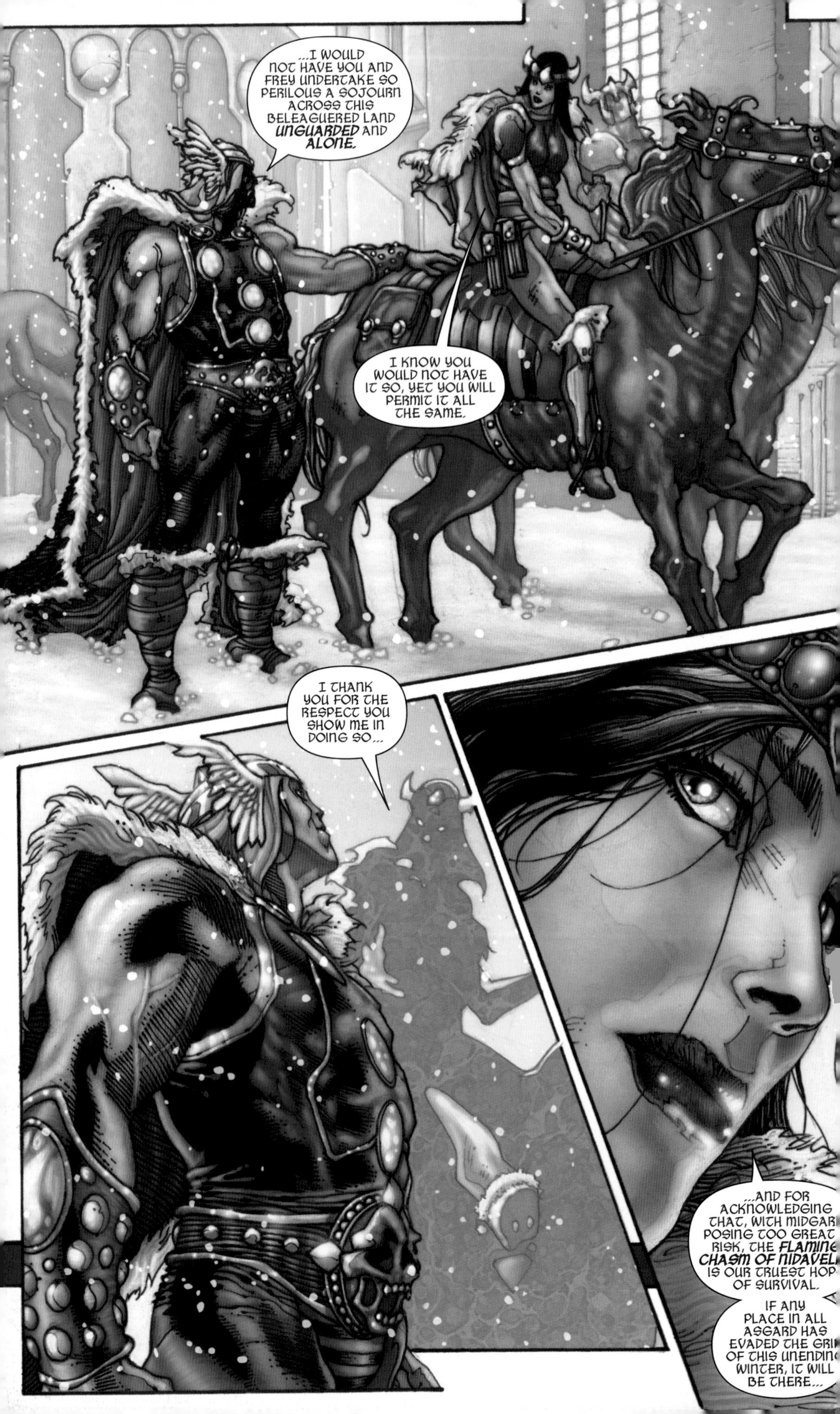
...I WOULD NOT HAVE YOU AND FREY UNDERTAKE SO PERILOUS A SOJOURN ACROSS THIS BELEAGUERED LAND **UNGUARDED** AND **ALONE**.
I KNOW YOU WOULD NOT HAVE IT SO, YET YOU WILL PERMIT IT ALL THE SAME.
I THANK YOU FOR THE RESPECT YOU SHOW ME IN DOING SO...
...AND FOR ACKNOWLEDGING THAT, WITH MIDGAR POSING TOO GREAT RISK, THE **FLAMING CHASM OF NIDAVEL** IS OUR TRUEST HOP OF SURVIVAL.
IF ANY PLACE IN ALL ASGARD HAS EVADED THE GRI OF THIS UNENDIN WINTER, IT WILL BE THERE...

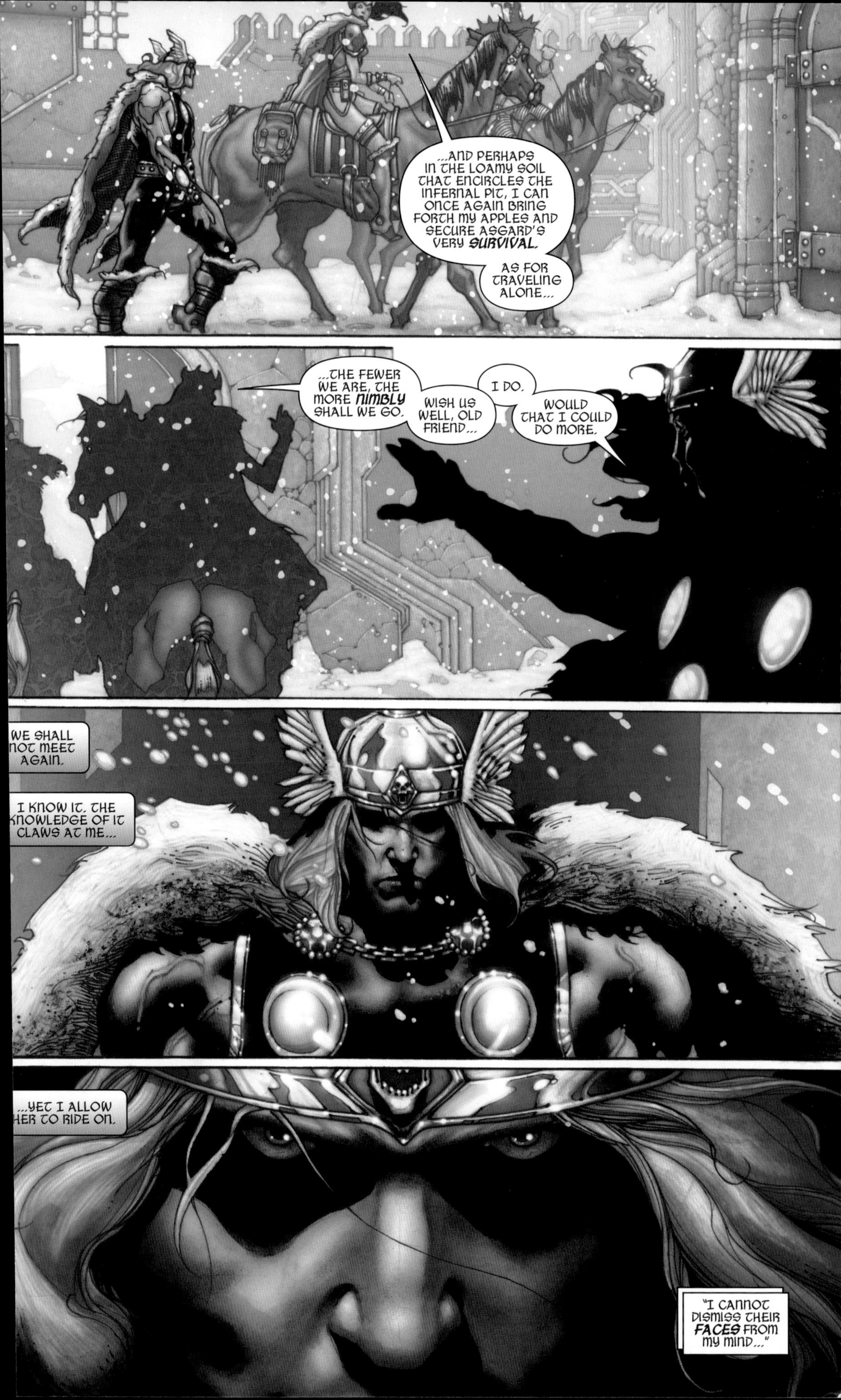
...AND PERHAPS IN THE LOAMY SOIL THAT ENCIRCLES THE INFERNAL PIT, I CAN ONCE AGAIN BRING FORTH MY APPLES AND SECURE ASGARD'S VERY SURVIVAL.
AS FOR TRAVELING ALONE...
...THE FEWER WE ARE, THE MORE NIMBLY SHALL WE GO.
WISH US WELL, OLD FRIEND...
I DO.
WOULD THAT I COULD DO MORE.
WE SHALL NOT MEET AGAIN.
I KNOW IT. THE KNOWLEDGE OF IT CLAWS AT ME...
...YET I ALLOW HER TO RIDE ON.
"I CANNOT DISMISS THEIR FACES FROM MY MIND..."

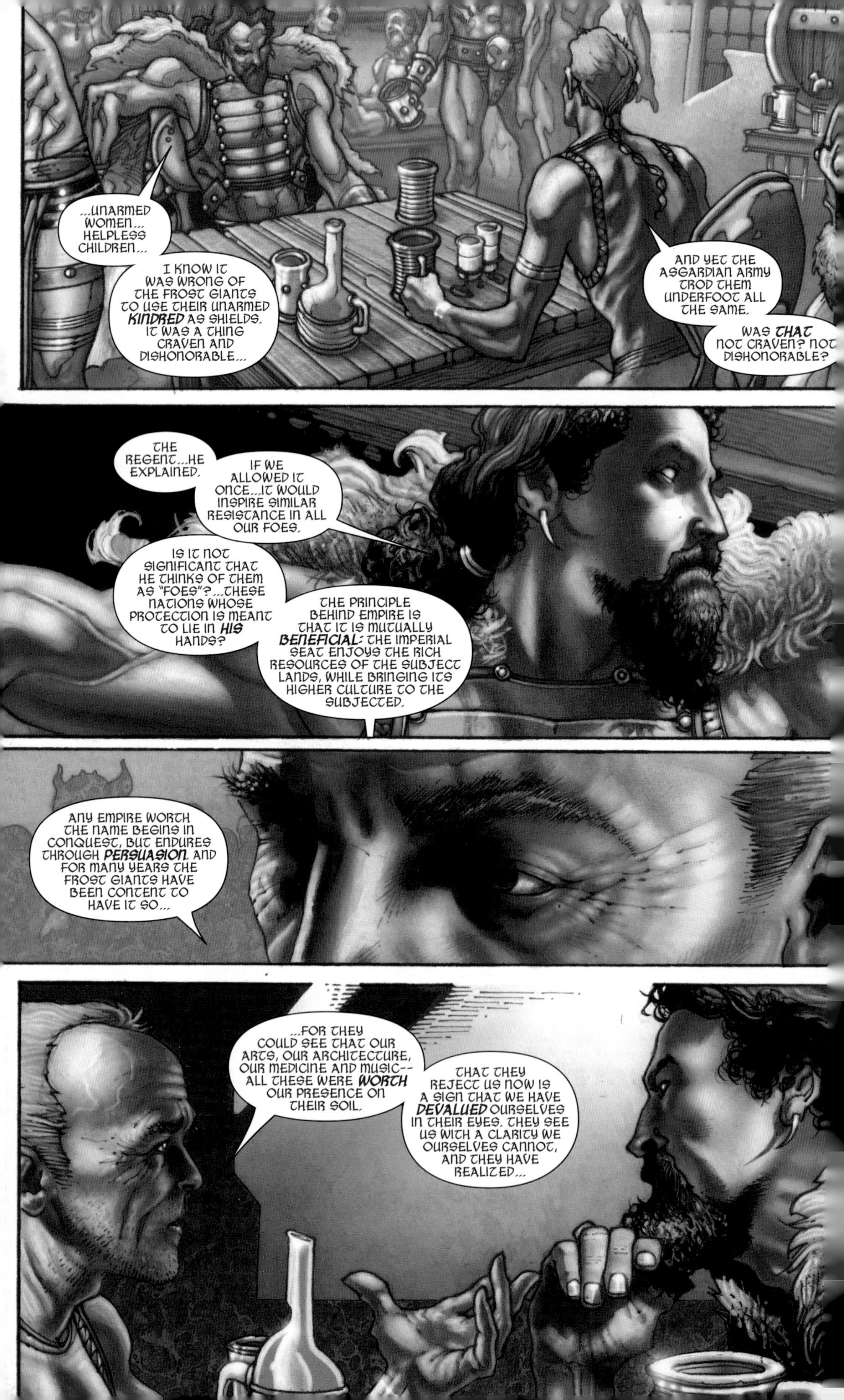
...UNARMED WOMEN... HELPLESS CHILDREN...
I KNOW IT WAS WRONG OF THE FROST GIANTS TO USE THEIR UNARMED KINDRED AS SHIELDS. IT WAS A THING CRAVEN AND DISHONORABLE...
AND YET THE ASGARDIAN ARMY TROD THEM UNDERFOOT ALL THE SAME.
WAS THAT NOT CRAVEN? NOT DISHONORABLE?
THE REGENT...HE EXPLAINED.
IF WE ALLOWED IT ONCE...IT WOULD INSPIRE SIMILAR RESISTANCE IN ALL OUR FOES.
IS IT NOT SIGNIFICANT THAT HE THINKS OF THEM AS "FOES"?...THESE NATIONS WHOSE PROTECTION IS MEANT TO LIE IN HIS HANDS?
THE PRINCIPLE BEHIND EMPIRE IS THAT IT IS MUTUALLY BENEFICIAL: THE IMPERIAL SEAT ENJOYS THE RICH RESOURCES OF THE SUBJECT LANDS, WHILE BRINGING ITS HIGHER CULTURE TO THE SUBJECTED.
ANY EMPIRE WORTH THE NAME BEGINS IN CONQUEST, BUT ENDURES THROUGH PERSUASION. AND FOR MANY YEARS THE FROST GIANTS HAVE BEEN CONTENT TO HAVE IT SO...
...FOR THEY COULD SEE THAT OUR ARTS, OUR ARCHITECTURE, OUR MEDICINE AND MUSIC--ALL THESE WERE WORTH OUR PRESENCE ON THEIR SOIL.
THAT THEY REJECT US NOW IS A SIGN THAT WE HAVE DEVALUED OURSELVES IN THEIR EYES. THEY SEE US WITH A CLARITY WE OURSELVES CANNOT, AND THEY HAVE REALIZED...

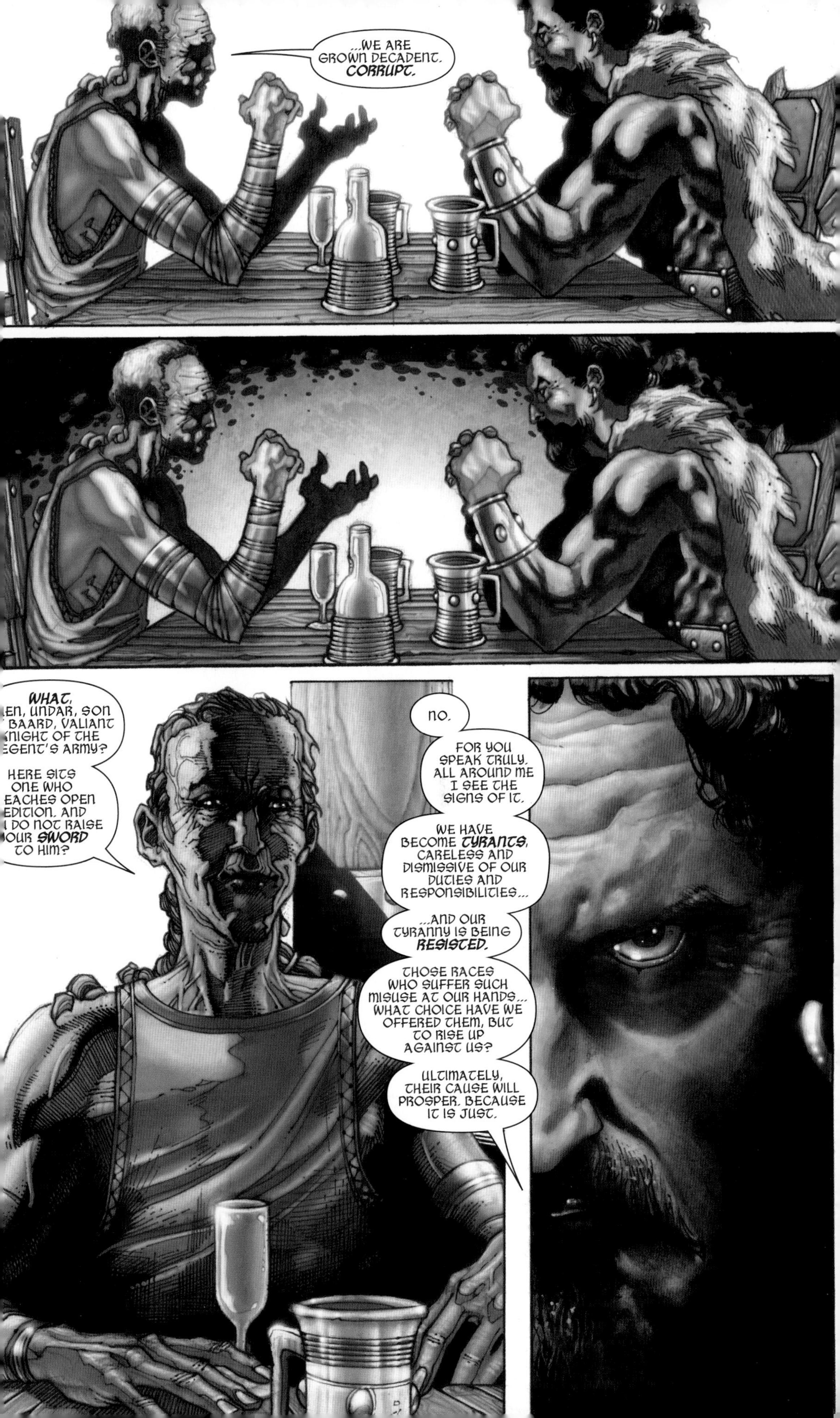
...WE ARE GROWN DECADENT. CORRUPT.
WHAT, EN, UNDAR, SON BAARD, VALIANT KNIGHT OF THE EGENT'S ARMY?
HERE SITS ONE WHO EACHES OPEN EDITION. AND DO NOT RAISE OUR SWORD TO HIM?
NO.
FOR YOU SPEAK TRULY. ALL AROUND ME I SEE THE SIGNS OF IT.
WE HAVE BECOME TYRANTS, CARELESS AND DISMISSIVE OF OUR DUTIES AND RESPONSIBILITIES...
...AND OUR TYRANNY IS BEING RESISTED.
THOSE RACES WHO SUFFER SUCH MISUSE AT OUR HANDS... WHAT CHOICE HAVE WE OFFERED THEM, BUT TO RISE UP AGAINST US?
ULTIMATELY, THEIR CAUSE WILL PROSPER. BECAUSE IT IS JUST.

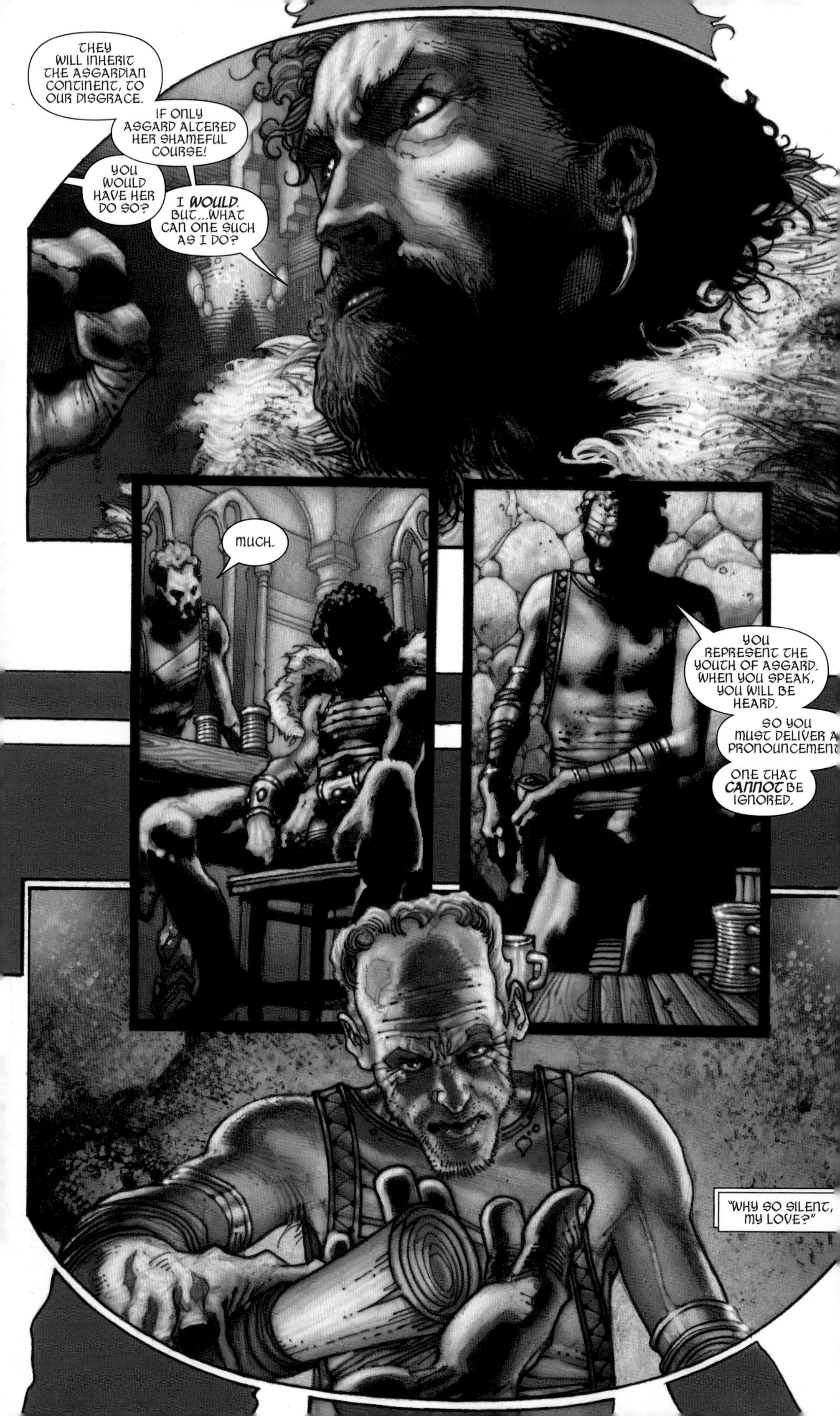
THEY WILL INHERIT THE ASGARDIAN CONTINENT, TO OUR DISGRACE.
IF ONLY ASGARD ALTERED HER SHAMEFUL COURSE!
YOU WOULD HAVE HER DO SO?
I **WOULD**. BUT...WHAT CAN ONE SUCH AS I DO?
MUCH.
YOU REPRESENT THE YOUTH OF ASGARD. WHEN YOU SPEAK, YOU WILL BE HEARD.
SO YOU MUST DELIVER A PRONOUNCEMENT.
ONE THAT **CANNOT** BE IGNORED.
"WHY SO SILENT, MY LOVE?"

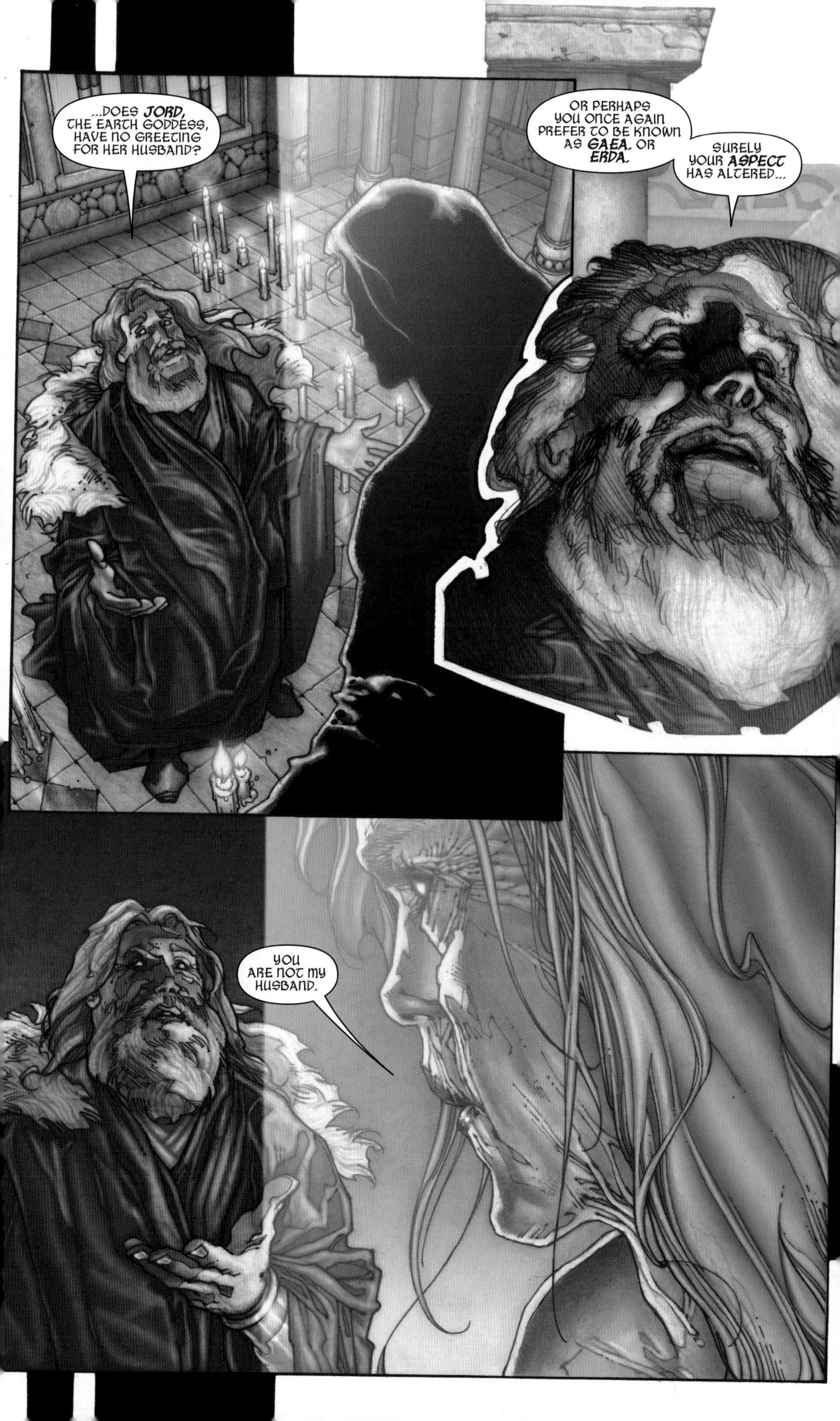
...DOES JORD, THE EARTH GODDESS, HAVE NO GREETING FOR HER HUSBAND?
OR PERHAPS YOU ONCE AGAIN PREFER TO BE KNOWN AS GAEA, OR ERDA.
SURELY YOUR ASPECT HAS ALTERED...
YOU ARE NOT MY HUSBAND.

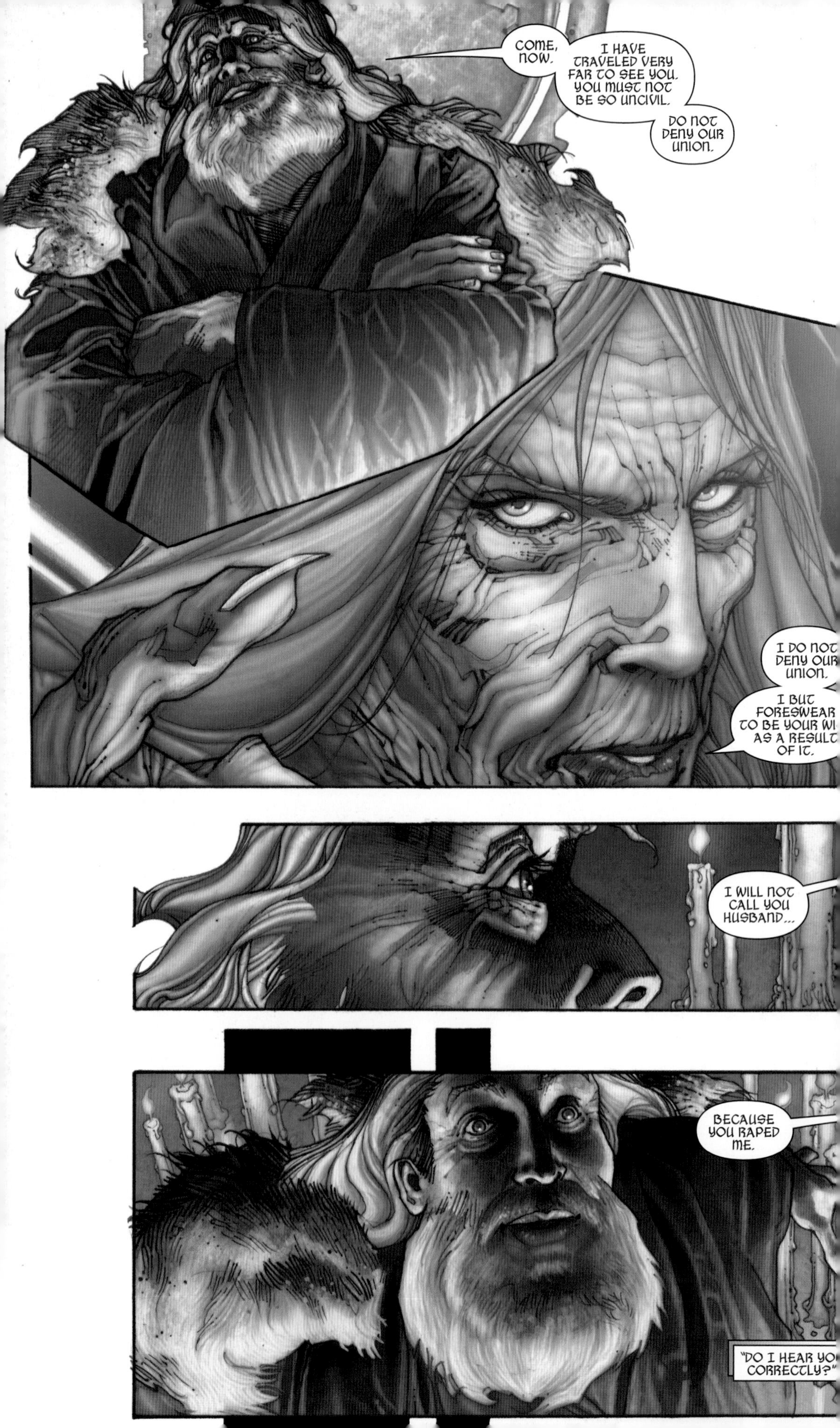
COME, NOW.
I HAVE TRAVELED VERY FAR TO SEE YOU. YOU MUST NOT BE SO UNCIVIL.
DO NOT DENY OUR UNION.
I DO NOT DENY OUR UNION.
I BUT FORESWEAR TO BE YOUR WI AS A RESULT OF IT.
I WILL NOT CALL YOU HUSBAND...
BECAUSE YOU RAPED ME.
"DO I HEAR YO CORRECTLY?"

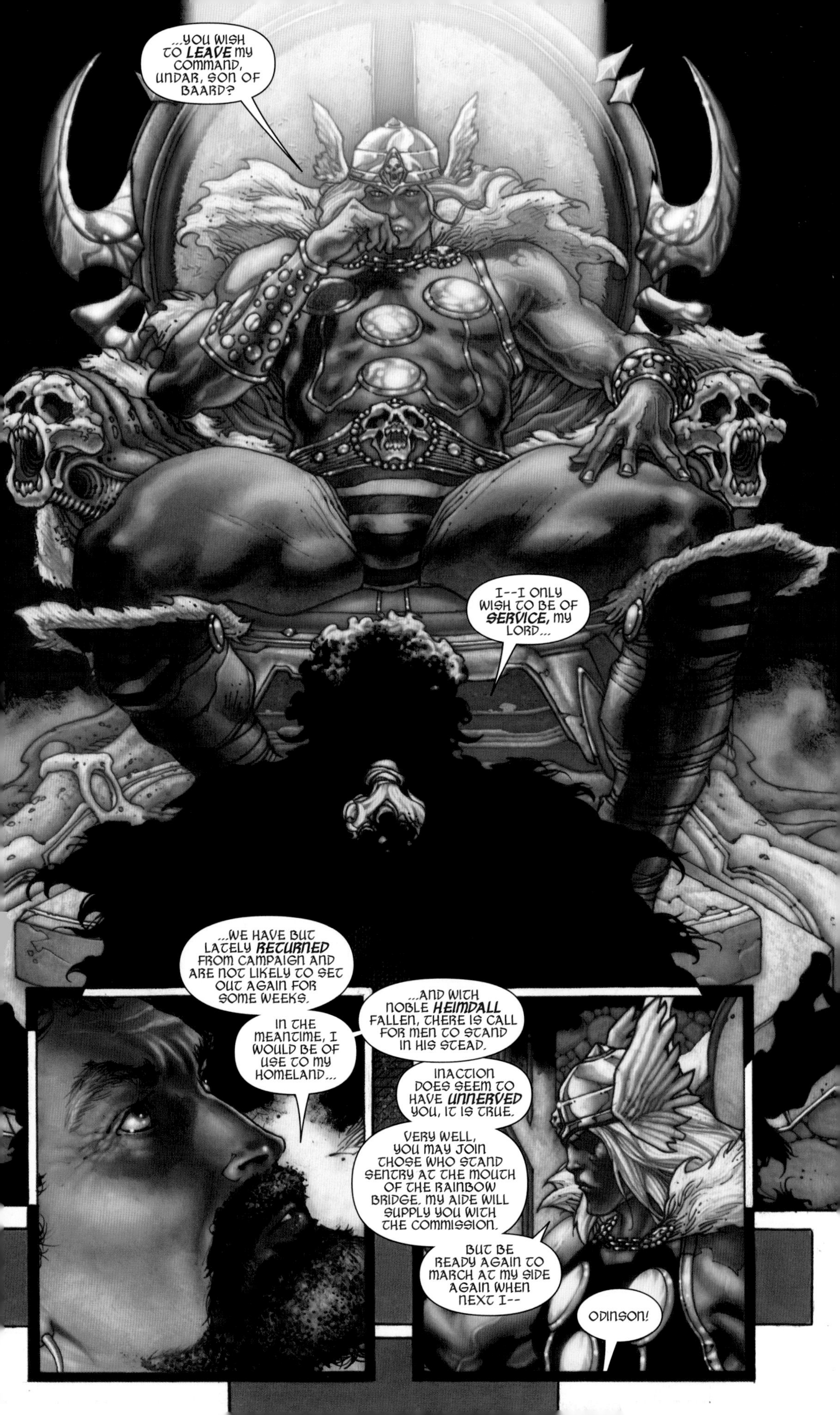

...YOU WISH TO LEAVE MY COMMAND, UNDAR, SON OF BAARD?
I--I ONLY WISH TO BE OF SERVICE, MY LORD...
...WE HAVE BUT LATELY RETURNED FROM CAMPAIGN AND ARE NOT LIKELY TO SET OUT AGAIN FOR SOME WEEKS.
IN THE MEANTIME, I WOULD BE OF USE TO MY HOMELAND...
...AND WITH NOBLE HEIMDALL FALLEN, THERE IS CALL FOR MEN TO STAND IN HIS STEAD.
INACTION DOES SEEM TO HAVE UNNERVED YOU, IT IS TRUE.
VERY WELL, YOU MAY JOIN THOSE WHO STAND SENTRY AT THE MOUTH OF THE RAINBOW BRIDGE. MY AIDE WILL SUPPLY YOU WITH THE COMMISSION.
BUT BE READY AGAIN TO MARCH AT MY SIDE AGAIN WHEN NEXT I--
ODINSON!

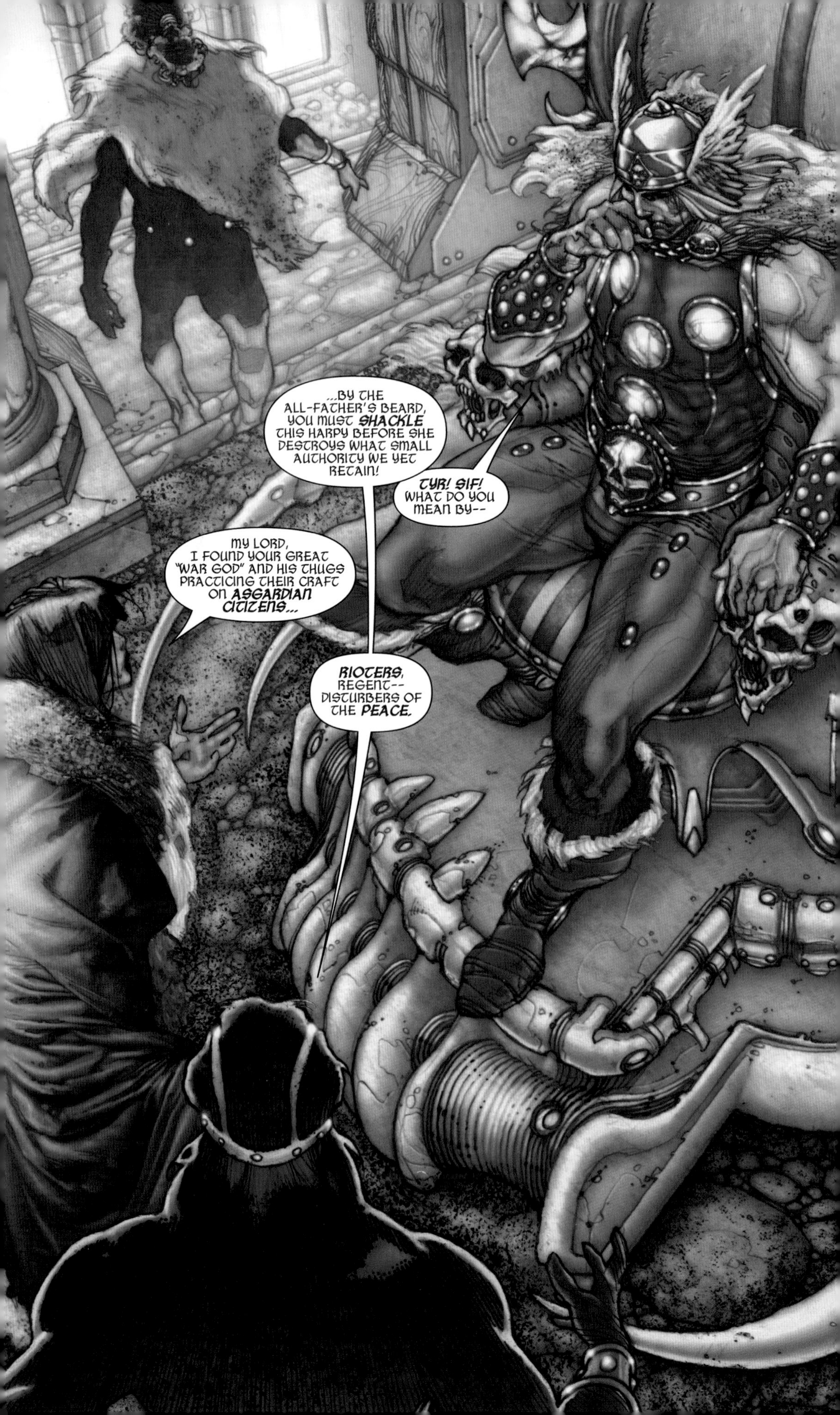
...BY THE ALL-FATHER'S BEARD, YOU MUST SHACKLE THIS HARPY BEFORE SHE DESTROYS WHAT SMALL AUTHORITY WE YET RETAIN!
TYR! SIF! WHAT DO YOU MEAN BY--
MY LORD, I FOUND YOUR GREAT "WAR GOD" AND HIS THUGS PRACTICING THEIR CRAFT ON ASGARDIAN CITIZENS...
RIOTERS, REGENT-- DISTURBERS OF THE PEACE.

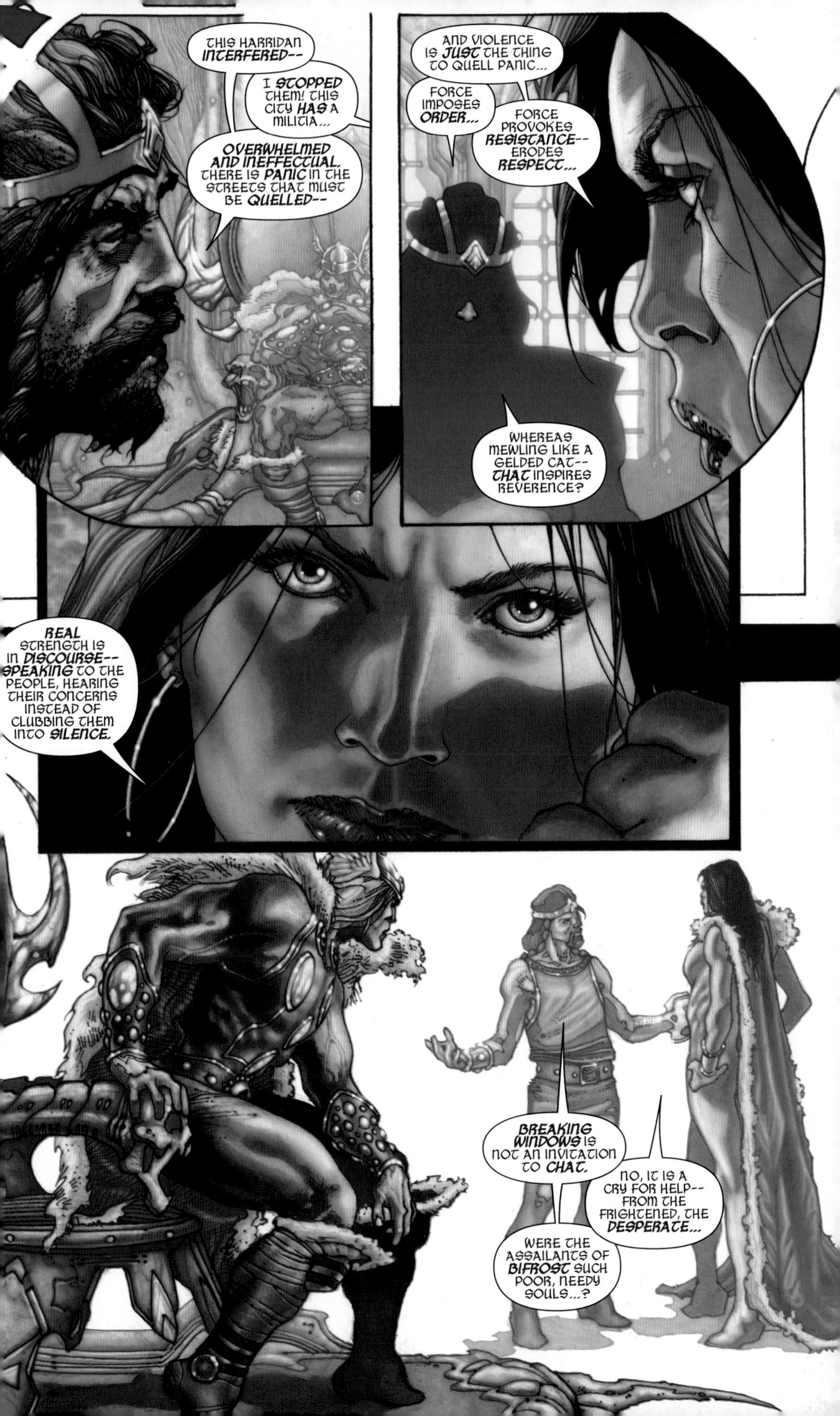
THIS HARRIDAN INTERFERED--
I STOPPED THEM! THIS CITY HAS A MILITIA...
OVERWHELMED AND INEFFECTUAL. THERE IS PANIC IN THE STREETS THAT MUST BE QUELLED--
AND VIOLENCE IS JUST THE THING TO QUELL PANIC...
FORCE IMPOSES ORDER...
FORCE PROVOKES RESISTANCE-- ERODES RESPECT...
WHEREAS MEWLING LIKE A GELDED CAT-- THAT INSPIRES REVERENCE?
REAL STRENGTH IS IN DISCOURSE-- SPEAKING TO THE PEOPLE, HEARING THEIR CONCERNS INSTEAD OF CLUBBING THEM INTO SILENCE.
BREAKING WINDOWS IS NOT AN INVITATION TO CHAT.
NO, IT IS A CRY FOR HELP-- FROM THE FRIGHTENED, THE DESPERATE...
WERE THE ASSAILANTS OF BIFROST SUCH POOR, NEEDY SOULS...?

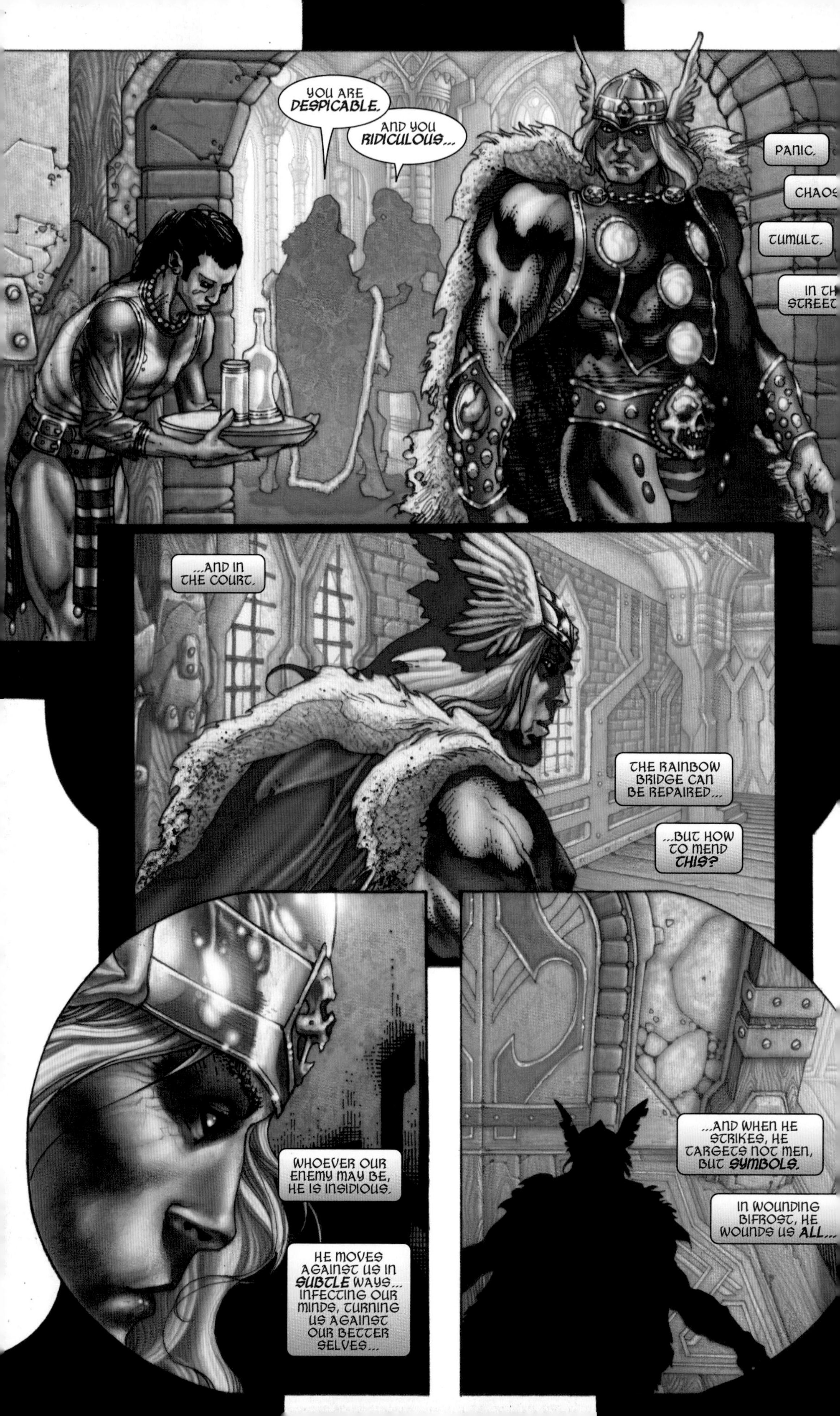
YOU ARE DESPICABLE.
AND YOU RIDICULOUS...
PANIC.
CHAOS
TUMULT.
IN THE STREET
...AND IN THE COURT.
THE RAINBOW BRIDGE CAN BE REPAIRED...
...BUT HOW TO MEND THIS?
WHOEVER OUR ENEMY MAY BE, HE IS INSIDIOUS.
HE MOVES AGAINST US IN SUBTLE WAYS... INFECTING OUR MINDS, TURNING US AGAINST OUR BETTER SELVES...
...AND WHEN HE STRIKES, HE TARGETS NOT MEN, BUT SYMBOLS.
IN WOUNDING BIFROST, HE WOUNDS US ALL...

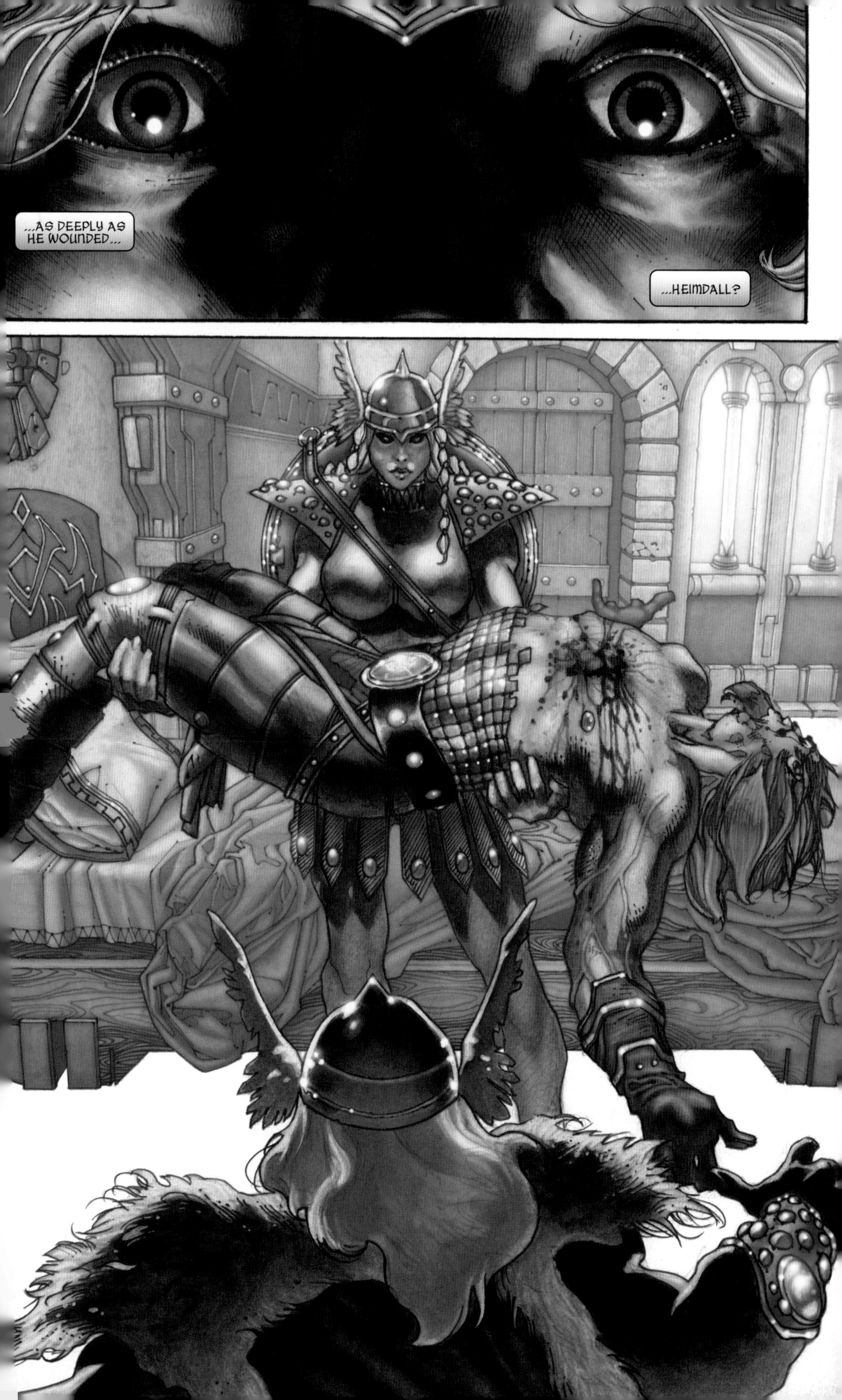
...AS DEEPLY AS HE WOUNDED...
...HEIMDALL?

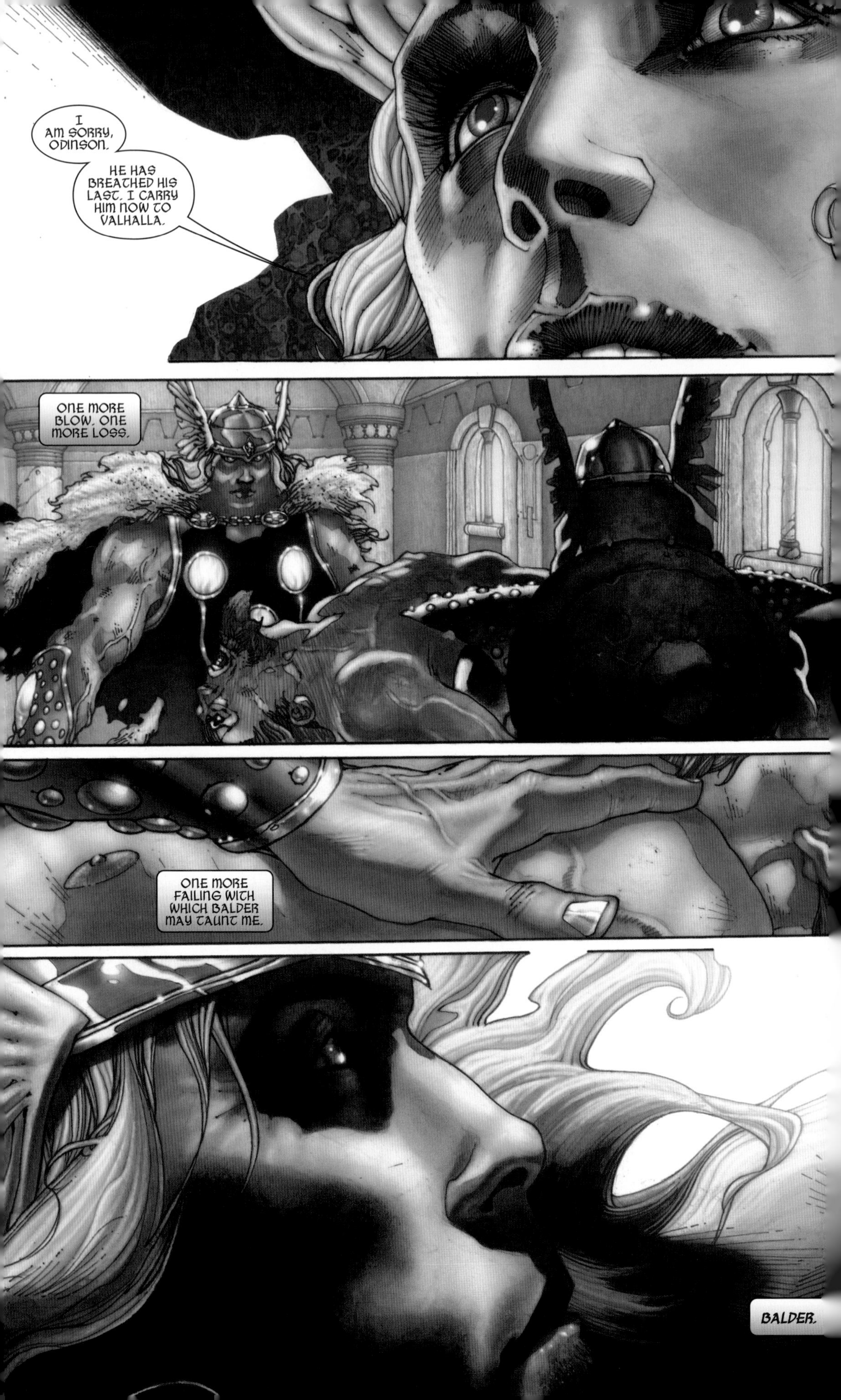
I AM SORRY, ODINSON.
HE HAS BREATHED HIS LAST. I CARRY HIM NOW TO VALHALLA.
ONE MORE BLOW. ONE MORE LOSS.
ONE MORE FAILING WITH WHICH BALDER MAY TAUNT ME.
BALDER.

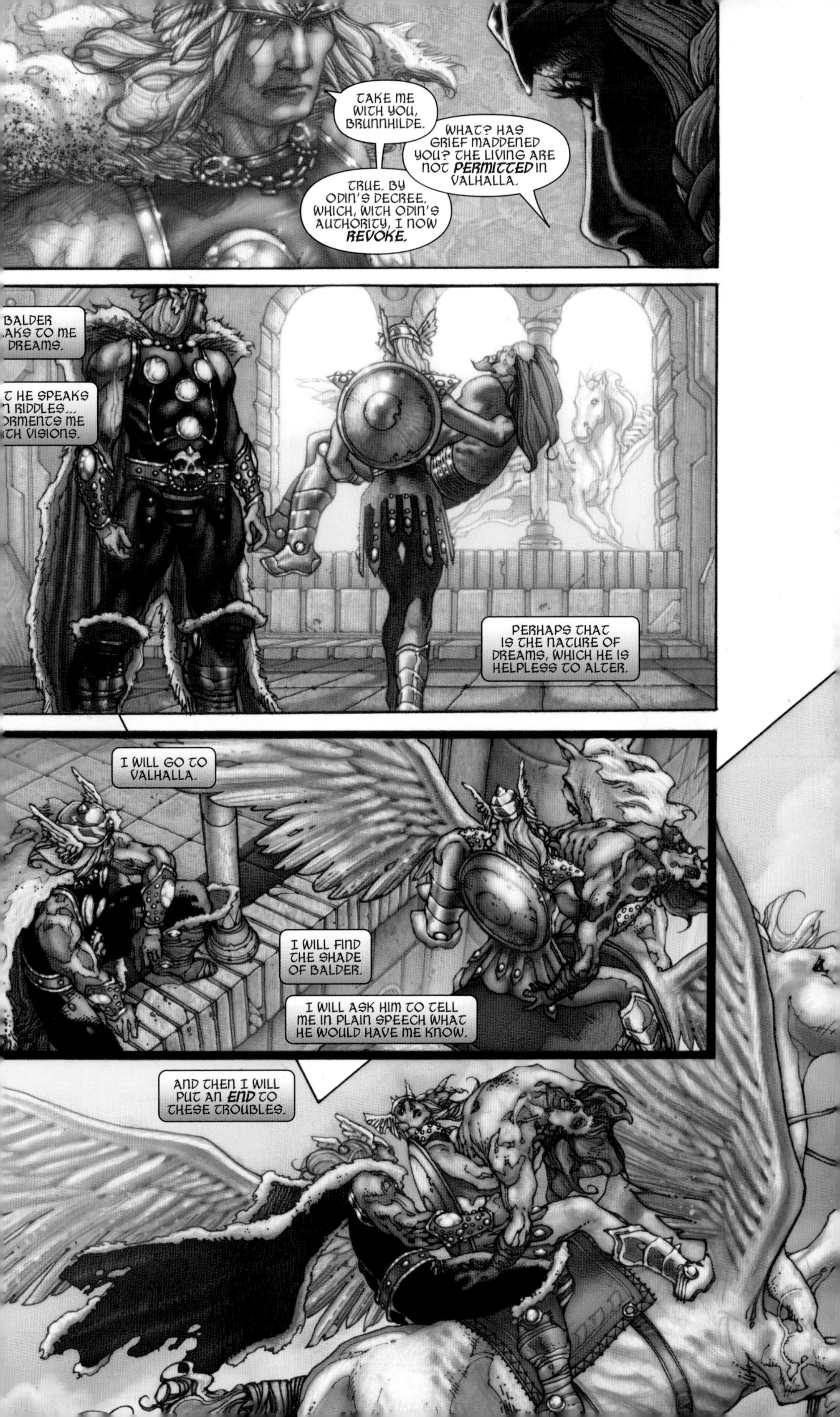
TAKE ME WITH YOU, BRUNNHILDE.
WHAT? HAS GRIEF MADDENED YOU? THE LIVING ARE NOT *PERMITTED* IN VALHALLA.
TRUE. BY ODIN'S DECREE. WHICH, WITH ODIN'S AUTHORITY, I NOW *REVOKE.*
BALDER AKS TO ME DREAMS.
T HE SPEAKS N RIDDLES... ORMENTS ME TH VISIONS.
PERHAPS THAT IS THE NATURE OF DREAMS, WHICH HE IS HELPLESS TO ALTER.
I WILL GO TO VALHALLA.
I WILL FIND THE SHADE OF BALDER.
I WILL ASK HIM TO TELL ME IN PLAIN SPEECH WHAT HE WOULD HAVE ME KNOW.
AND THEN I WILL PUT AN *END* TO THESE TROUBLES.

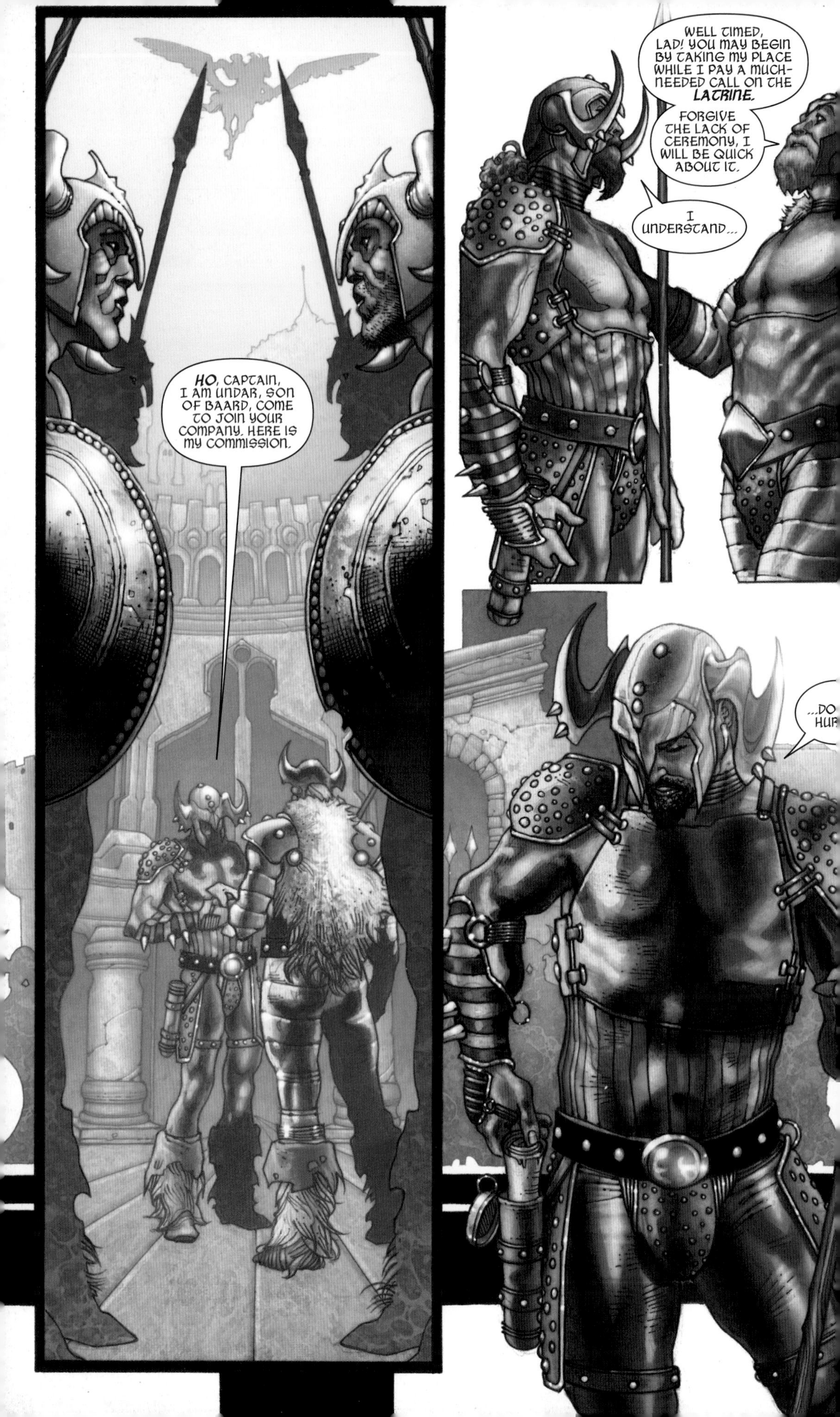
HO, CAPTAIN, I AM UNDAR, SON OF BAARD, COME TO JOIN YOUR COMPANY. HERE IS MY COMMISSION.
WELL TIMED, LAD! YOU MAY BEGIN BY TAKING MY PLACE WHILE I PAY A MUCH-NEEDED CALL ON THE LATRINE.
FORGIVE THE LACK OF CEREMONY, I WILL BE QUICK ABOUT IT.
I UNDERSTAND...
...DO
HUR

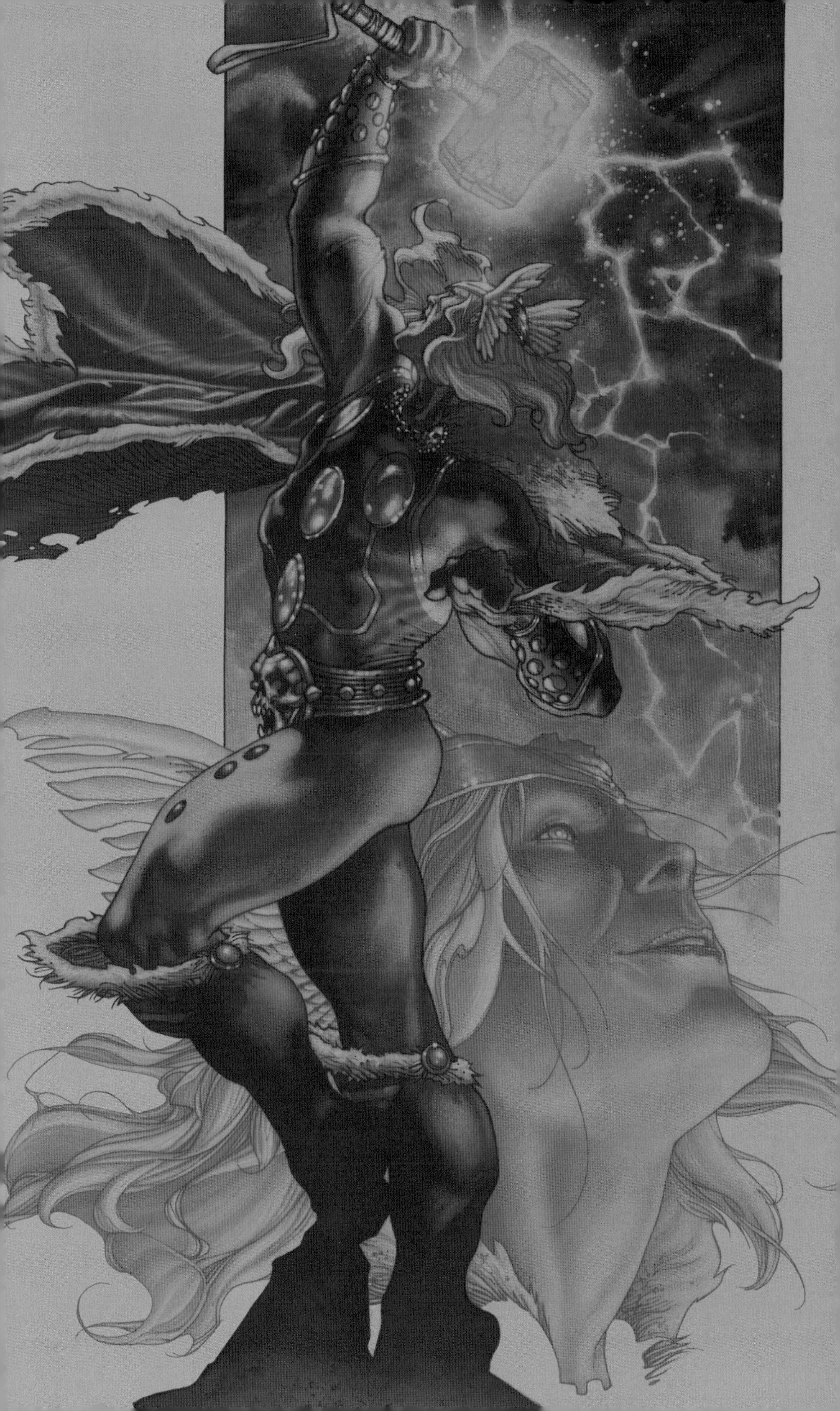

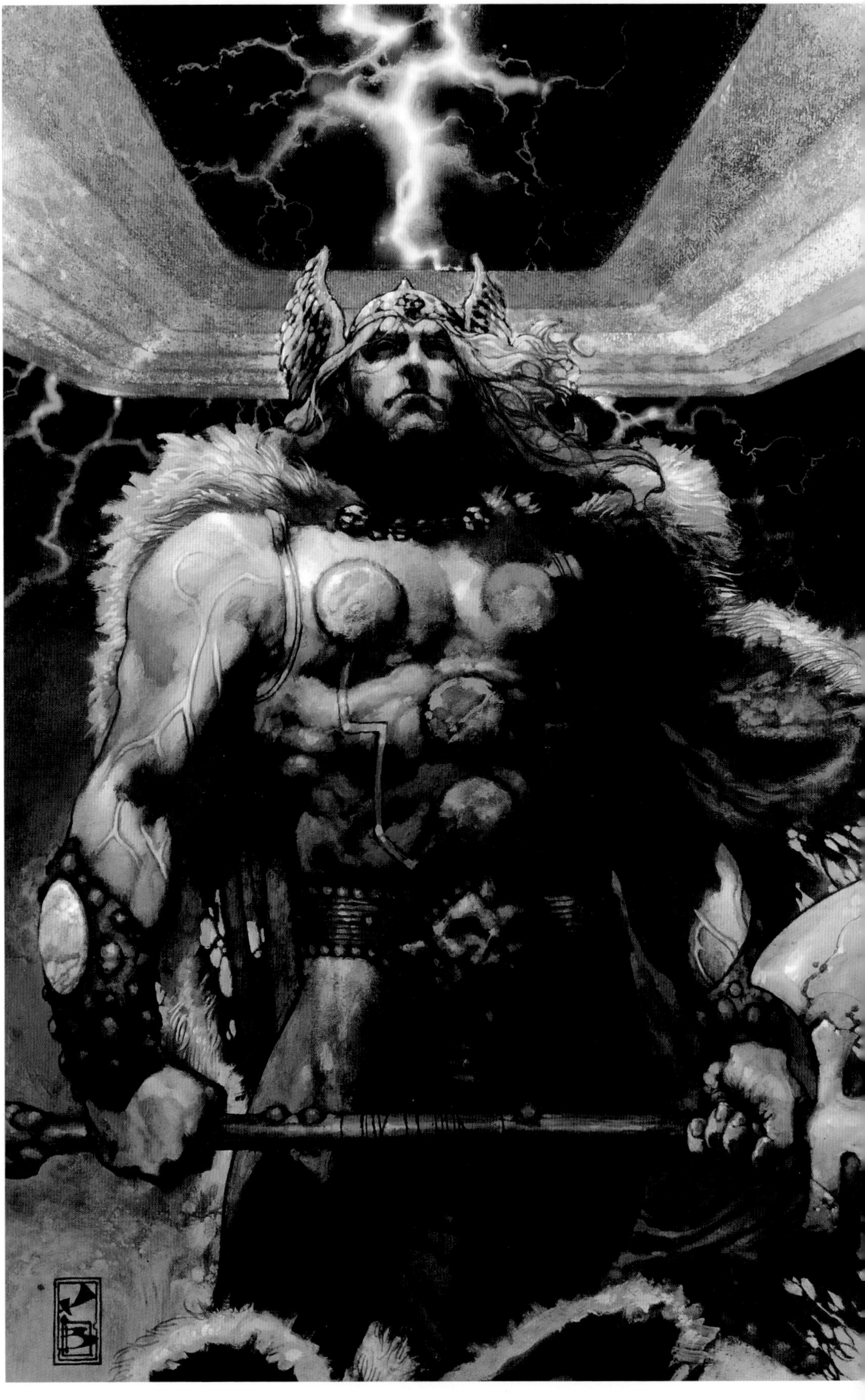

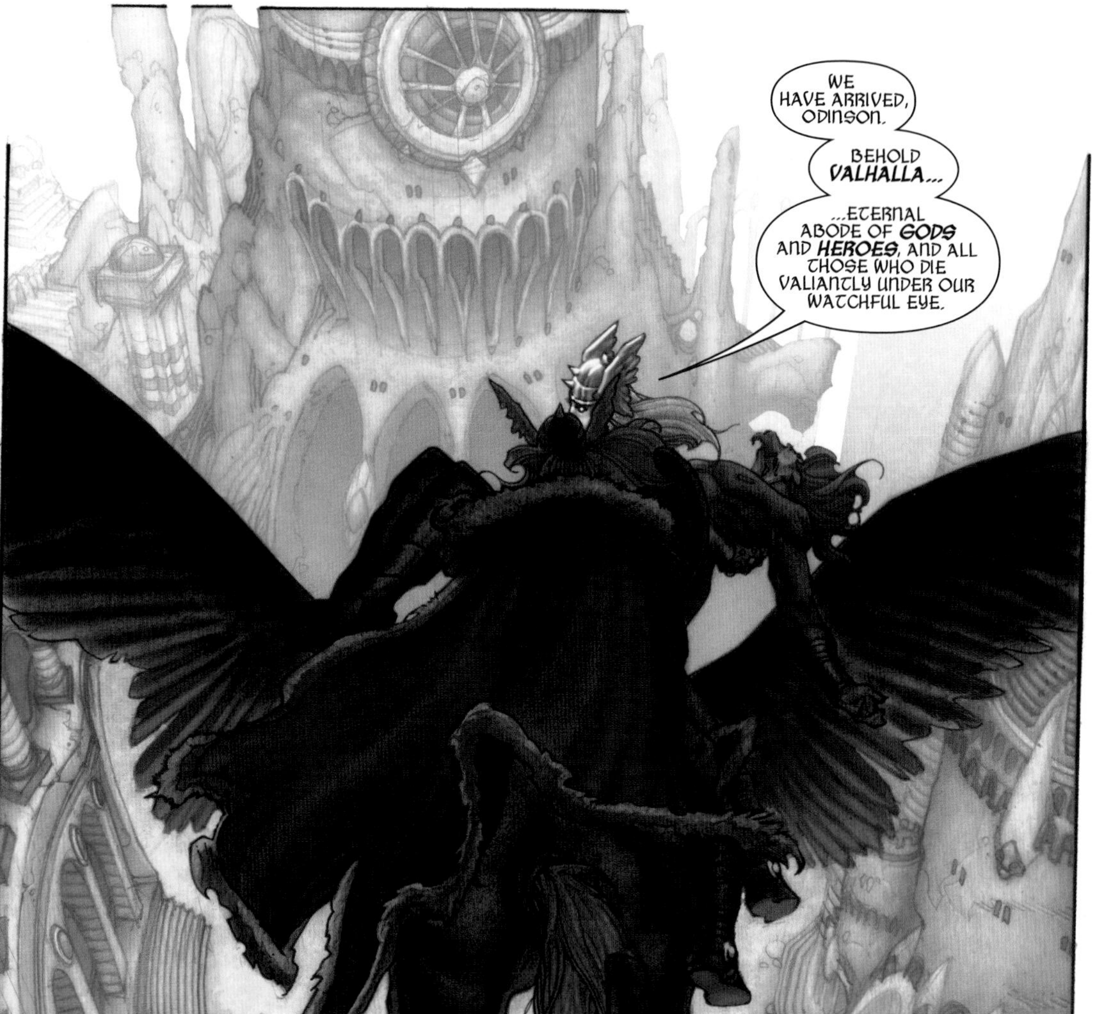
WE HAVE ARRIVED, ODINSON.
BEHOLD VALHALLA...
...ETERNAL ABODE OF GODS AND HEROES, AND ALL THOSE WHO DIE VALIANTLY UNDER OUR WATCHFUL EYE.

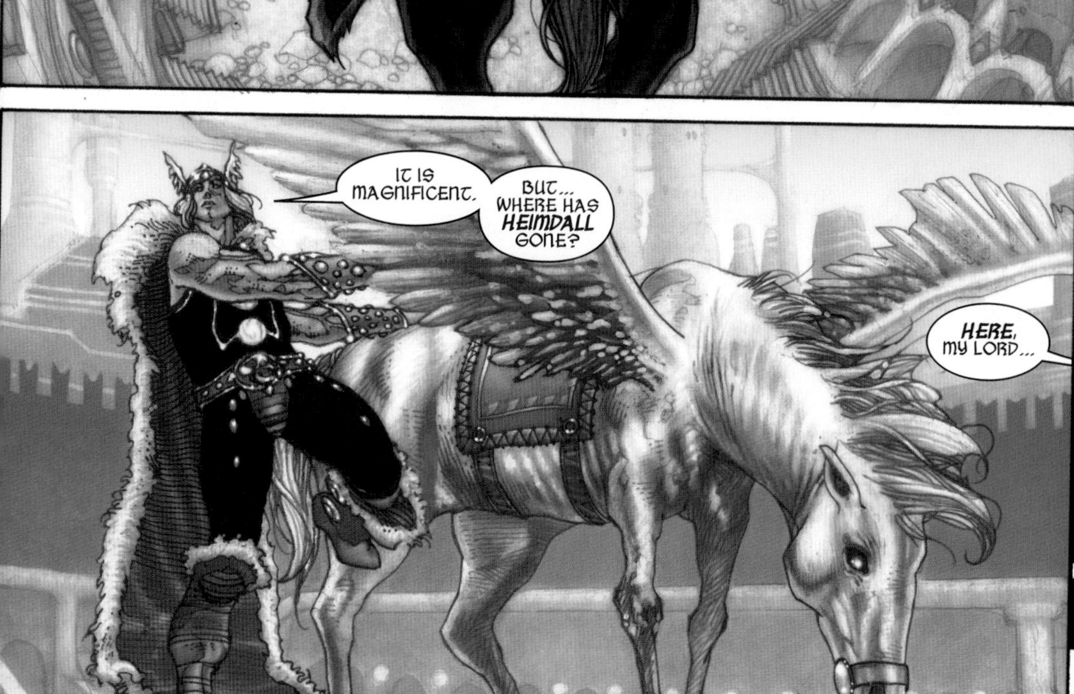
IT IS MAGNIFICENT.
BUT... WHERE HAS HEIMDALL GONE?
HERE, MY LORD...

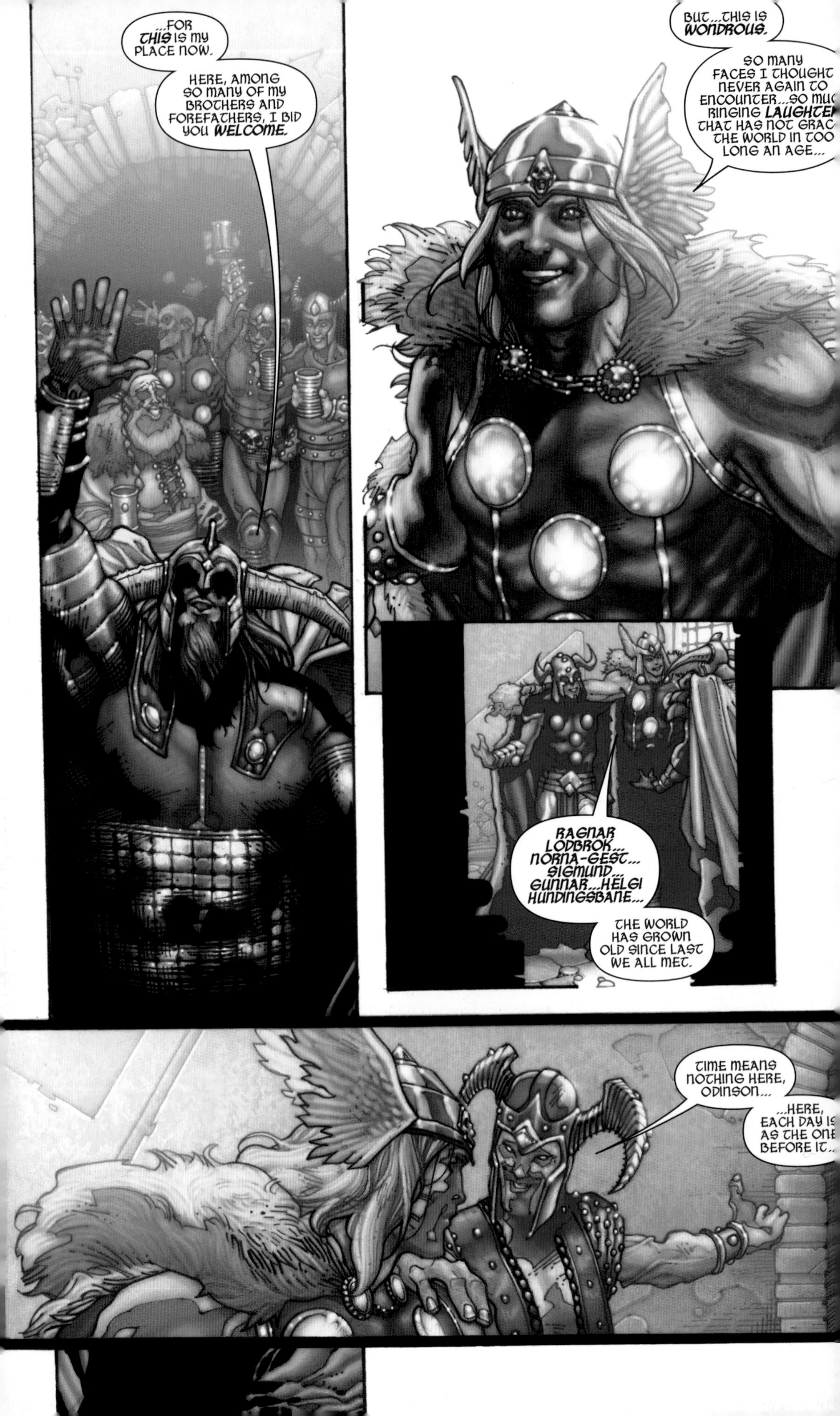
...FOR THIS IS MY PLACE NOW.
HERE, AMONG SO MANY OF MY BROTHERS AND FOREFATHERS, I BID YOU WELCOME.
BUT...THIS IS WONDROUS.
SO MANY FACES I THOUGHT NEVER AGAIN TO ENCOUNTER...SO MUC RINGING LAUGHTEI THAT HAS NOT GRAC THE WORLD IN TOO LONG AN AGE...
RAGNAR LODBROK... NORNA-GEST... SIGMUND... GUNNAR...HELGI HUNDINGSBANE...
THE WORLD HAS GROWN OLD SINCE LAST WE ALL MET.
TIME MEANS NOTHING HERE, ODINSON...
...HERE, EACH DAY IS AS THE ONE BEFORE IT...

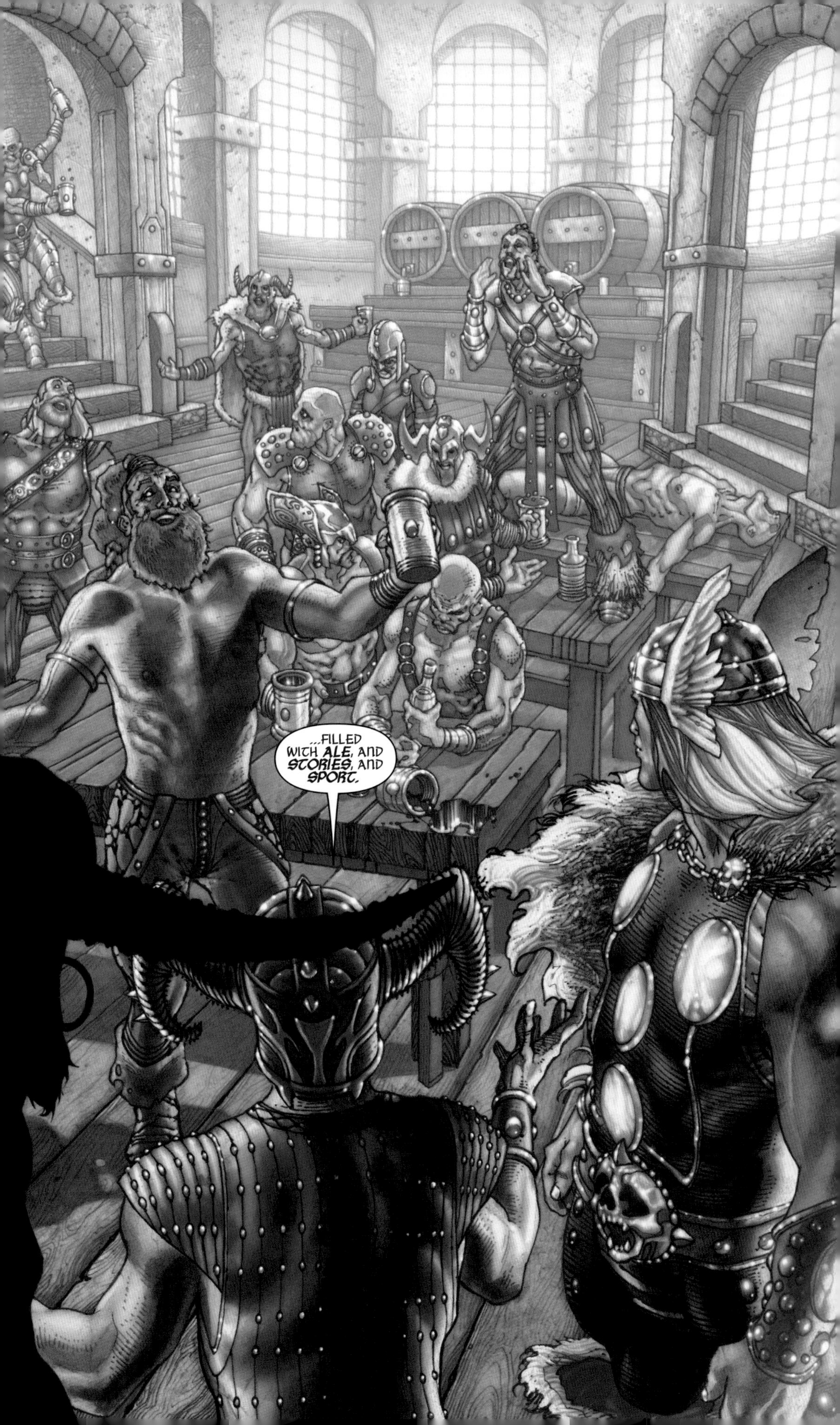
...FILLED WITH ALE, AND STORIES, AND SPORT.

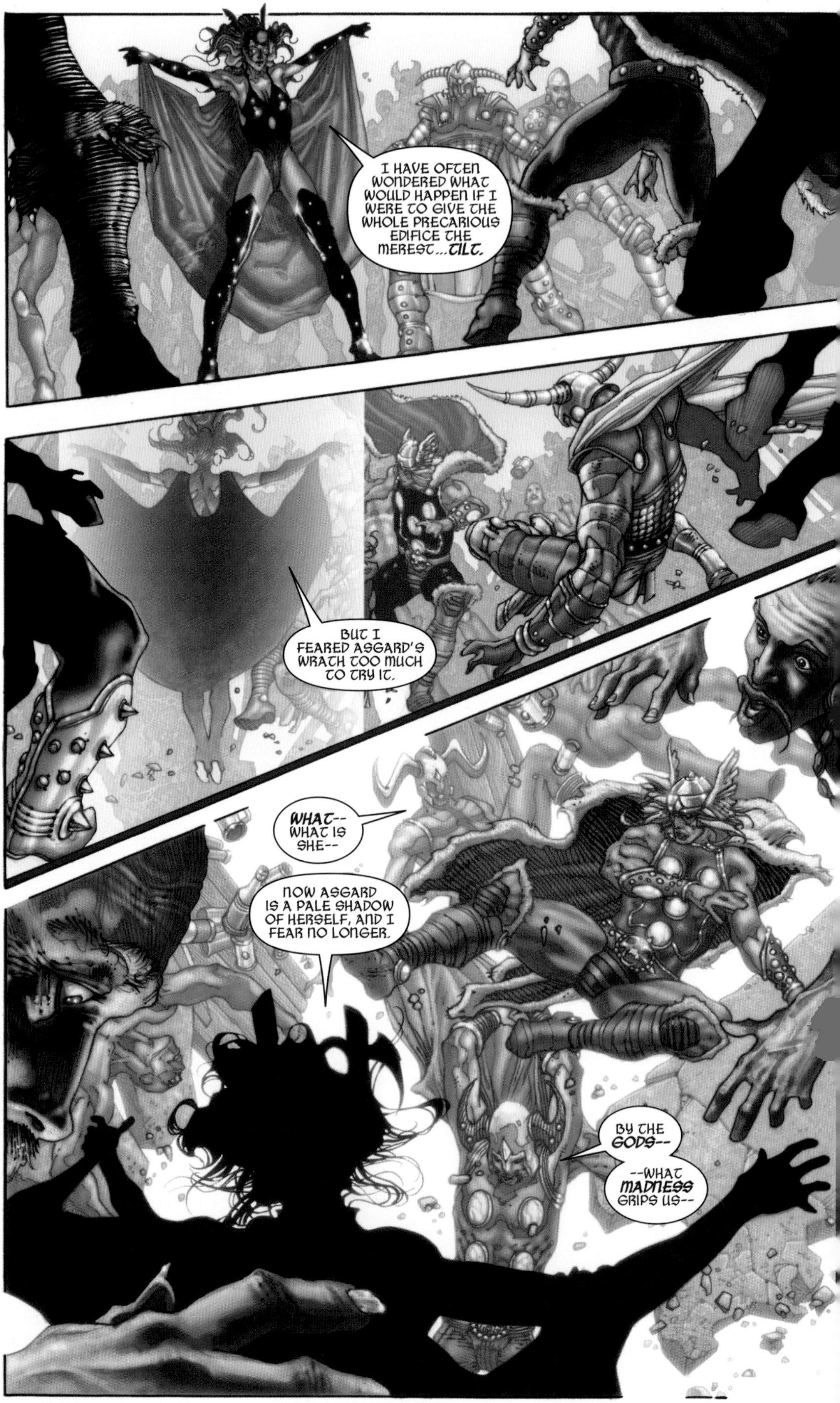
I HAVE OFTEN WONDERED WHAT WOULD HAPPEN IF I WERE TO GIVE THE WHOLE PRECARIOUS EDIFICE THE MEREST... TILT.
BUT I FEARED ASGARD'S WRATH TOO MUCH TO TRY IT.
WHAT-- WHAT IS SHE--
NOW ASGARD IS A PALE SHADOW OF HERSELF, AND I FEAR NO LONGER.
BY THE GODS--
--WHAT MADNESS GRIPS US--

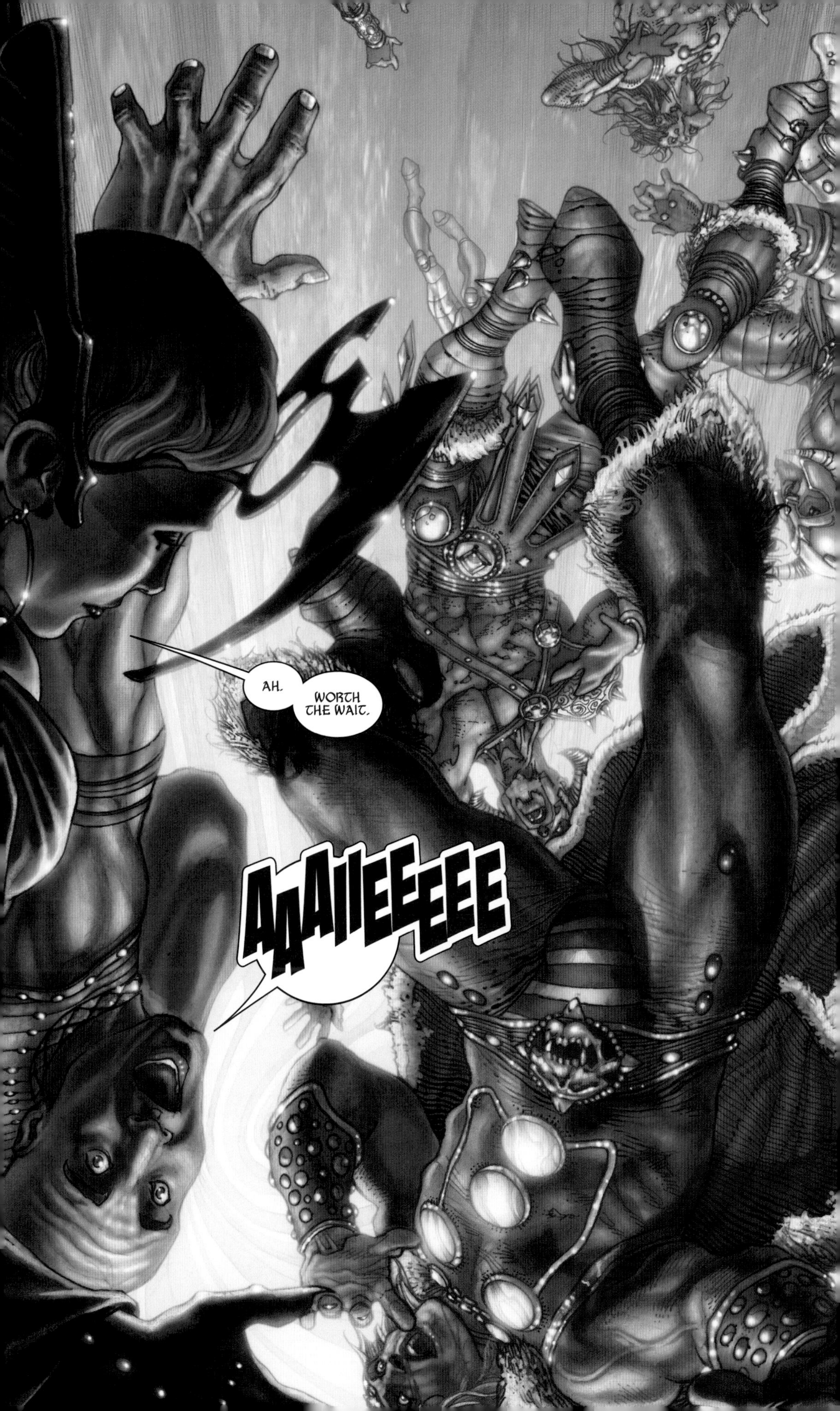
AH.
WORTH THE WAIT.
AAAIIEEEEEE

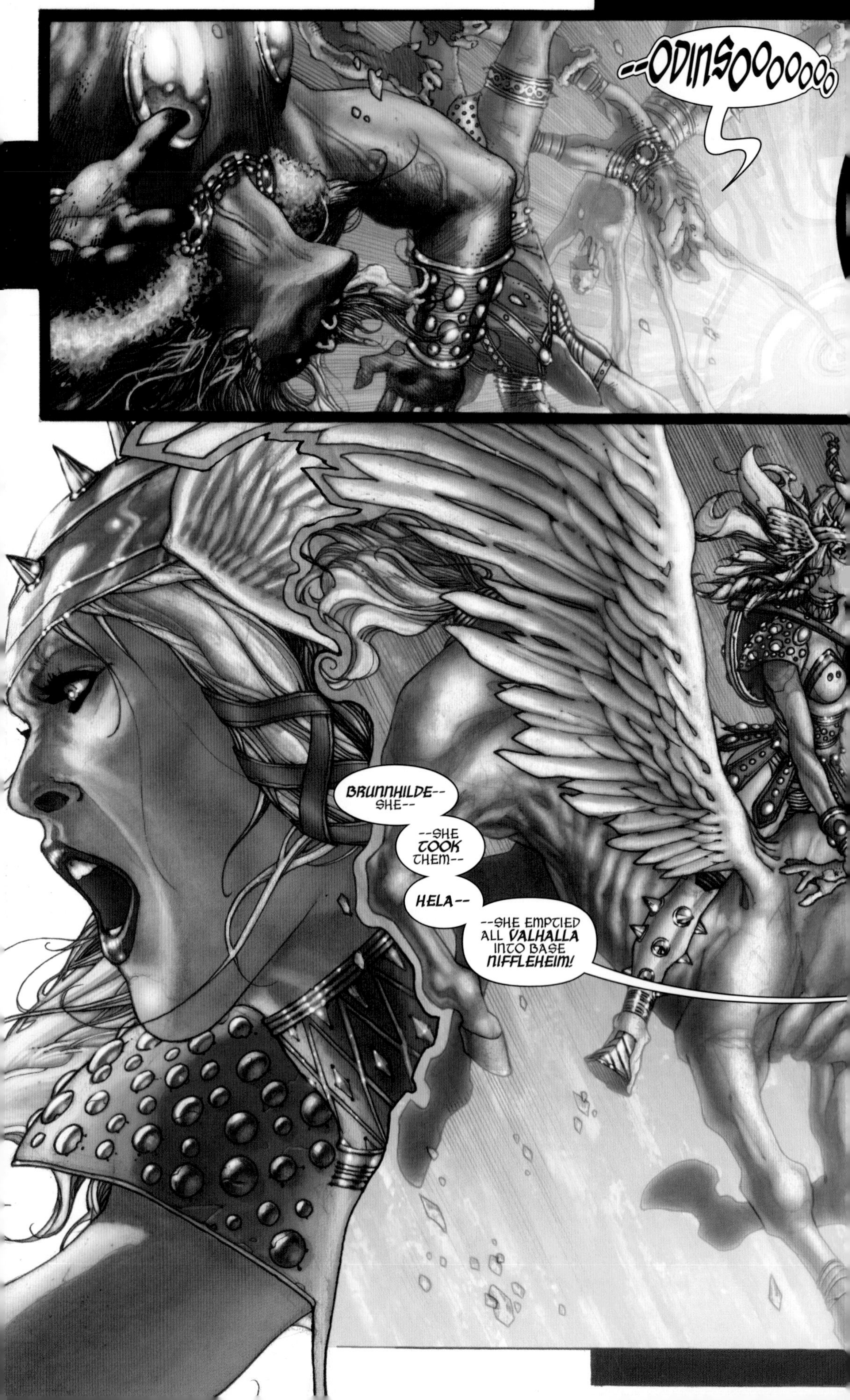
--ODINSOOOOOOO
BRUNNHILDE-- SHE--
--SHE TOOK THEM--
HELA--
--SHE EMPTIED ALL VALHALLA INTO BASE NIFFLEHEIM!

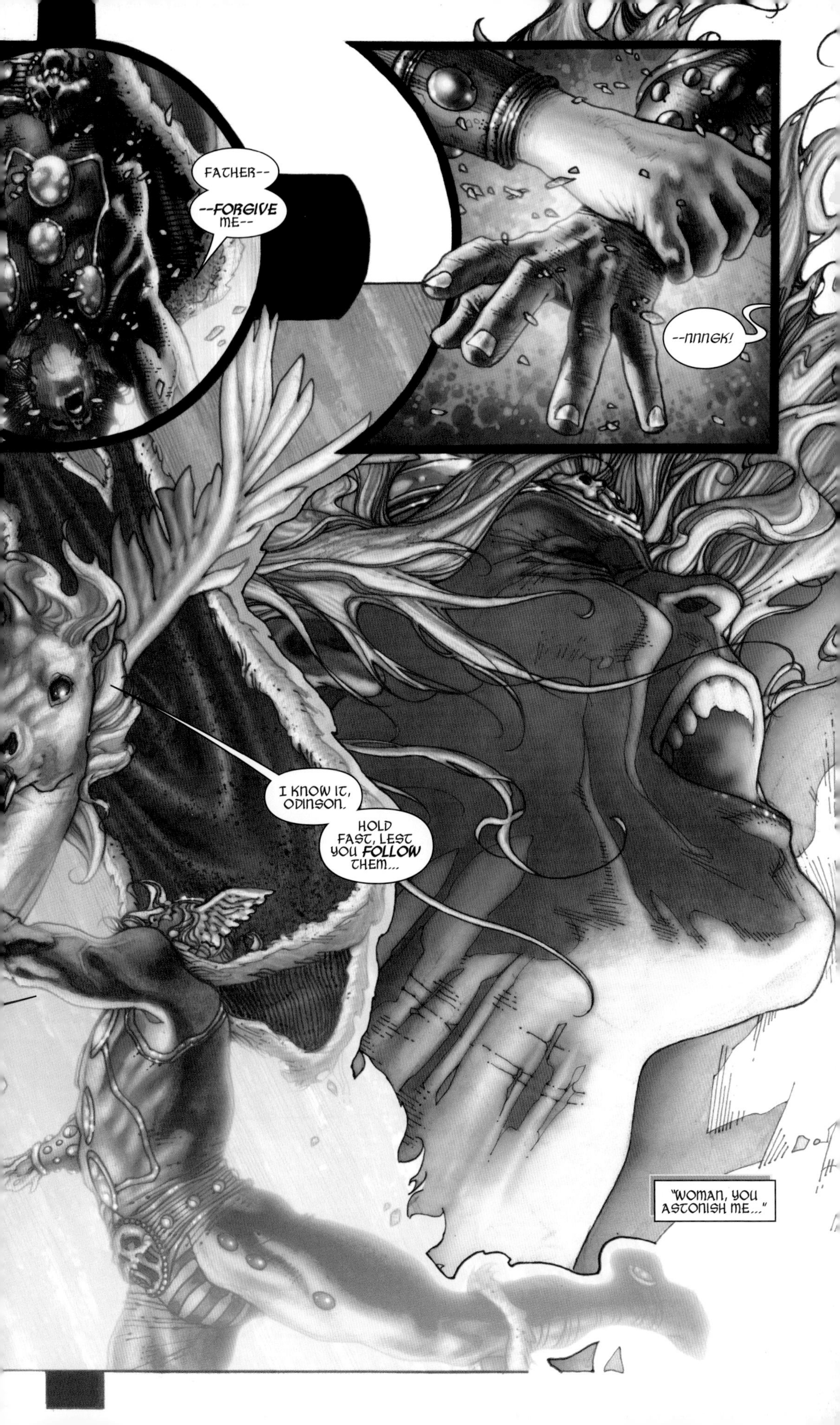
FATHER--
--**FORGIVE** ME--
--NNNGK!
I KNOW IT, ODINSON.
HOLD FAST, LEST YOU **FOLLOW** THEM...
"WOMAN, YOU ASTONISH ME..."

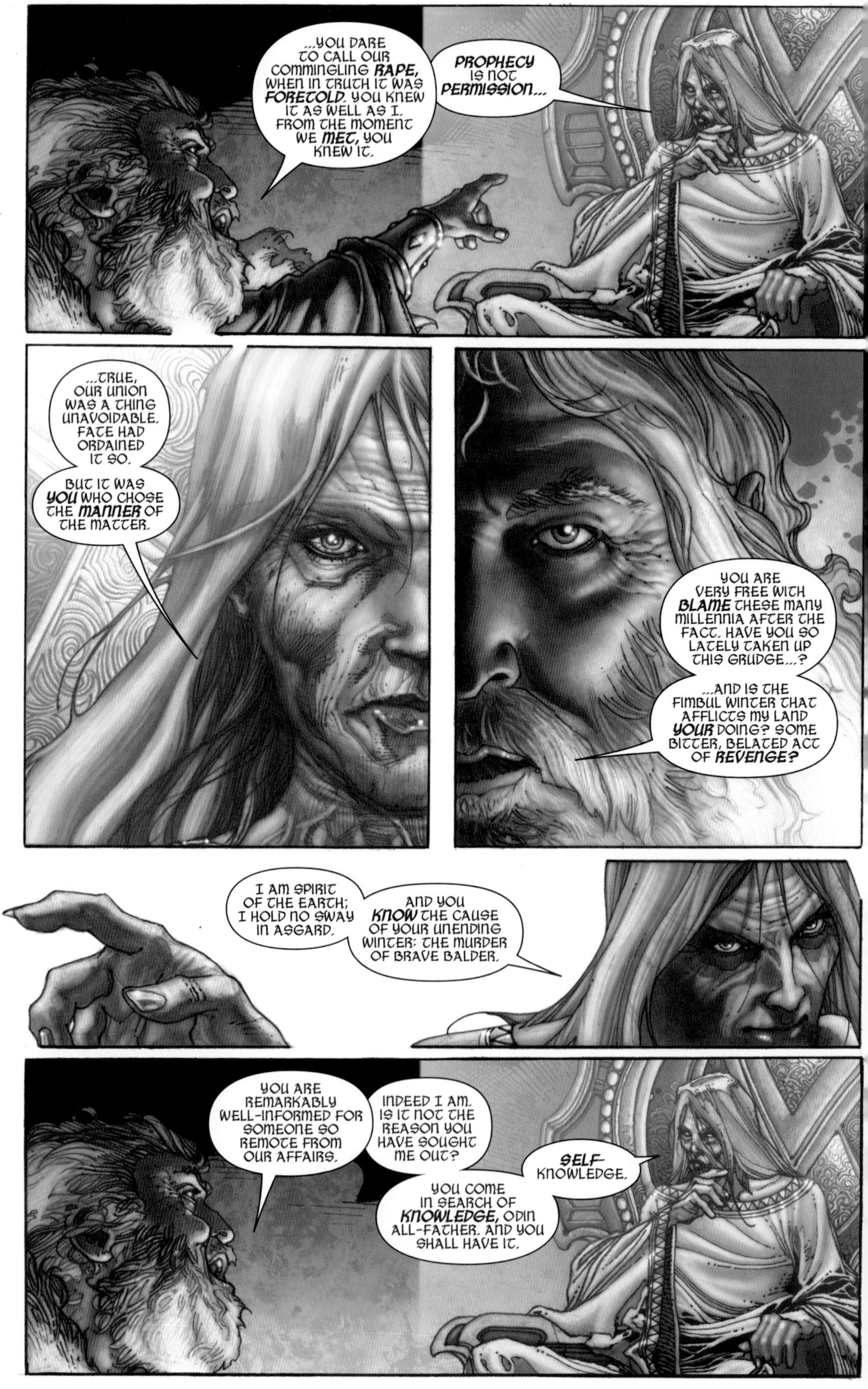
...YOU DARE TO CALL OUR COMMINGLING RAPE, WHEN IN TRUTH IT WAS FORETOLD. YOU KNEW IT AS WELL AS I. FROM THE MOMENT WE MET, YOU KNEW IT.
PROPHECY IS NOT PERMISSION...
...TRUE, OUR UNION WAS A THING UNAVOIDABLE. FATE HAD ORDAINED IT SO.
BUT IT WAS YOU WHO CHOSE THE MANNER OF THE MATTER.
YOU ARE VERY FREE WITH BLAME THESE MANY MILLENNIA AFTER THE FACT. HAVE YOU SO LATELY TAKEN UP THIS GRUDGE...?
...AND IS THE FIMBUL WINTER THAT AFFLICTS MY LAND YOUR DOING? SOME BITTER, BELATED ACT OF REVENGE?
I AM SPIRIT OF THE EARTH; I HOLD NO SWAY IN ASGARD.
AND YOU KNOW THE CAUSE OF YOUR UNENDING WINTER: THE MURDER OF BRAVE BALDER.
YOU ARE REMARKABLY WELL-INFORMED FOR SOMEONE SO REMOTE FROM OUR AFFAIRS.
INDEED I AM. IS IT NOT THE REASON YOU HAVE SOUGHT ME OUT?
YOU COME IN SEARCH OF KNOWLEDGE, ODIN ALL-FATHER. AND YOU SHALL HAVE IT.
SELF-KNOWLEDGE.

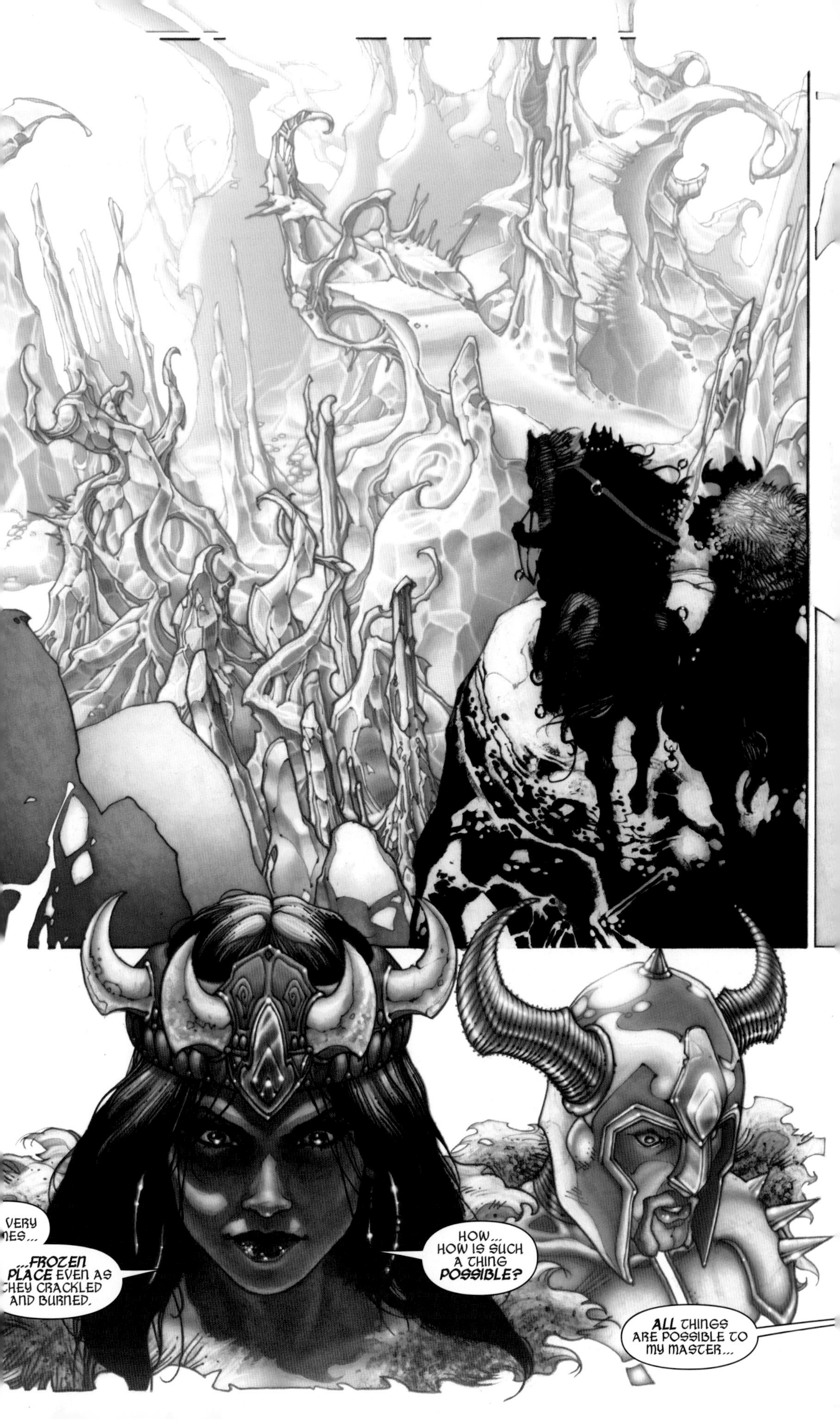

VERY
NES...
...FROZEN PLACE EVEN AS THEY CRACKLED AND BURNED.
HOW... HOW IS SUCH A THING POSSIBLE?
ALL THINGS ARE POSSIBLE TO MY MASTER...

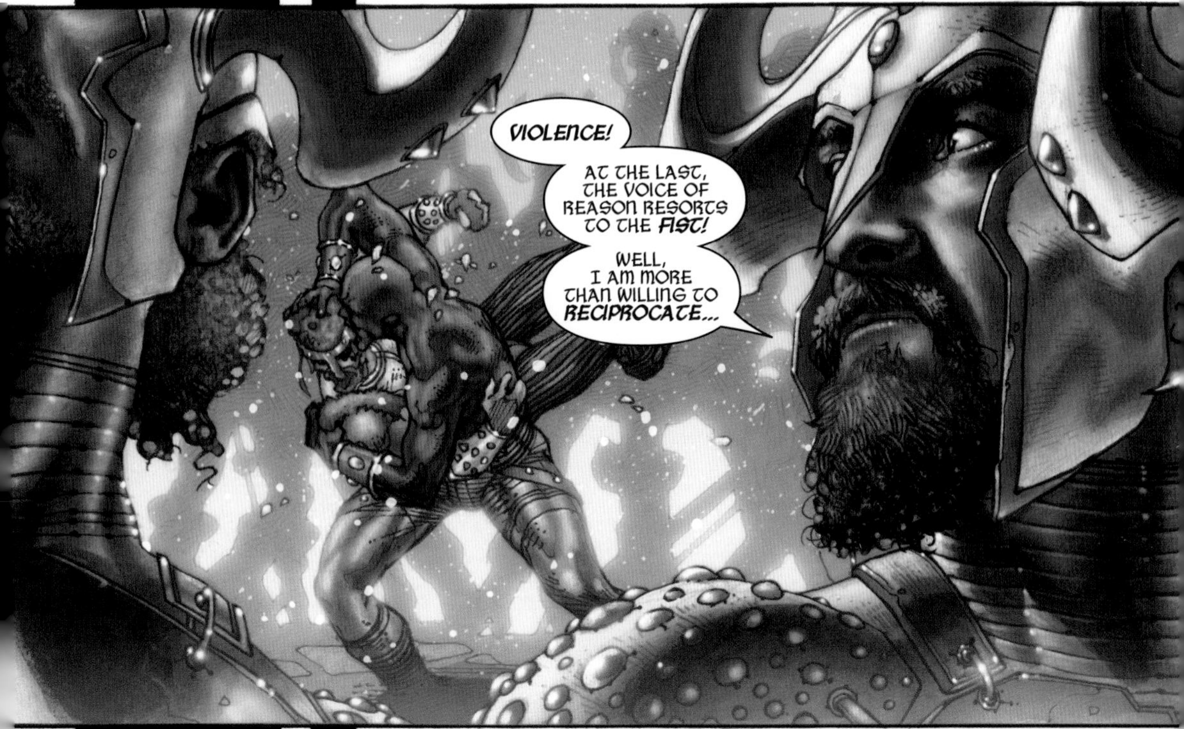
VIOLENCE!
AT THE LAST, THE VOICE OF REASON RESORTS TO THE FIST!
WELL, I AM MORE THAN WILLING TO RECIPROCATE...

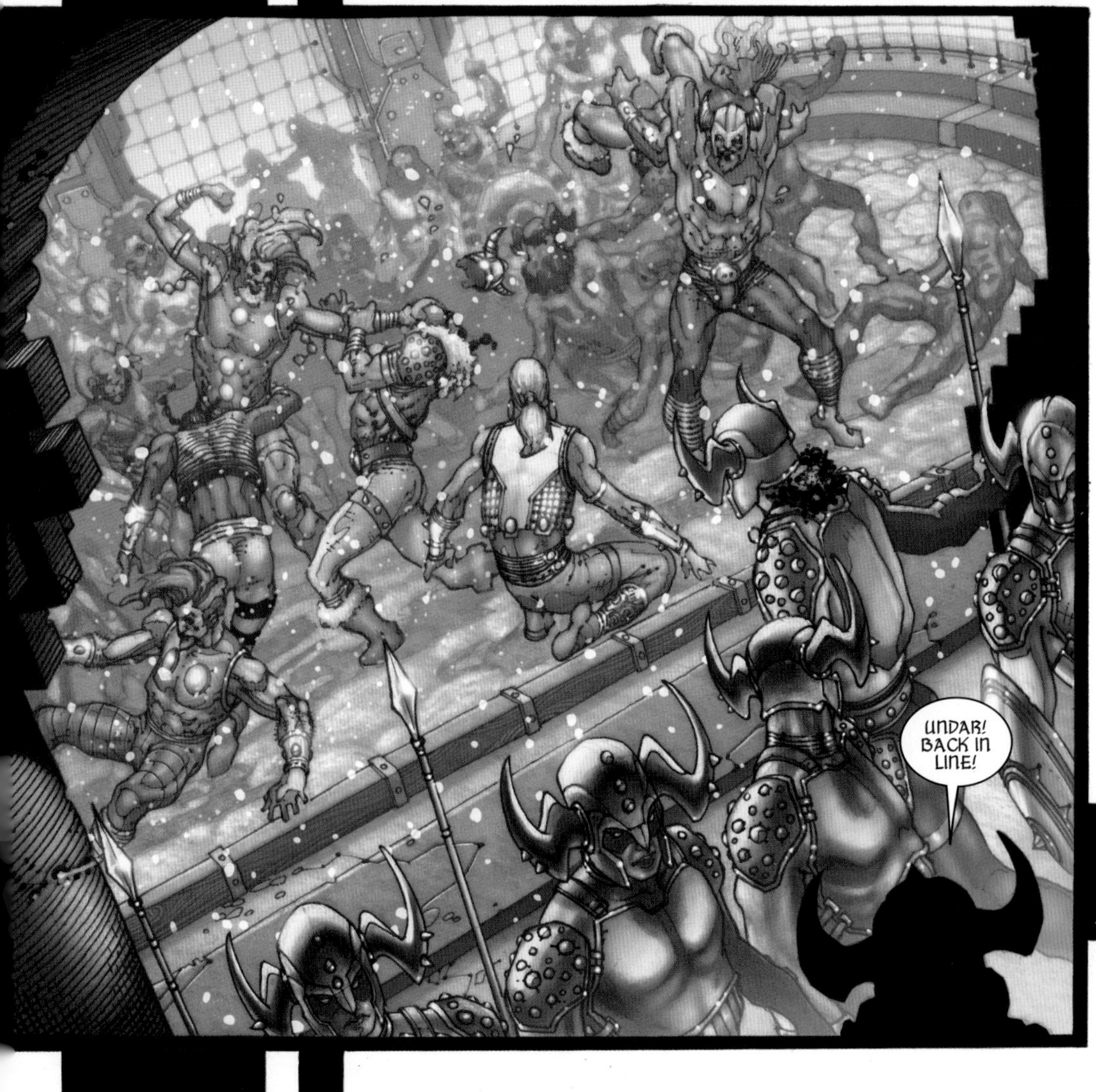
UNDAR! BACK IN LINE!

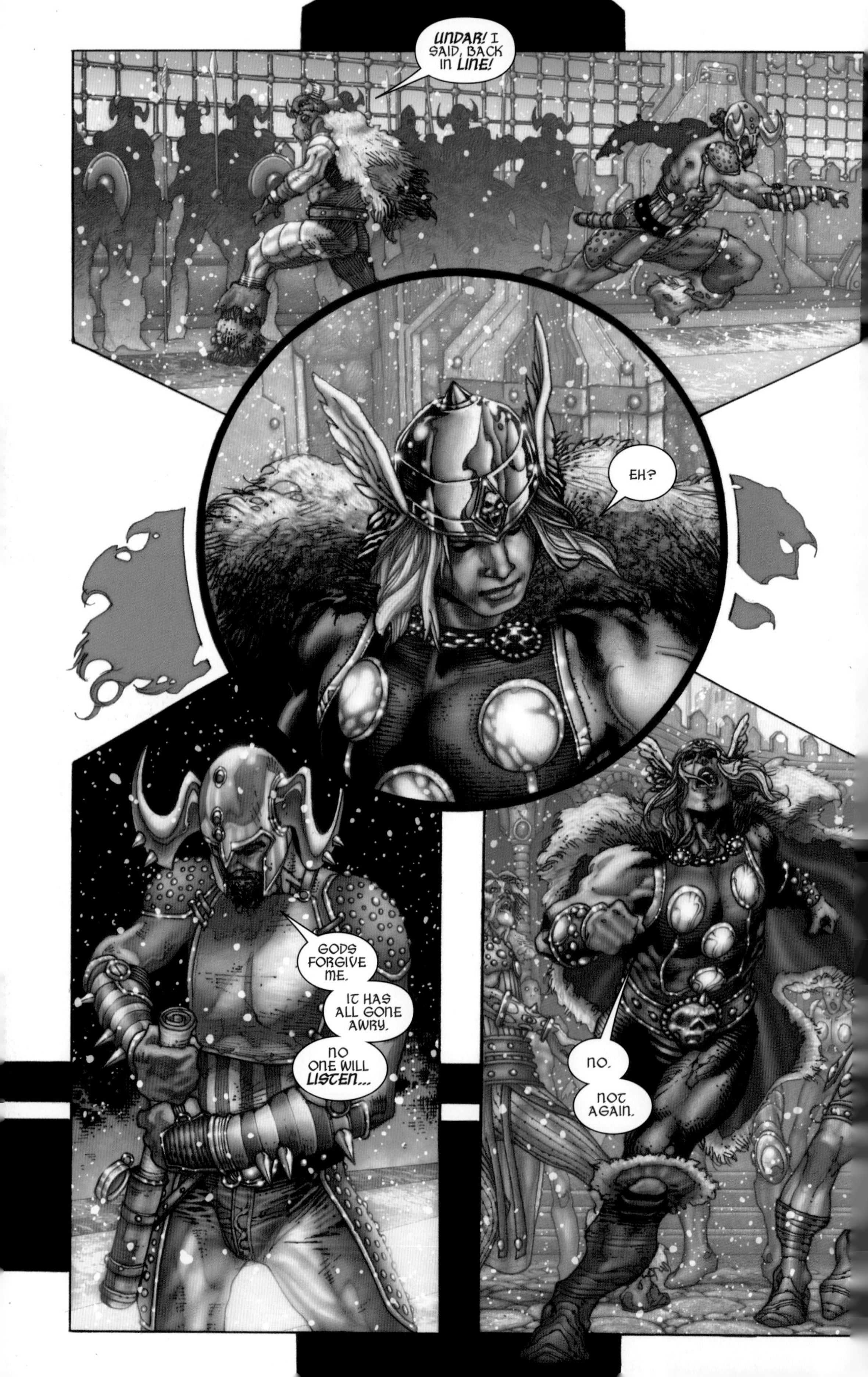
UNDAR! I SAID, BACK IN LINE!
EH?
GODS FORGIVE ME.
IT HAS ALL GONE AWRY.
NO ONE WILL LISTEN...
NO.
NOT AGAIN.

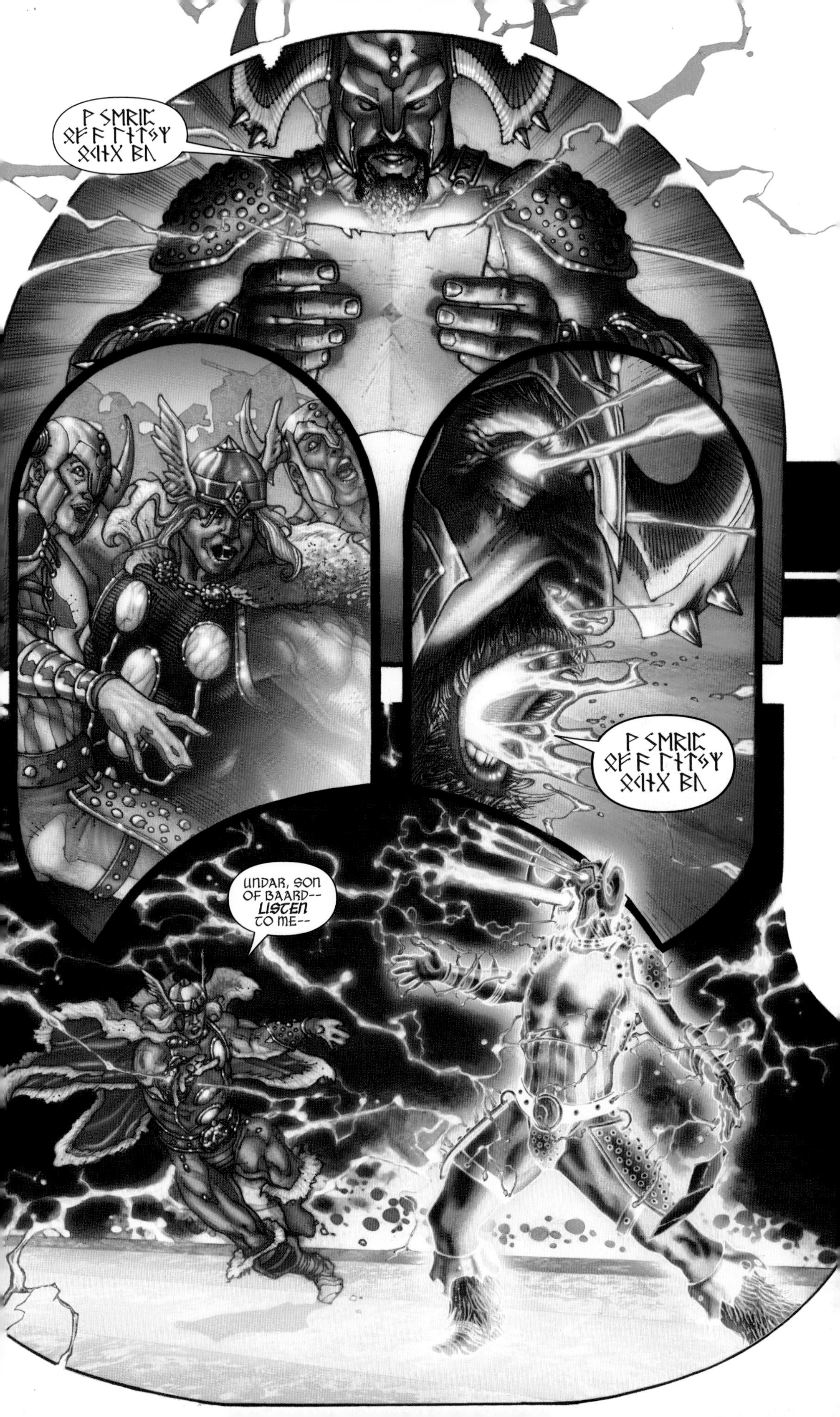
UNDAR, SON OF BAARD-- **LISTEN** TO ME--

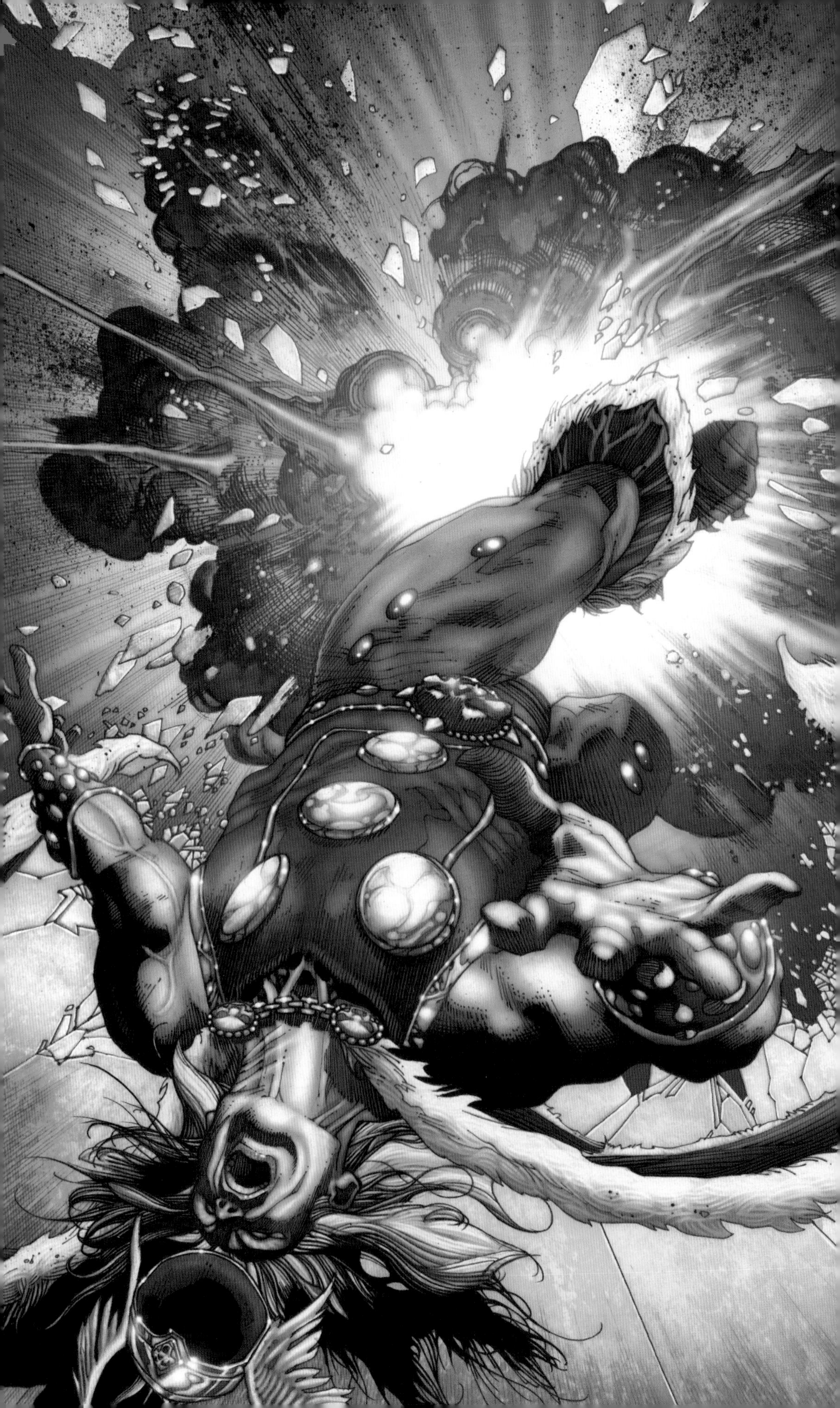

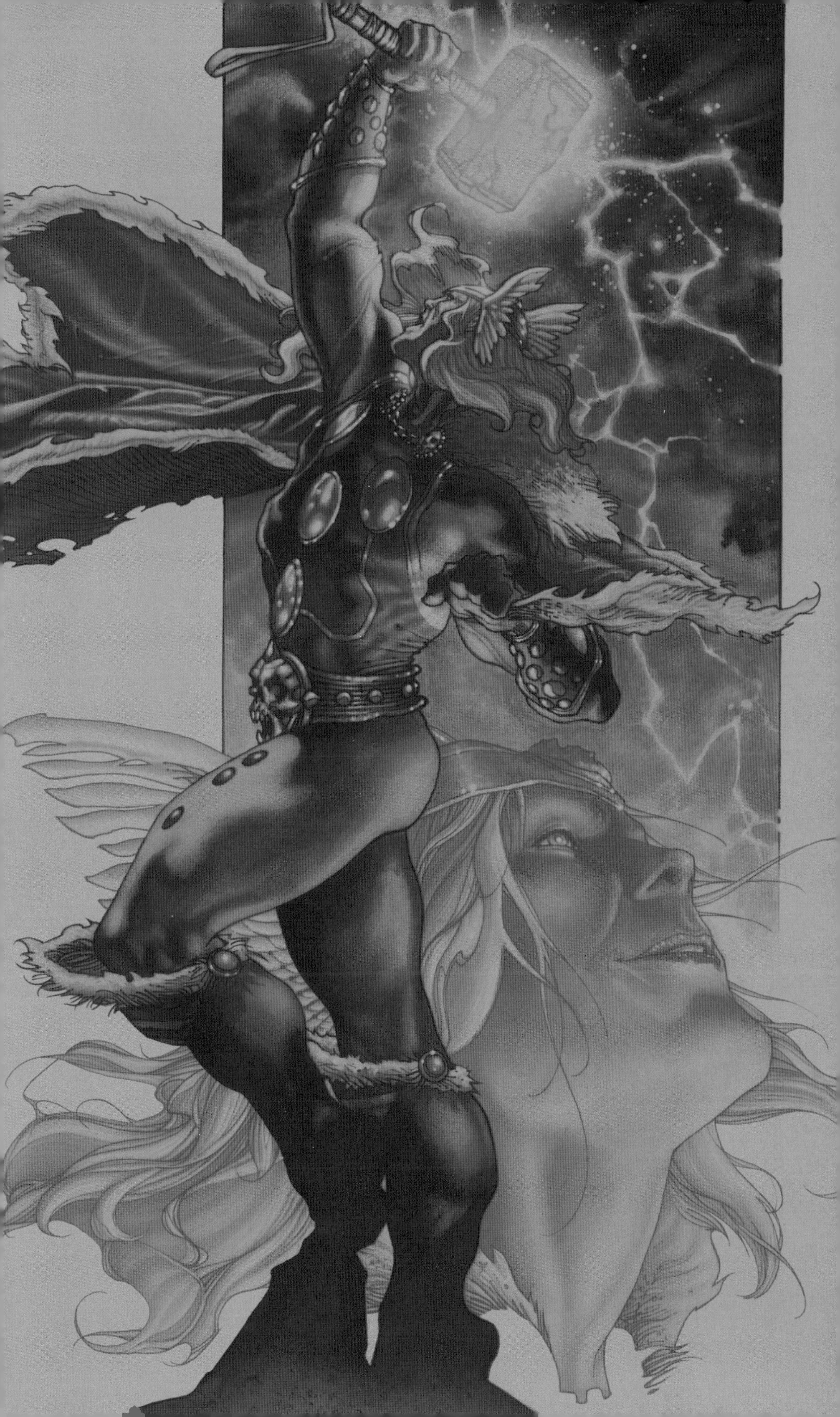

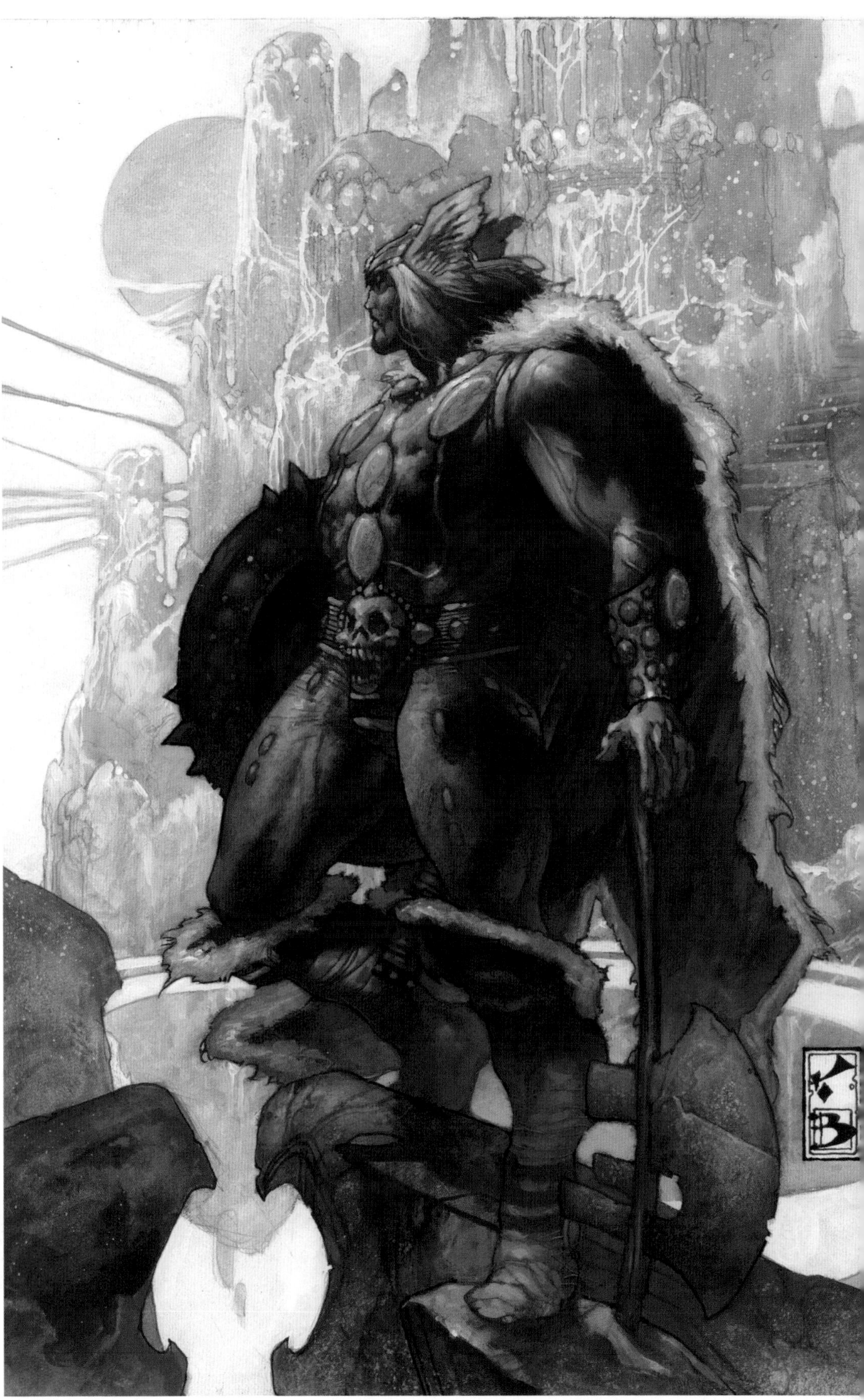

WOE TO ASGARD.
WOE TO THE SON OF ODIN.
WOE.
WOE.
HO, GOD OF THUNDER...

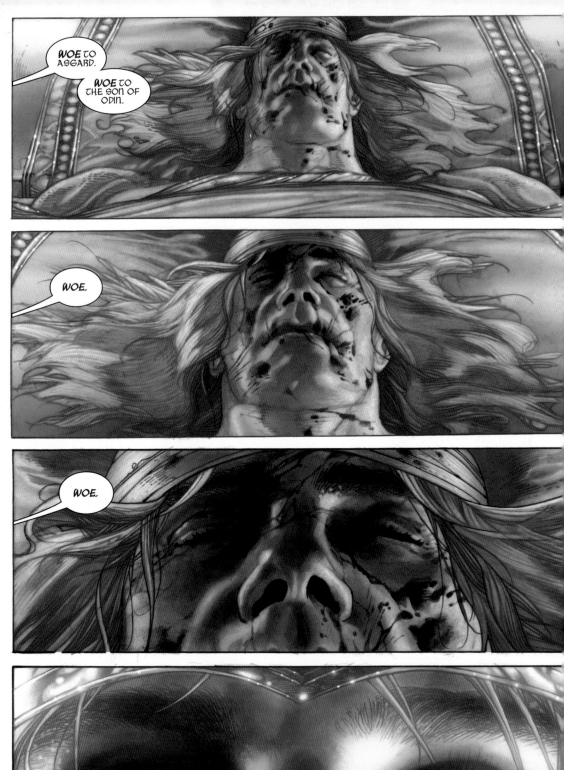

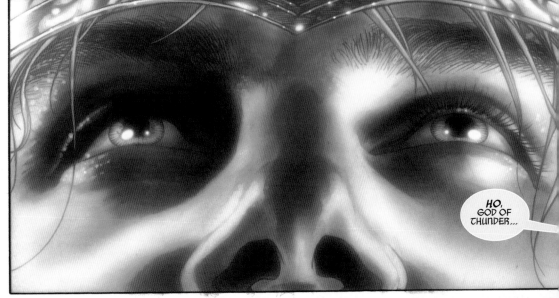

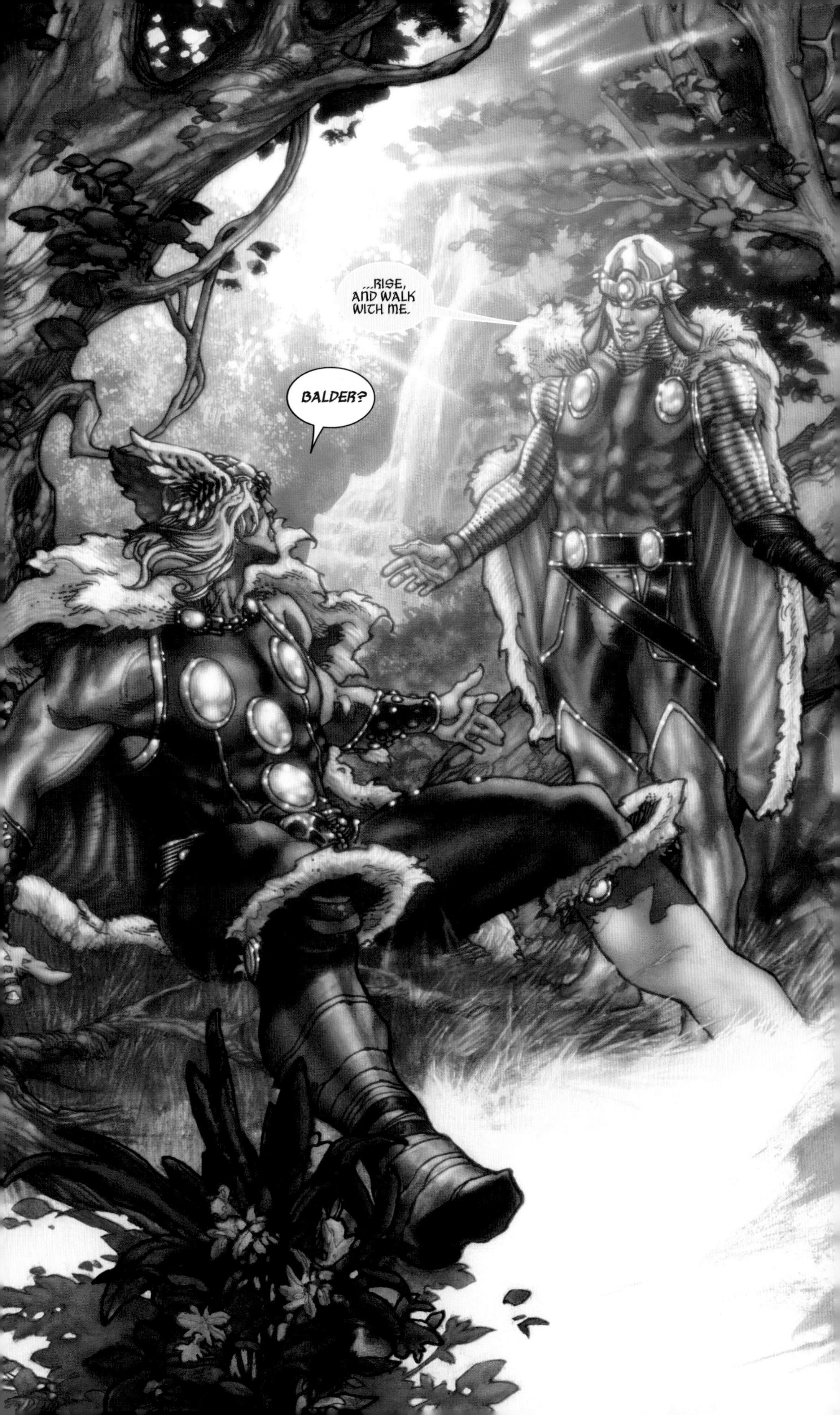
BALDER?
...RISE, AND WALK WITH ME.

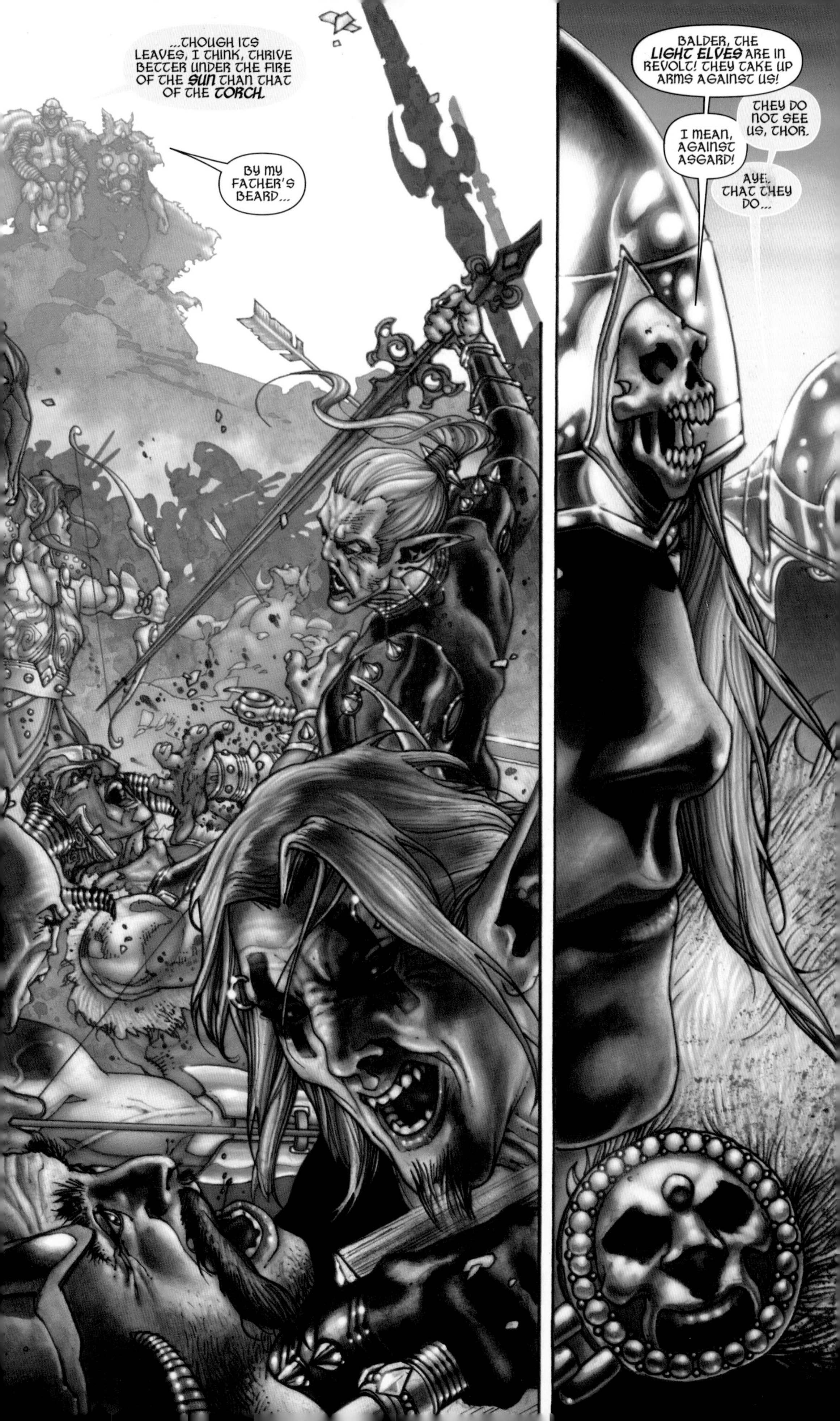
...THOUGH ITS LEAVES, I THINK, THRIVE BETTER UNDER THE FIRE OF THE SUN THAN THAT OF THE TORCH.
BY MY FATHER'S BEARD...
BALDER, THE LIGHT ELVES ARE IN REVOLT! THEY TAKE UP ARMS AGAINST US!
I MEAN, AGAINST ASGARD!
THEY DO NOT SEE US, THOR.
AYE. THAT THEY DO...

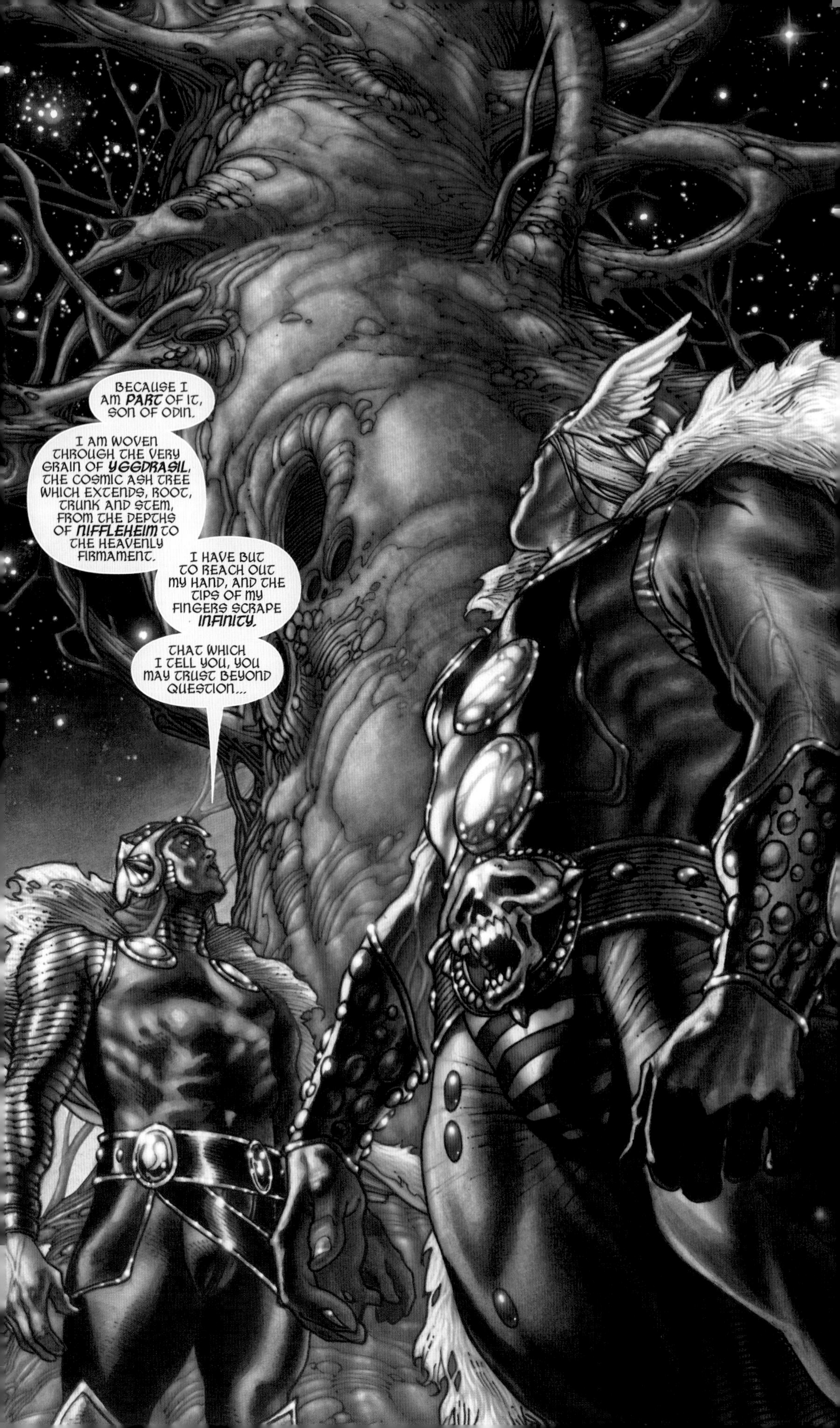
BECAUSE I AM PART OF IT, SON OF ODIN.
I AM WOVEN THROUGH THE VERY GRAIN OF YGGDRASIL, THE COSMIC ASH TREE WHICH EXTENDS, ROOT, TRUNK AND STEM, FROM THE DEPTHS OF NIFFLEHEIM TO THE HEAVENLY FIRMAMENT.
I HAVE BUT TO REACH OUT MY HAND, AND THE TIPS OF MY FINGERS SCRAPE INFINITY.
THAT WHICH I TELL YOU, YOU MAY TRUST BEYOND QUESTION...

...WERE OUR LONG *FRIENDSHIP* NOT SUFFICIENT GUARANTEE.

BALDER...

...*WHAT ARE YOU?*

I AM LIFE.

BUT... YOU *DIED.*

I AM DEATH AS WELL.

I AM THE *CYCLE,* THOR...

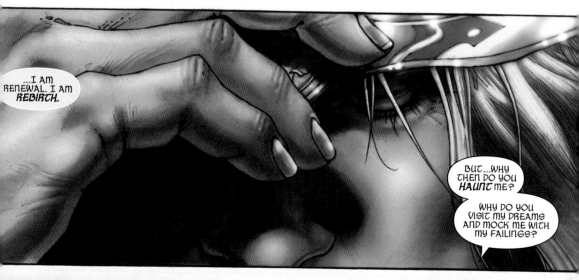

...I AM RENEWAL. I AM *REBIRTH.*

BUT...WHY THEN DO YOU *HAUNT* ME?

WHY DO YOU VISIT MY DREAMS AND MOCK ME WITH MY FAILINGS?

I DO NOT MOCK YOU.
I SEEK TO SET YOU ON YOUR PROPER PATH.
YOU STRIVE TO ACT AS WOULD YOUR **FATHER...**
...BUT YOU WERE NOT MEANT TO FILL HIS PLACE. RATHER HIS PLACE WAS MEANT TO ACCOMMODATE **YOU.**
I...DO NOT UNDERSTAND.
THERE ARE FORCES AGAINST WHICH WE ARE POWERLESS, OLD FRIEND...OUR ESSENTIAL **NATURES** BEING BUT ONE OF THEM.
YOU MUST EMBRACE THAT POWERLESSNESS.
SUBMIT TO THE INEVITABLE.
LET THE WHEEL TURN.
LET THE WHEEL TURN...

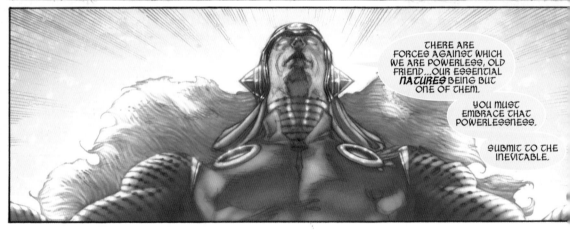

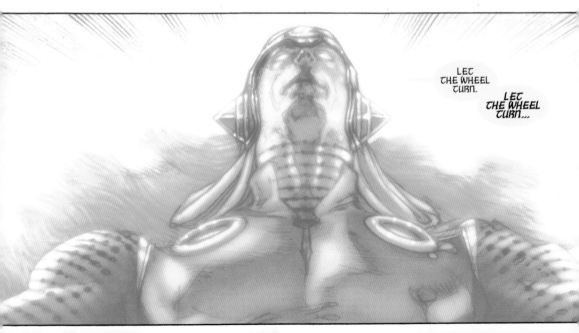

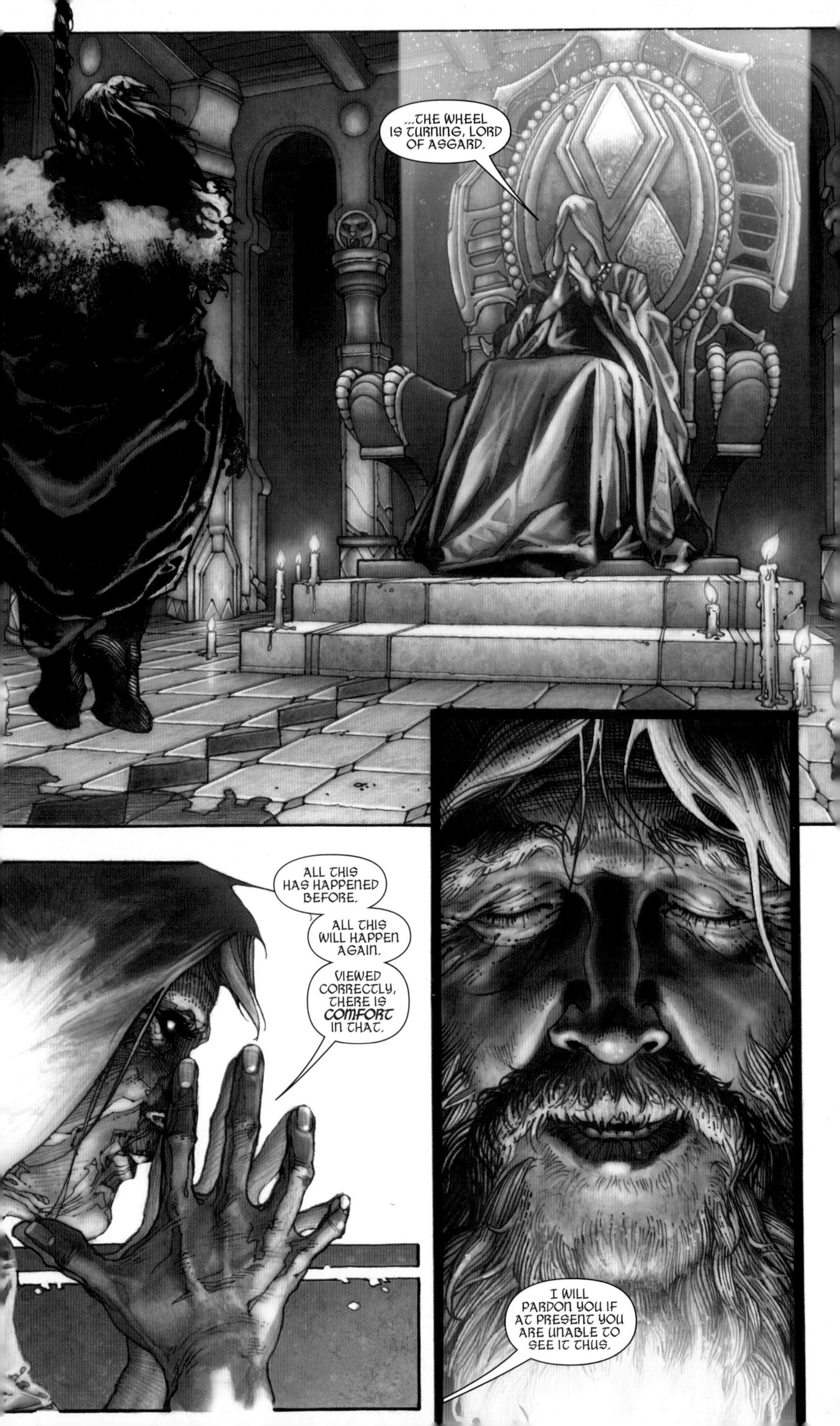
...THE WHEEL IS TURNING, LORD OF ASGARD.
ALL THIS HAS HAPPENED BEFORE.
ALL THIS WILL HAPPEN AGAIN.
VIEWED CORRECTLY, THERE IS **COMFORT** IN THAT.
I WILL PARDON YOU IF AT PRESENT YOU ARE UNABLE TO SEE IT THUS.

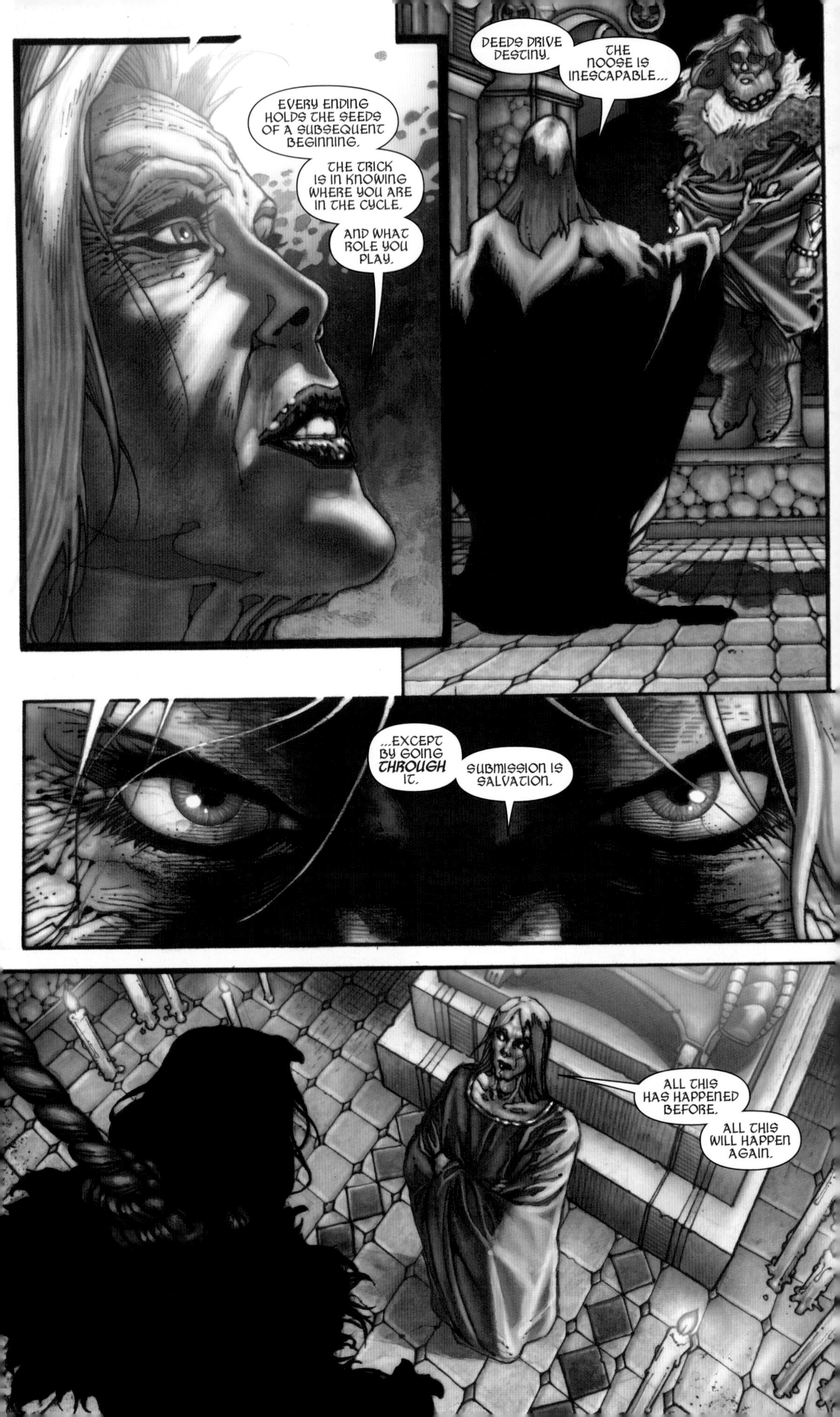
EVERY ENDING HOLDS THE SEEDS OF A SUBSEQUENT BEGINNING.
THE TRICK IS IN KNOWING WHERE YOU ARE IN THE CYCLE.
AND WHAT ROLE YOU PLAY.
DEEDS DRIVE DESTINY.
THE NOOSE IS INESCAPABLE...
...EXCEPT BY GOING **THROUGH** IT.
SUBMISSION IS SALVATION.
ALL THIS HAS HAPPENED BEFORE.
ALL THIS WILL HAPPEN AGAIN.

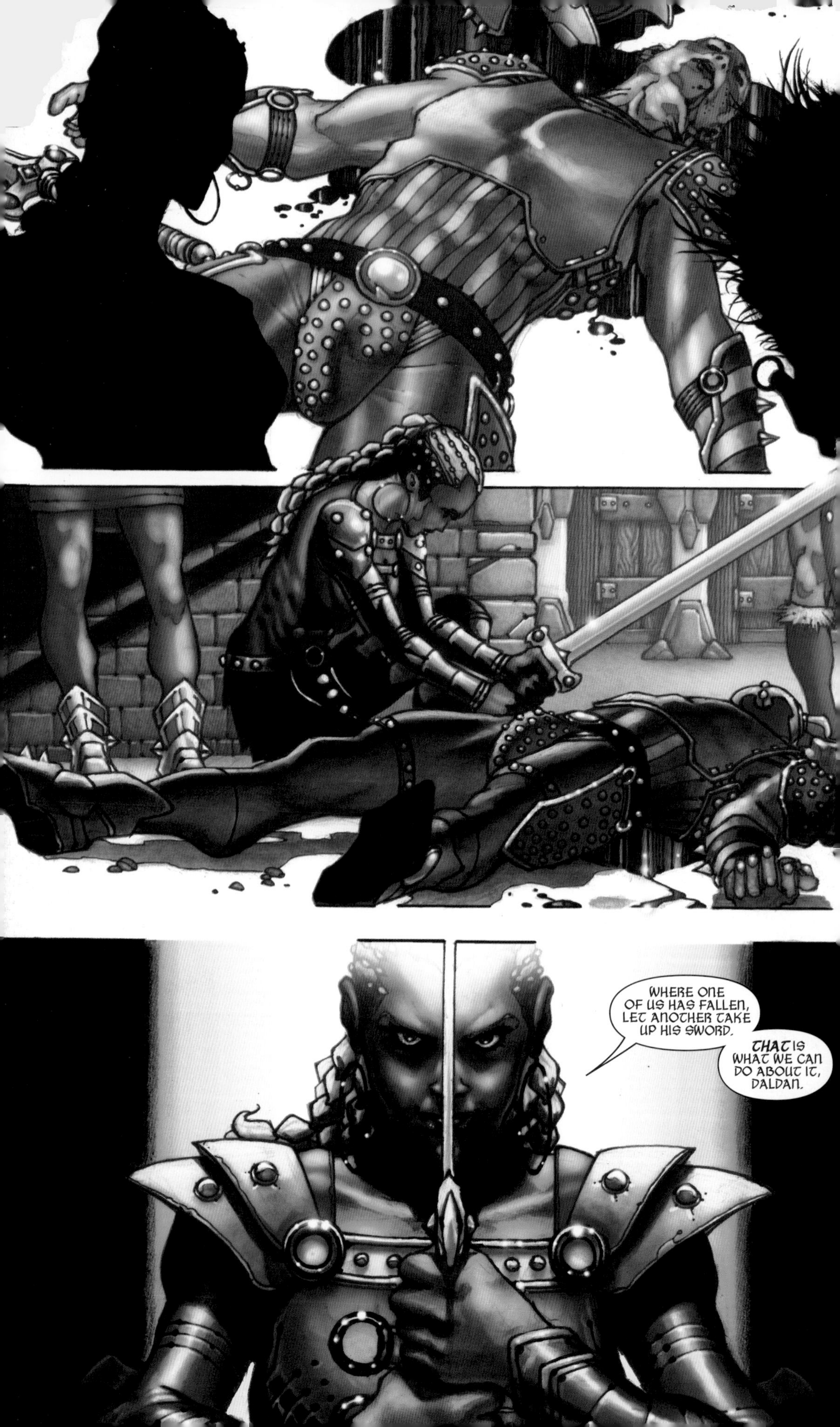
WHERE ONE OF US HAS FALLEN, LET ANOTHER TAKE UP HIS SWORD.
THAT IS WHAT WE CAN DO ABOUT IT, DALDAN.

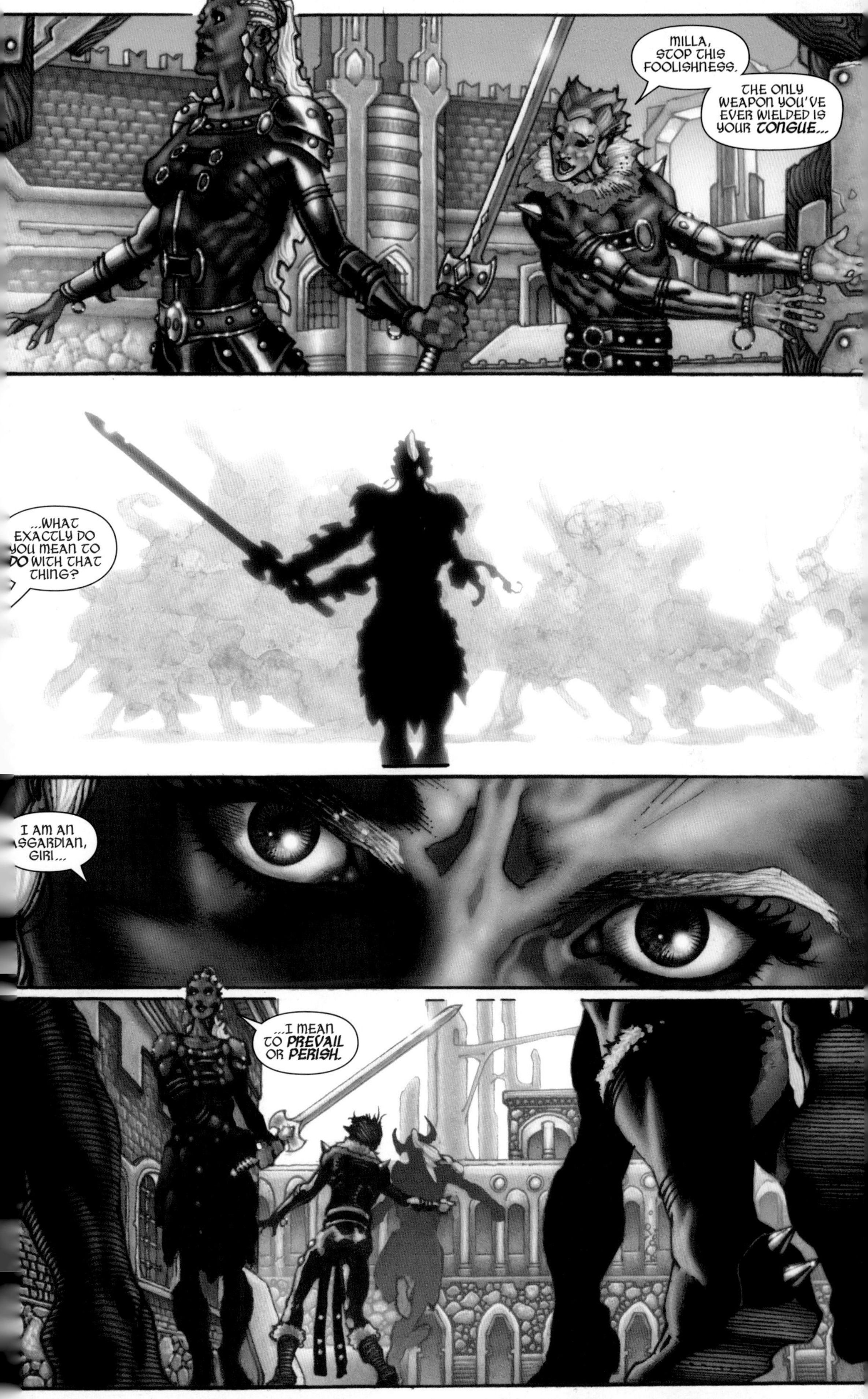
MILLA, STOP THIS FOOLISHNESS.
THE ONLY WEAPON YOU'VE EVER WIELDED IS YOUR TONGUE...
...WHAT EXACTLY DO YOU MEAN TO DO WITH THAT THING?
I AM AN ASGARDIAN, GIRL...
...I MEAN TO PREVAIL OR PERISH.

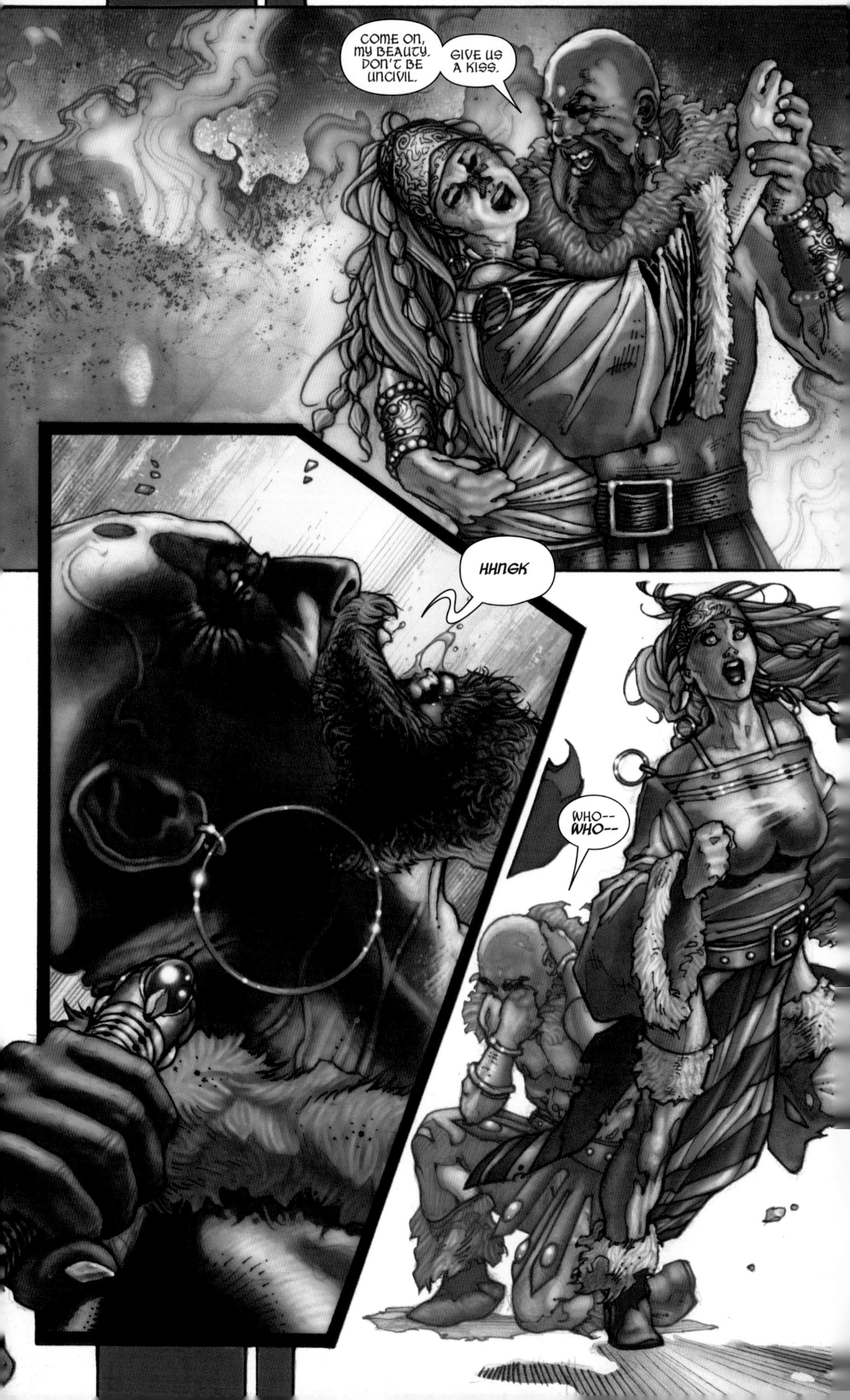
COME ON, MY BEAUTY. DON'T BE UNCIVIL.
GIVE US A KISS.
HHNGK
WHO-- WHO--

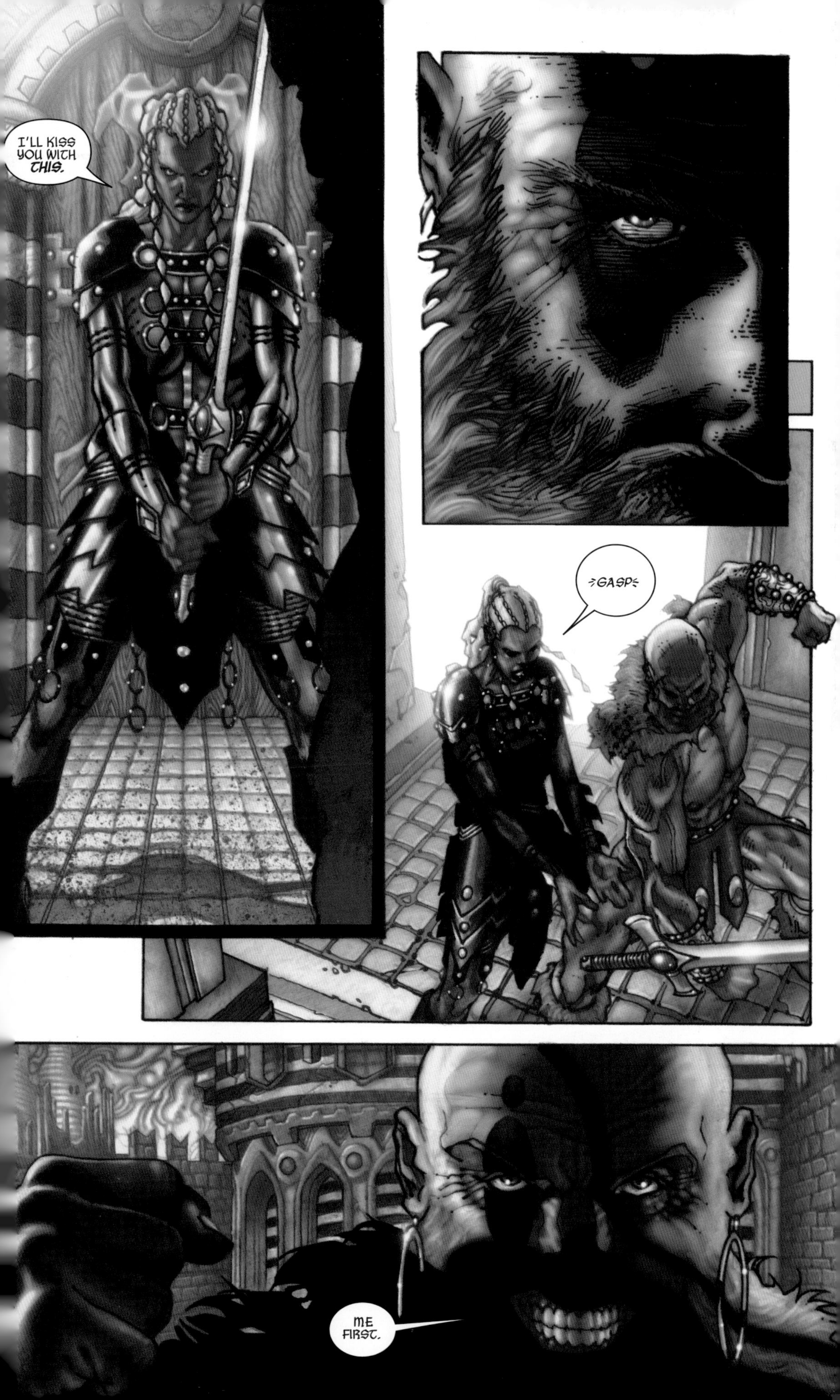
I'LL KISS YOU WITH THIS.
GASP
ME FIRST.

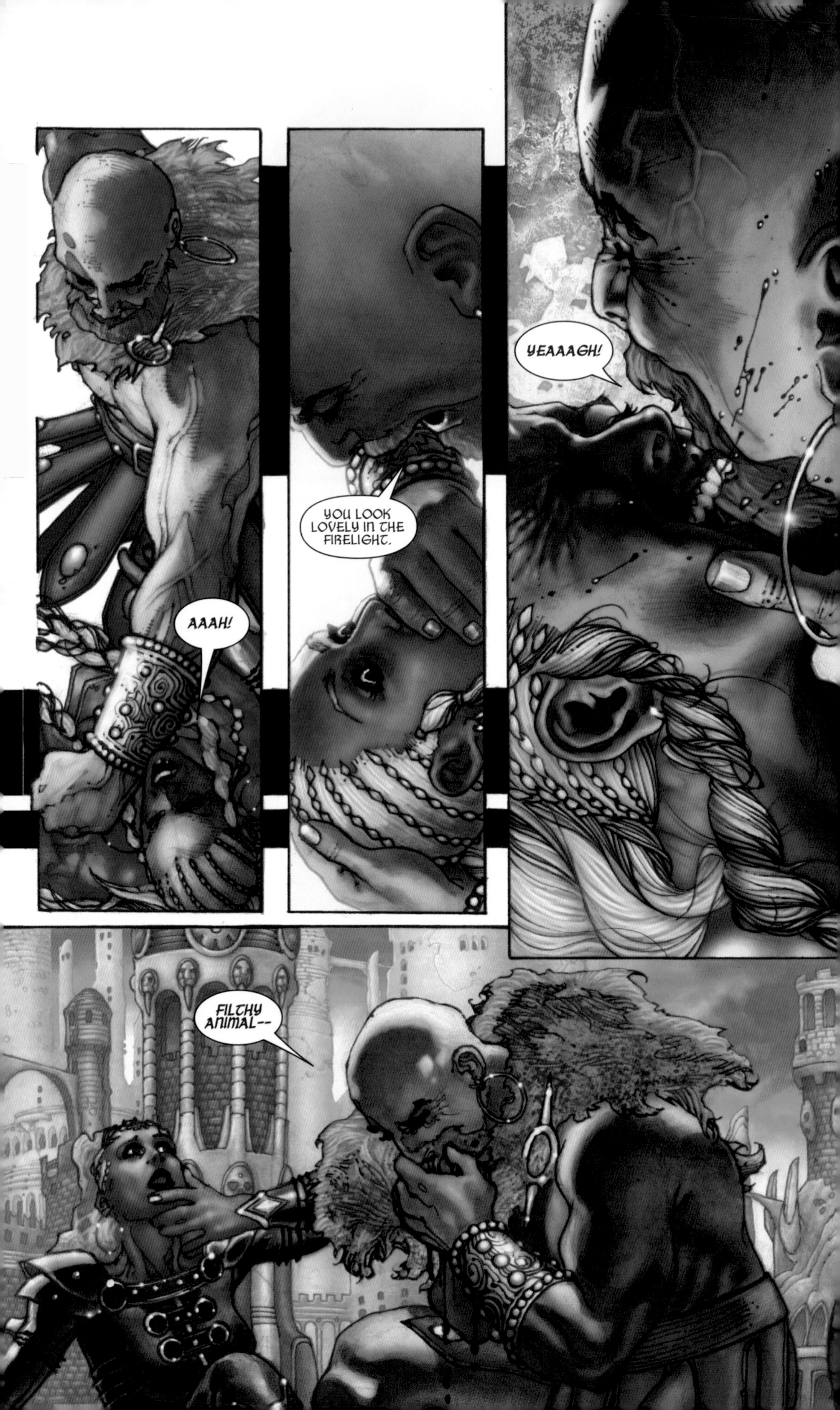
AAAH!
YOU LOOK LOVELY IN THE FIRELIGHT.
YEAAAGH!
FILTHY ANIMAL--

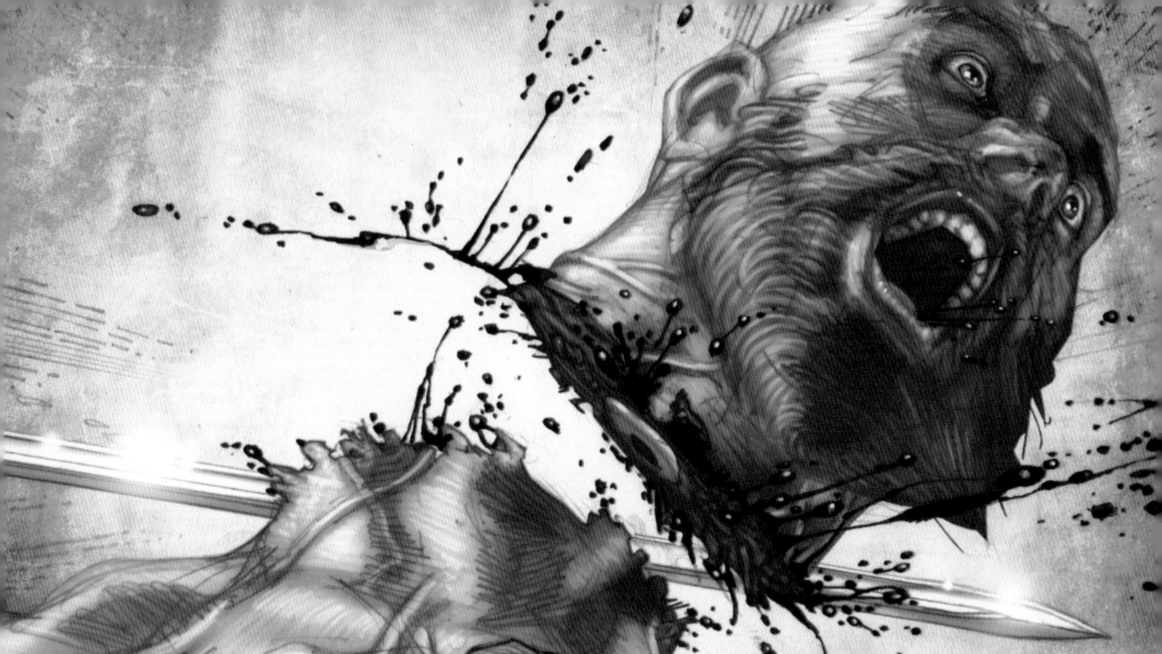

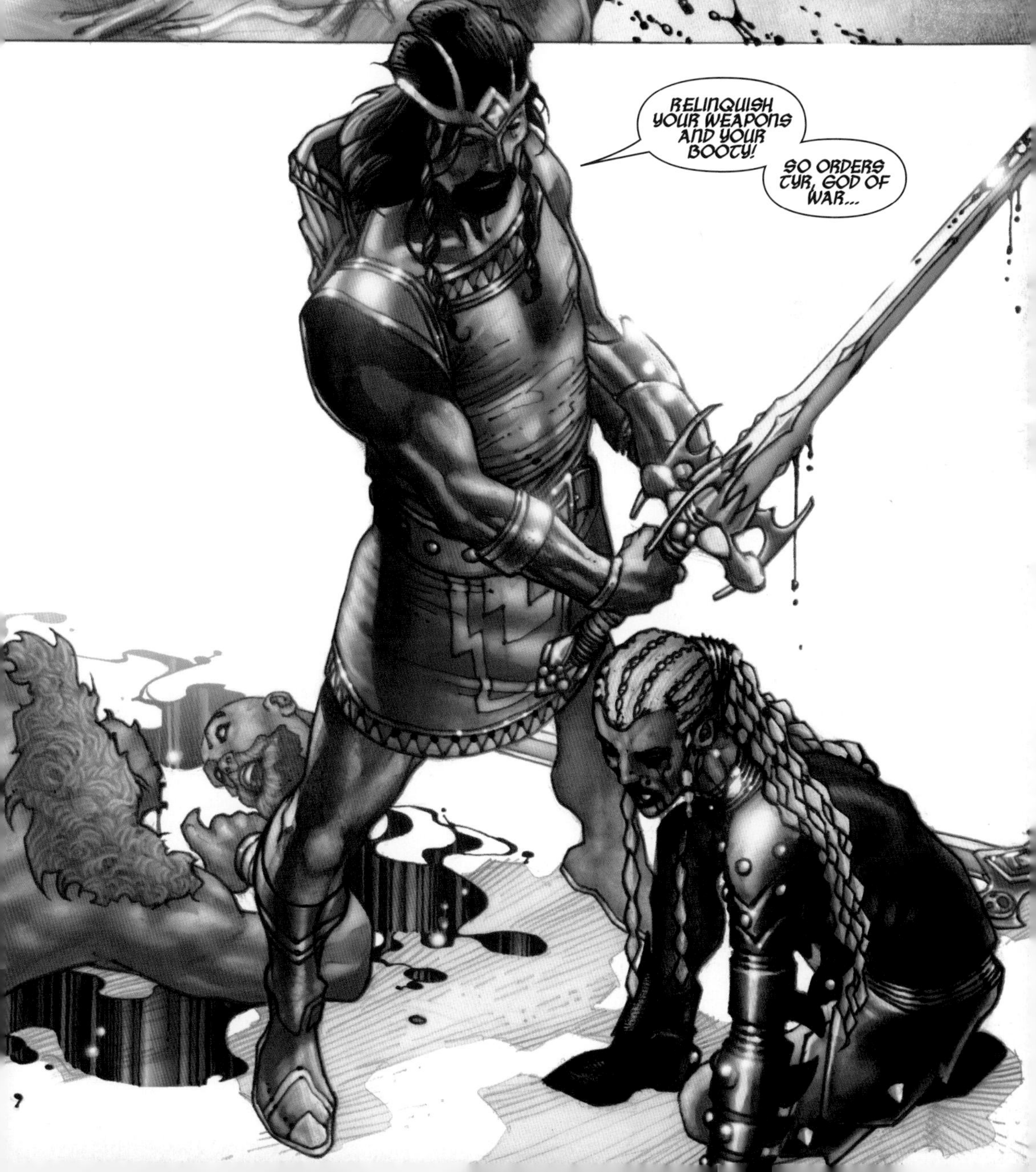
RELINQUISH YOUR WEAPONS AND YOUR BOOTY!
SO ORDERS TYR, GOD OF WAR...

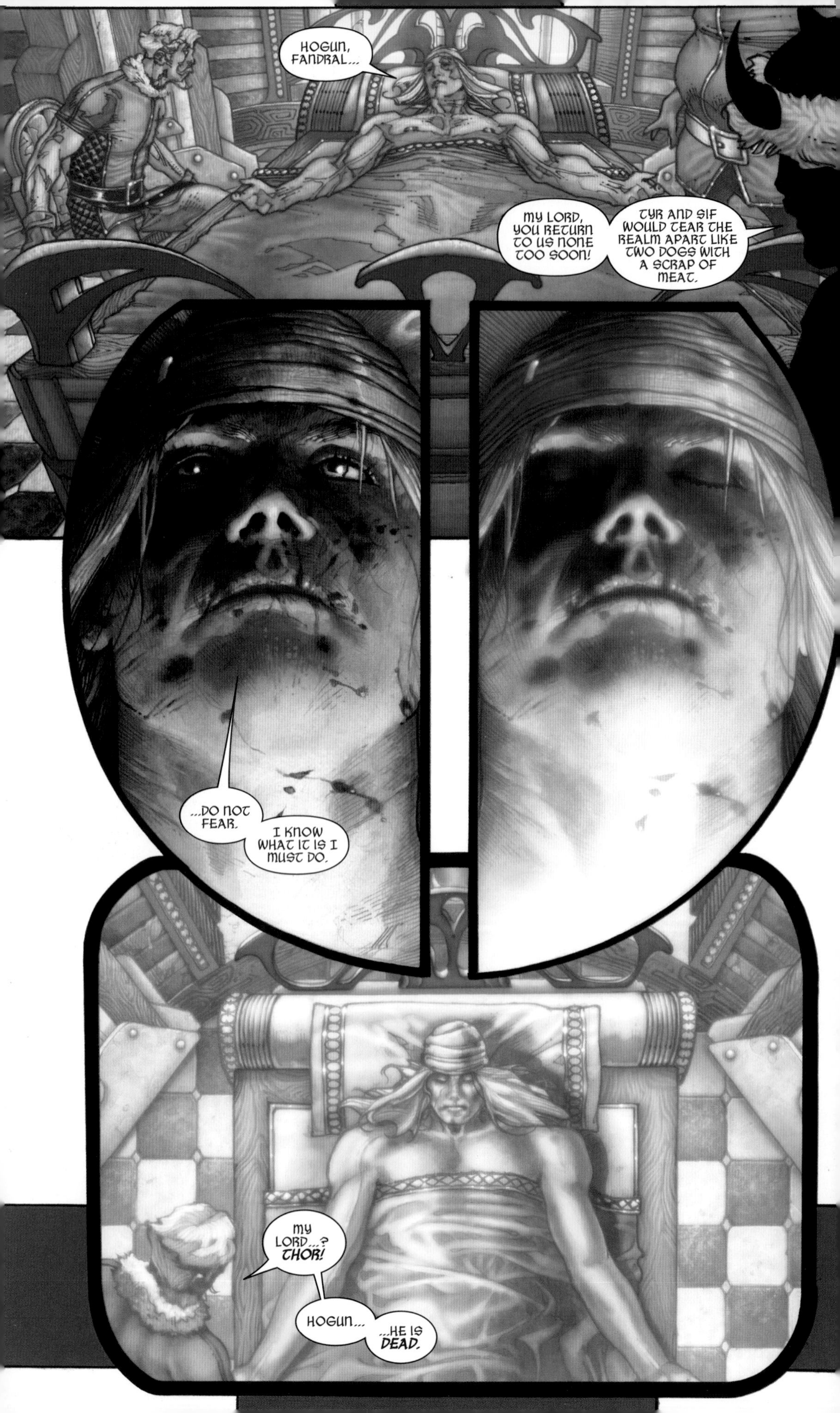
HOGUN, FANDRAL...
MY LORD, YOU RETURN TO US NONE TOO SOON!
TYR AND SIF WOULD TEAR THE REALM APART LIKE TWO DOGS WITH A SCRAP OF MEAT.
...DO NOT FEAR.
I KNOW WHAT IT IS I MUST DO.
MY LORD...? THOR!
HOGUN...
...HE IS DEAD.

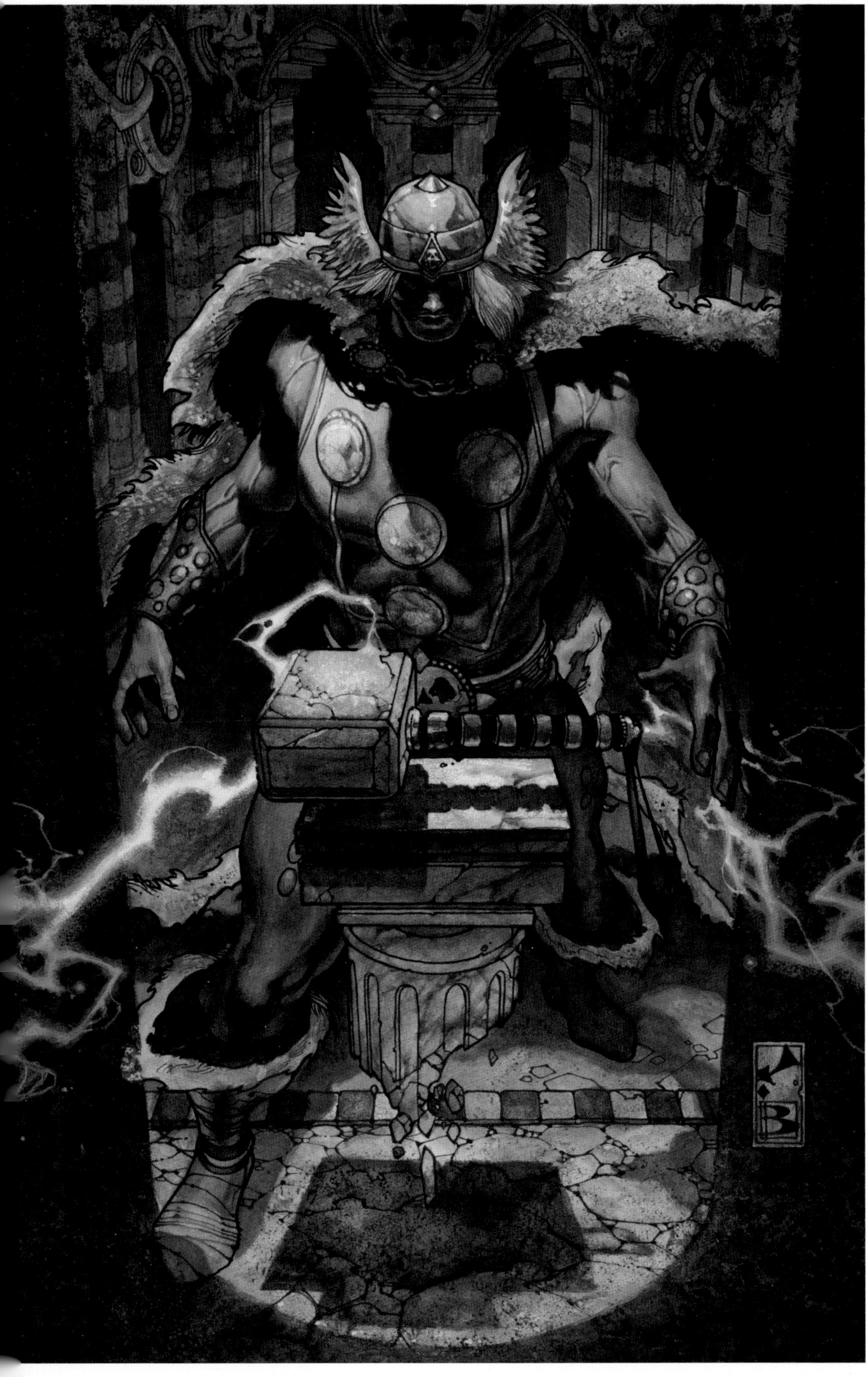

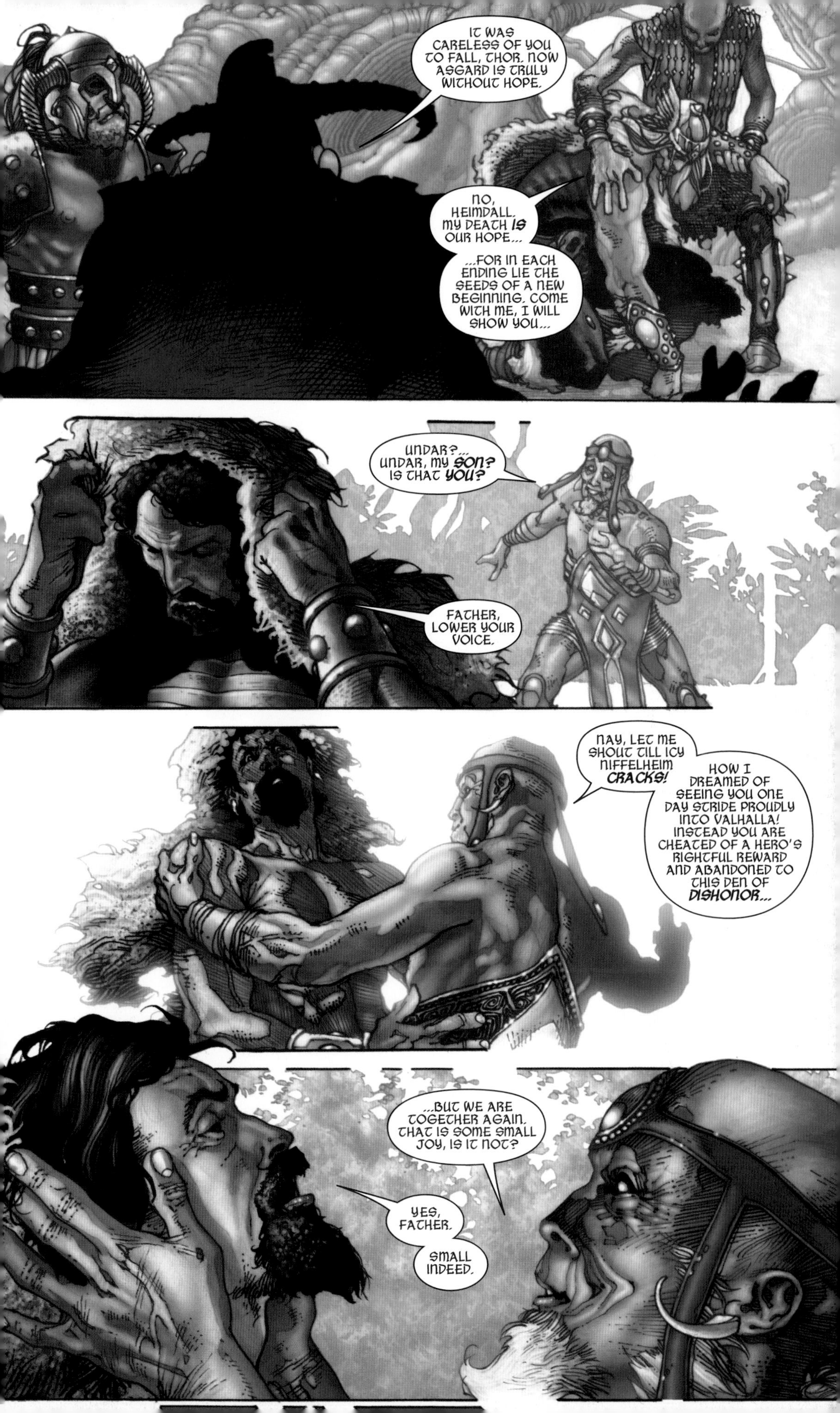
IT WAS CARELESS OF YOU TO FALL, THOR. NOW ASGARD IS TRULY WITHOUT HOPE.
NO, HEIMDALL. MY DEATH IS OUR HOPE...
...FOR IN EACH ENDING LIE THE SEEDS OF A NEW BEGINNING. COME WITH ME, I WILL SHOW YOU...
UNDAR?... UNDAR, MY SON? IS THAT YOU?
FATHER, LOWER YOUR VOICE.
NAY, LET ME SHOUT TILL ICY NIFFELHEIM CRACKS!
HOW I DREAMED OF SEEING YOU ONE DAY STRIDE PROUDLY INTO VALHALLA! INSTEAD YOU ARE CHEATED OF A HERO'S RIGHTFUL REWARD AND ABANDONED TO THIS DEN OF DISHONOR...
...BUT WE ARE TOGETHER AGAIN. THAT IS SOME SMALL JOY, IS IT NOT?
YES, FATHER.
SMALL INDEED.

...THESE ARE THE ROOTS OF *YGGDRASIL,* THE COSMIC ASH TREE WHOSE TRUNK RISES UP THROUGH ALL THE NINE WORLDS, AND WHOSE BRANCHES FLOWER IN THE SKY ABOVE *ASGARD CITY.*

THIS IS WHY I HAVE COME WILLINGLY TO *NIFFELHEIM,* TO LEAD YOU HERE.

WE WILL *CLIMB* THE ASH TREE BACK TO ASGARD.

CLIMB IT? ODINSON, ARE YOU *MAD?*

YGGDRASIL IS *IMPOSSIBLY* VAST. ITS SPAN IS BEYOND ALL MEASURE, MORTAL OR DIVINE. IN SOME PLACES IT EXISTS ONLY AS A *CONCEPT.*

WE OURSELVES ARE LITTLE MORE THAN *SHADOWS...*

...THIS THING *CANNOT* BE DONE.

VERY WELL THEN, SIGMUND.

STAY HERE.

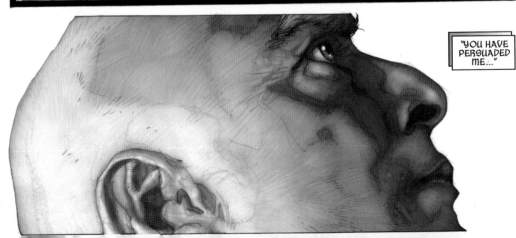

"YOU HAVE PERSUADED ME...."

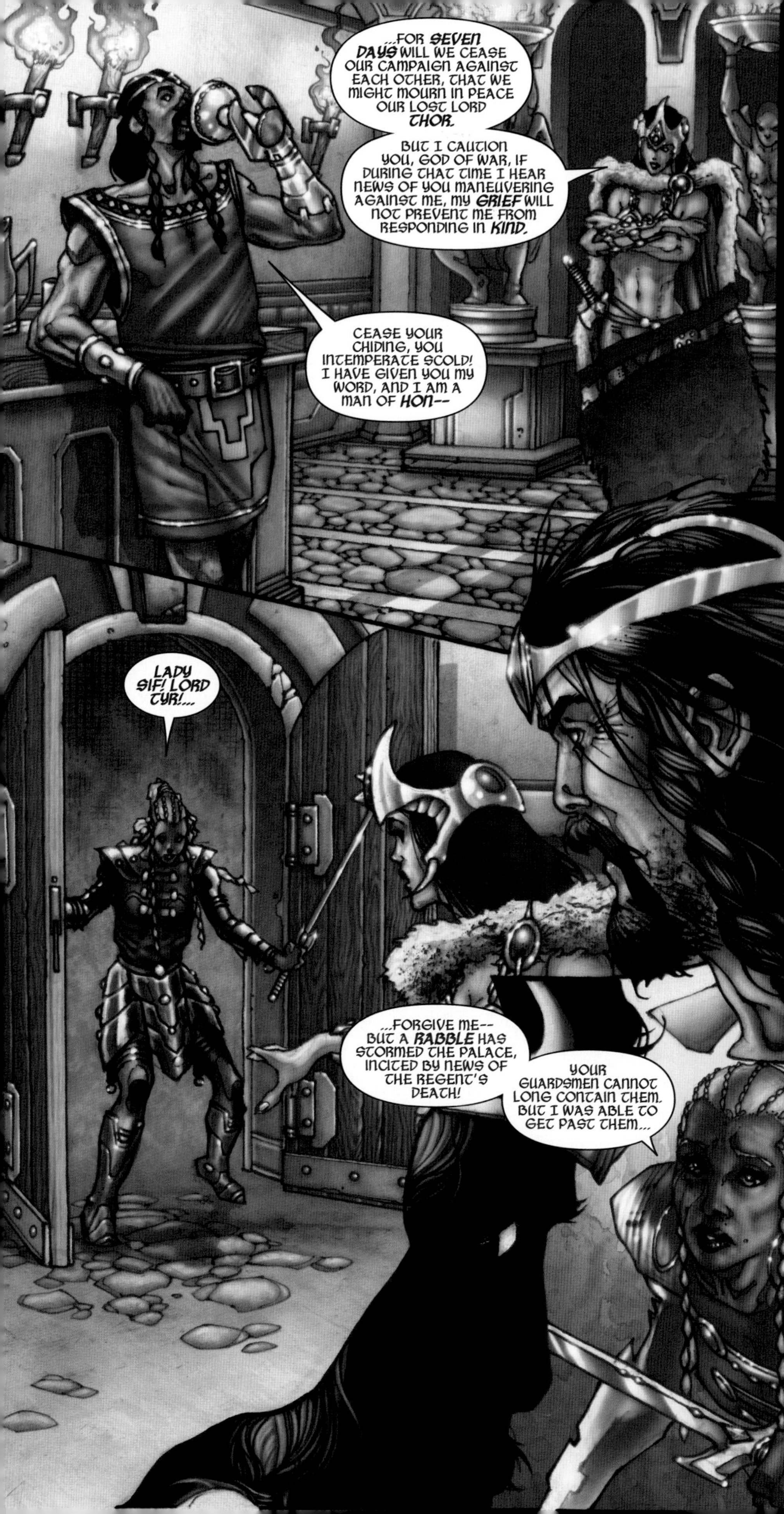
...FOR SEVEN DAYS WILL WE CEASE OUR CAMPAIGN AGAINST EACH OTHER, THAT WE MIGHT MOURN IN PEACE OUR LOST LORD THOR.
BUT I CAUTION YOU, GOD OF WAR, IF DURING THAT TIME I HEAR NEWS OF YOU MANEUVERING AGAINST ME, MY GRIEF WILL NOT PREVENT ME FROM RESPONDING IN KIND.
CEASE YOUR CHIDING, YOU INTEMPERATE SCOLD! I HAVE GIVEN YOU MY WORD, AND I AM A MAN OF HON--
LADY SIF! LORD TYR!...
...FORGIVE ME-- BUT A RABBLE HAS STORMED THE PALACE, INCITED BY NEWS OF THE REGENT'S DEATH!
YOUR GUARDSMEN CANNOT LONG CONTAIN THEM. BUT I WAS ABLE TO GET PAST THEM...

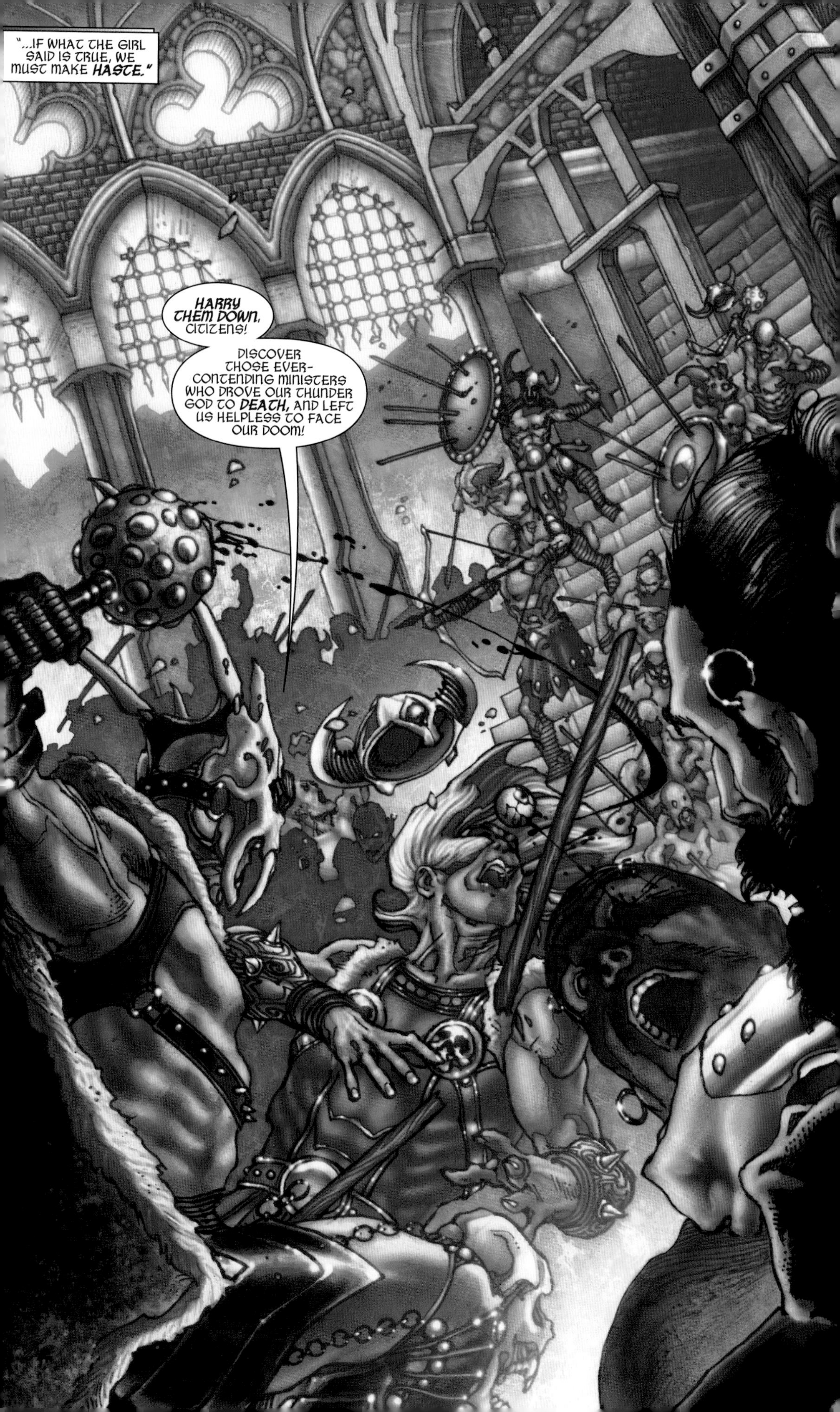
"...IF WHAT THE GIRL SAID IS TRUE, WE MUST MAKE HASTE."
HARRY THEM DOWN, CITIZENS!
DISCOVER THOSE EVER-CONTENDING MINISTERS WHO DROVE OUR THUNDER GOD TO DEATH, AND LEFT US HELPLESS TO FACE OUR DOOM!

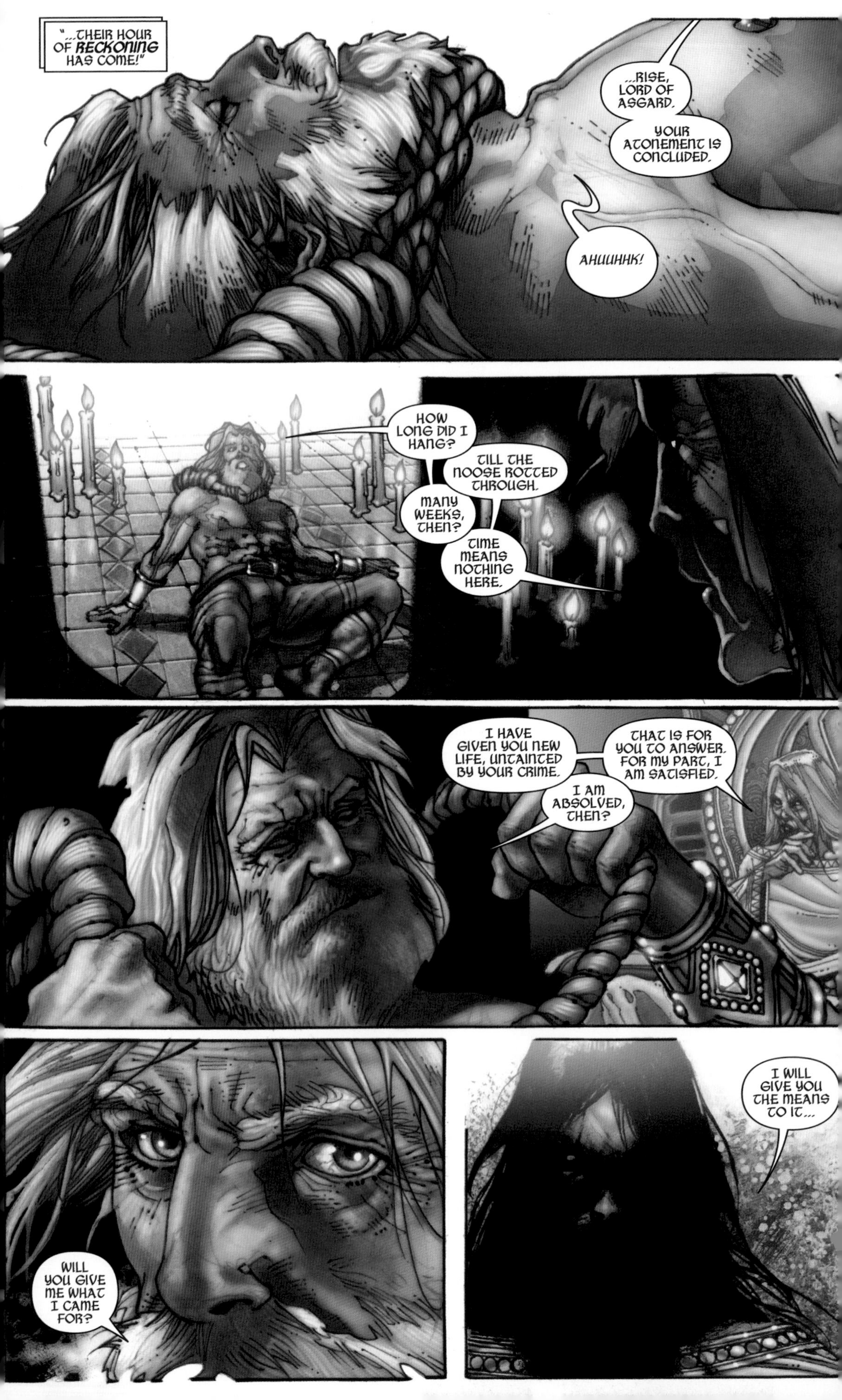
"...THEIR HOUR OF RECKONING HAS COME!"
...RISE, LORD OF ASGARD.
YOUR ATONEMENT IS CONCLUDED.
AHUUHHK!
HOW LONG DID I HANG?
TILL THE NOOSE ROTTED THROUGH.
MANY WEEKS, THEN?
TIME MEANS NOTHING HERE.
I HAVE GIVEN YOU NEW LIFE, UNTAINTED BY YOUR CRIME.
I AM ABSOLVED, THEN?
THAT IS FOR YOU TO ANSWER. FOR MY PART, I AM SATISFIED.
WILL YOU GIVE ME WHAT I CAME FOR?
I WILL GIVE YOU THE MEANS TO IT...

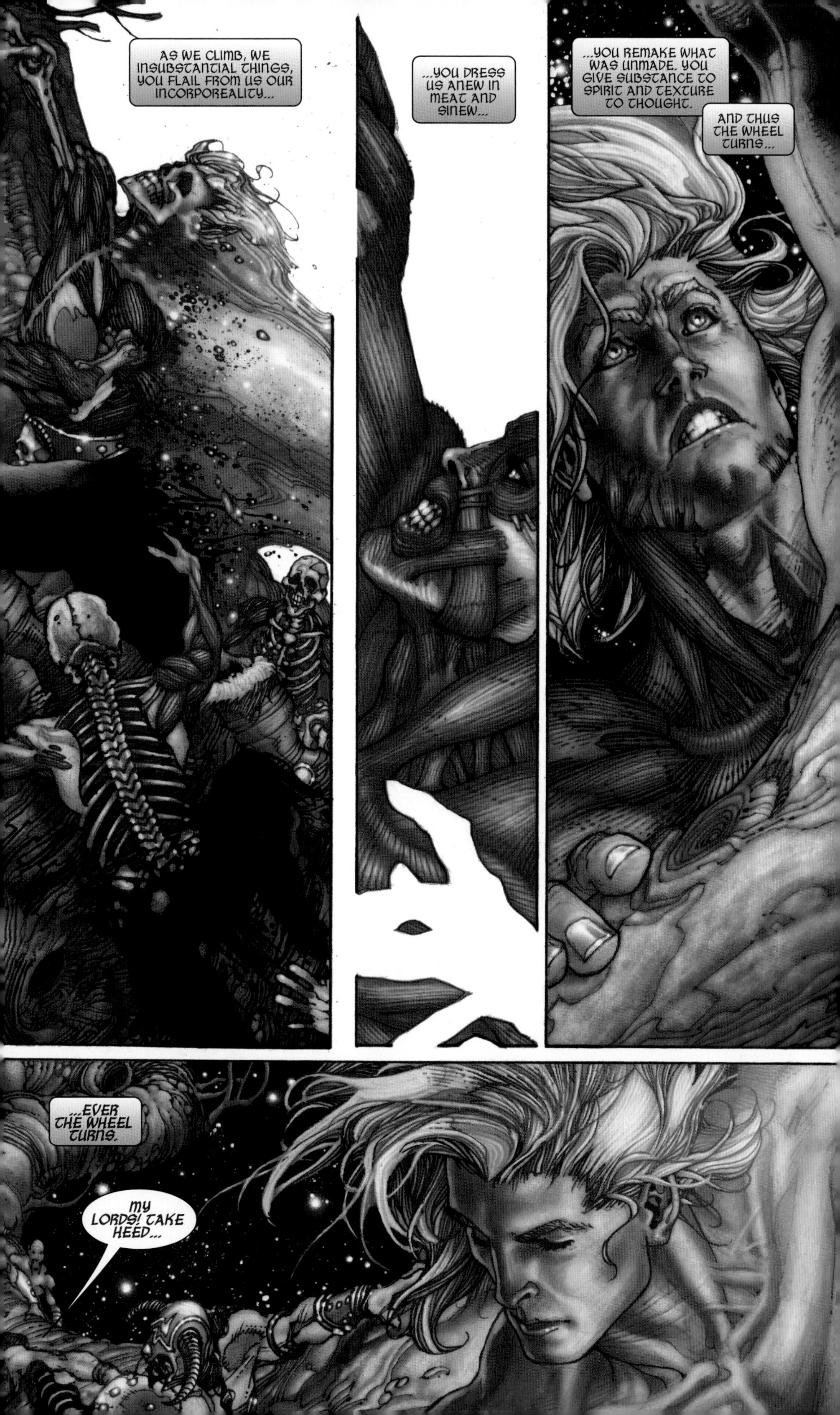
AS WE CLIMB, WE INSUBSTANTIAL THINGS, YOU FLAIL FROM US OUR INCORPOREALITY...
...YOU DRESS US ANEW IN MEAT AND SINEW...
...YOU REMAKE WHAT WAS UNMADE. YOU GIVE SUBSTANCE TO SPIRIT AND TEXTURE TO THOUGHT.
AND THUS THE WHEEL TURNS...
...EVER THE WHEEL TURNS.
MY LORDS! TAKE HEED...

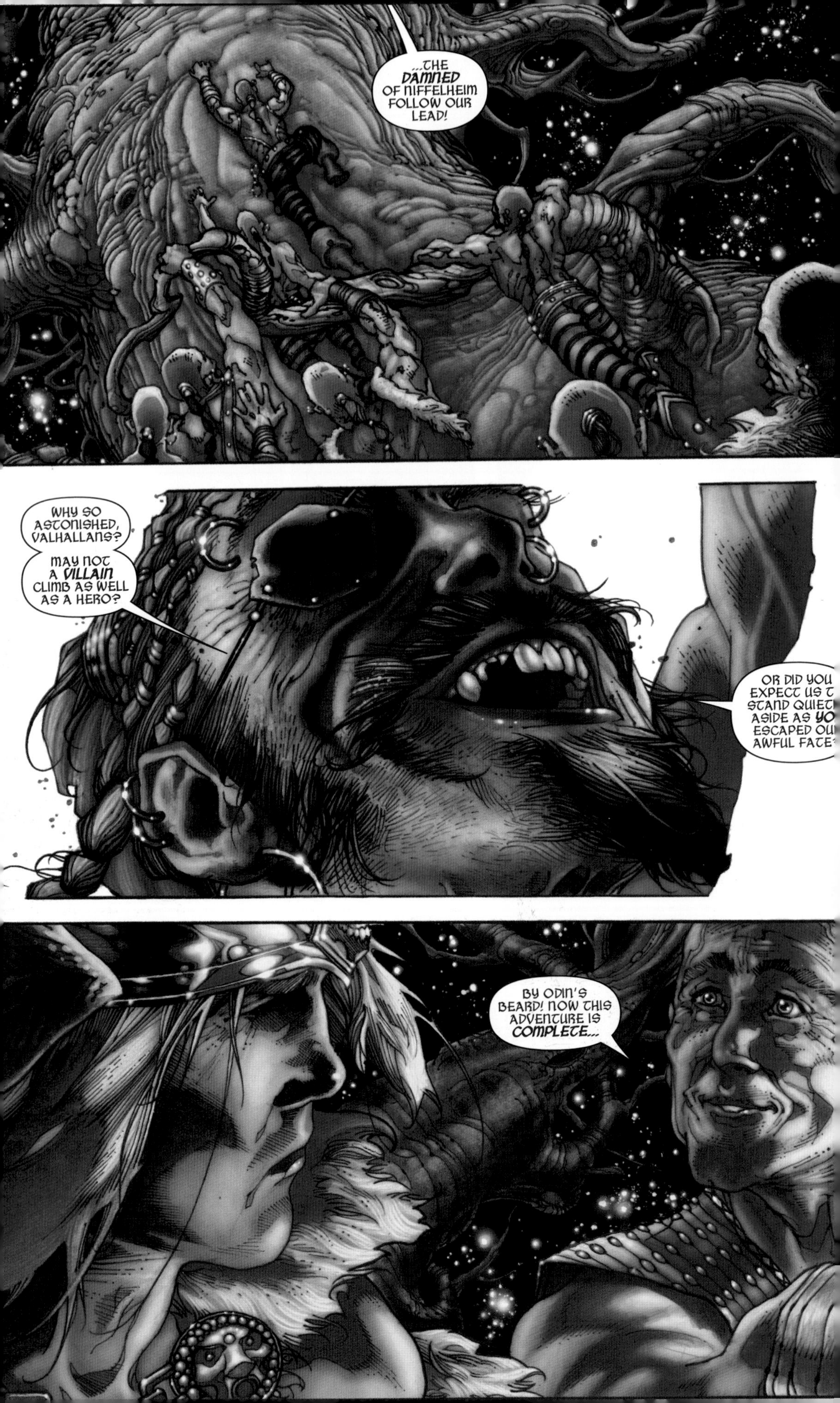

...THE DAMNED OF NIFFELHEIM FOLLOW OUR LEAD!
WHY SO ASTONISHED, VALHALLANS?
MAY NOT A VILLAIN CLIMB AS WELL AS A HERO?
OR DID YOU EXPECT US T STAND QUIET ASIDE AS YO ESCAPED OU AWFUL FATE
BY ODIN'S BEARD! NOW THIS ADVENTURE IS COMPLETE...

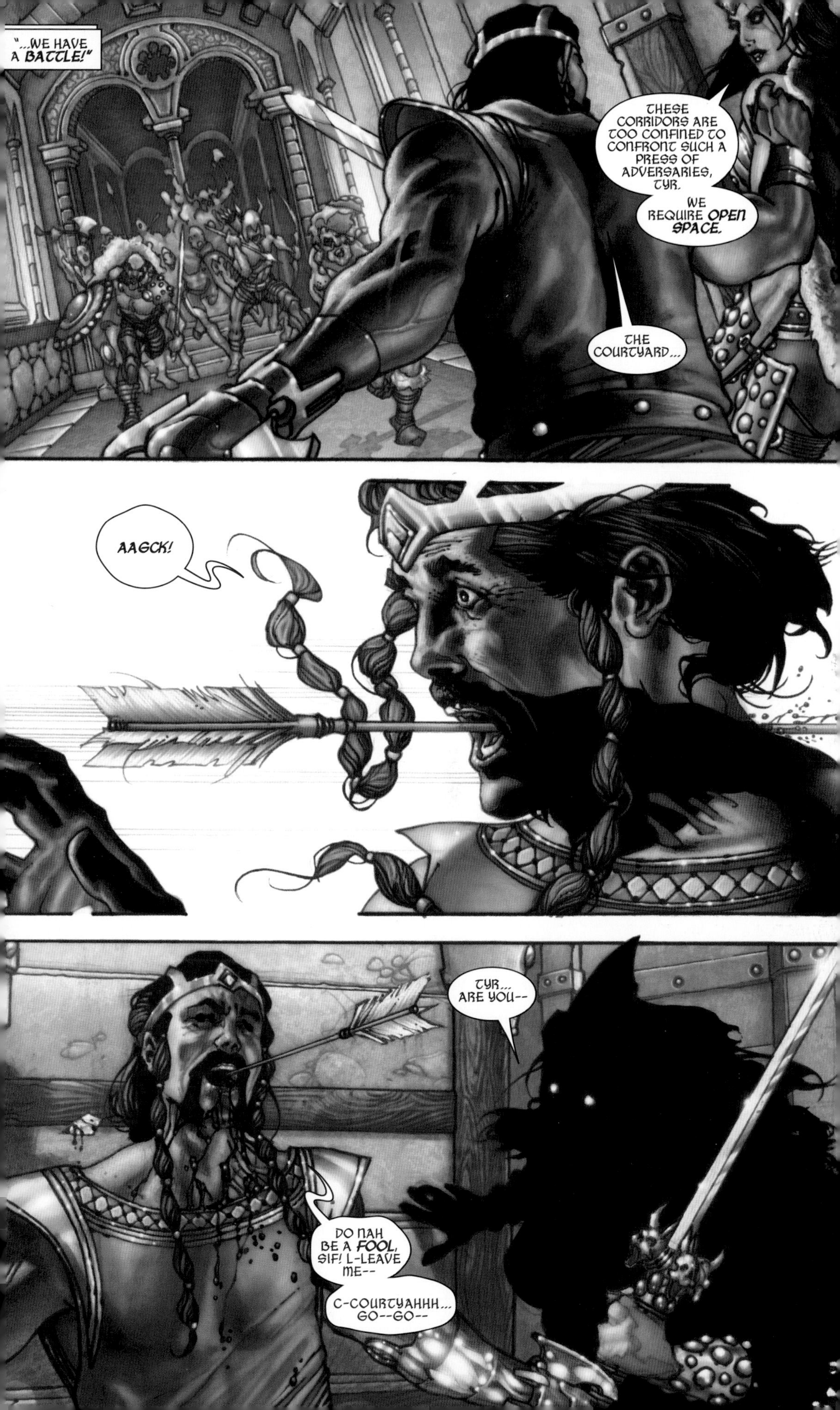
"...WE HAVE A BATTLE!"
THESE CORRIDORS ARE TOO CONFINED TO CONFRONT SUCH A PRESS OF ADVERSARIES, TYR.
WE REQUIRE OPEN SPACE.
THE COURTYARD...
AAGCK!
TYR... ARE YOU--
DO NAH BE A FOOL, SIF! L-LEAVE ME--
C-COURTYAHHH... GO--GO--

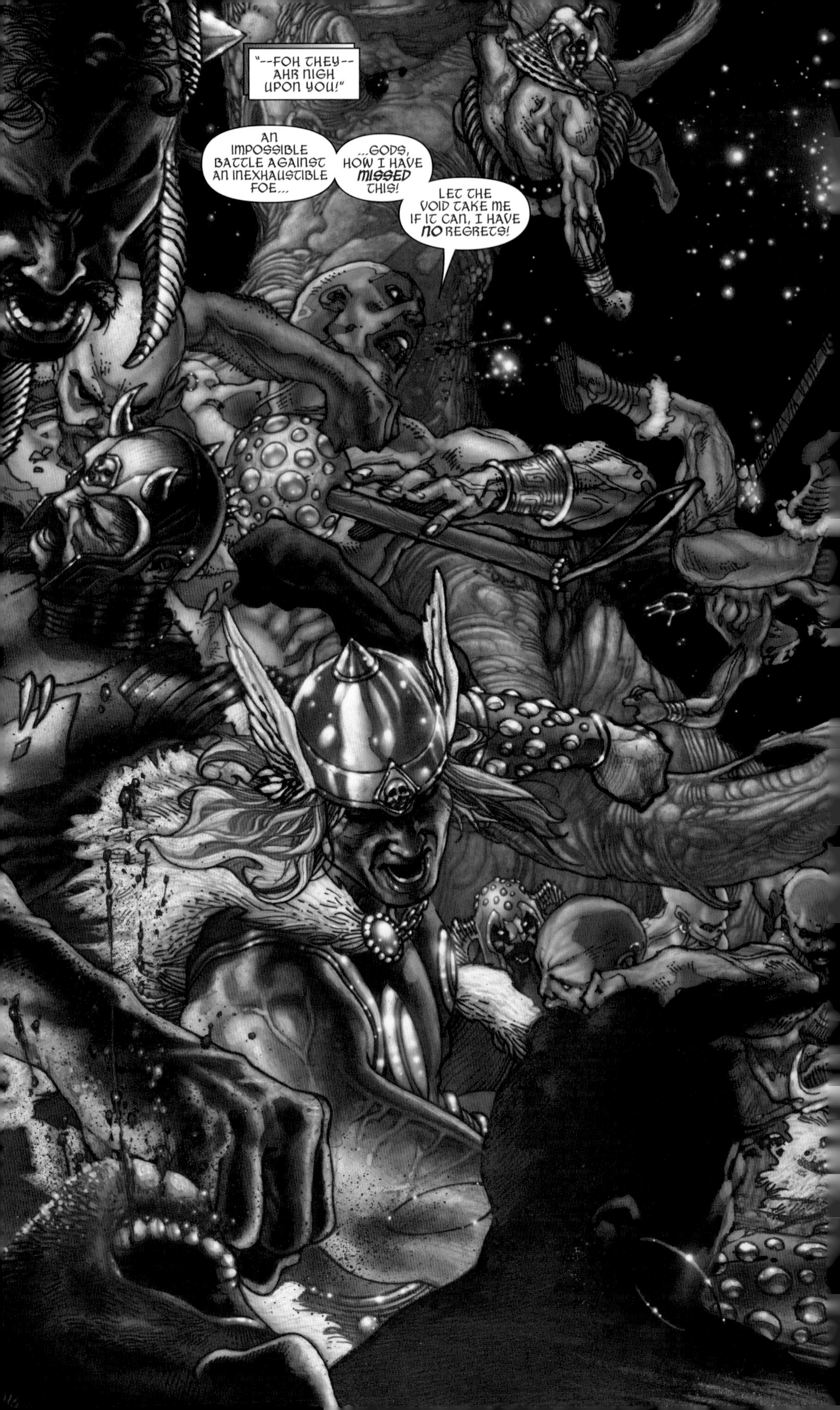
"--FOH THEY--
AHR NIGH
UPON YOU!"
AN IMPOSSIBLE BATTLE AGAINST AN INEXHAUSTIBLE FOE...
...GODS, HOW I HAVE MISSED THIS!
LET THE VOID TAKE ME IF IT CAN, I HAVE NO REGRETS!

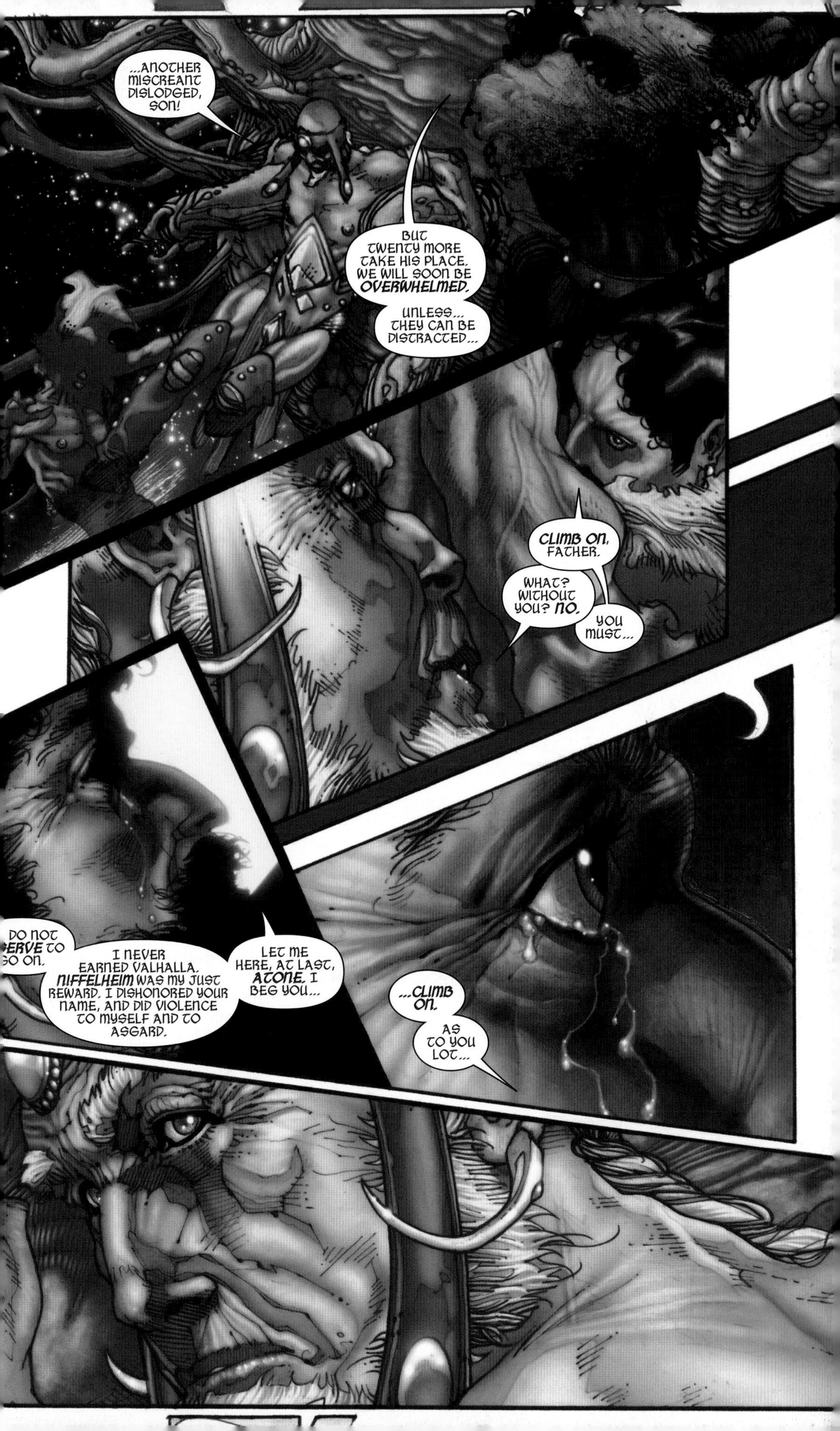

...ANOTHER MISCREANT DISLODGED, SON!
BUT TWENTY MORE TAKE HIS PLACE. WE WILL SOON BE **OVERWHELMED.**
UNLESS... THEY CAN BE DISTRACTED...
CLIMB ON, FATHER.
WHAT? WITHOUT YOU? **NO.**
YOU MUST...
DO NOT **ERVE** TO GO ON.
I NEVER EARNED VALHALLA. **NIFFELHEIM** WAS MY JUST REWARD. I DISHONORED YOUR NAME, AND DID VIOLENCE TO MYSELF AND TO ASGARD.
LET ME HERE, AT LAST, **ATONE.** I BEG YOU...
...CLIMB ON.
AS TO YOU LOT...

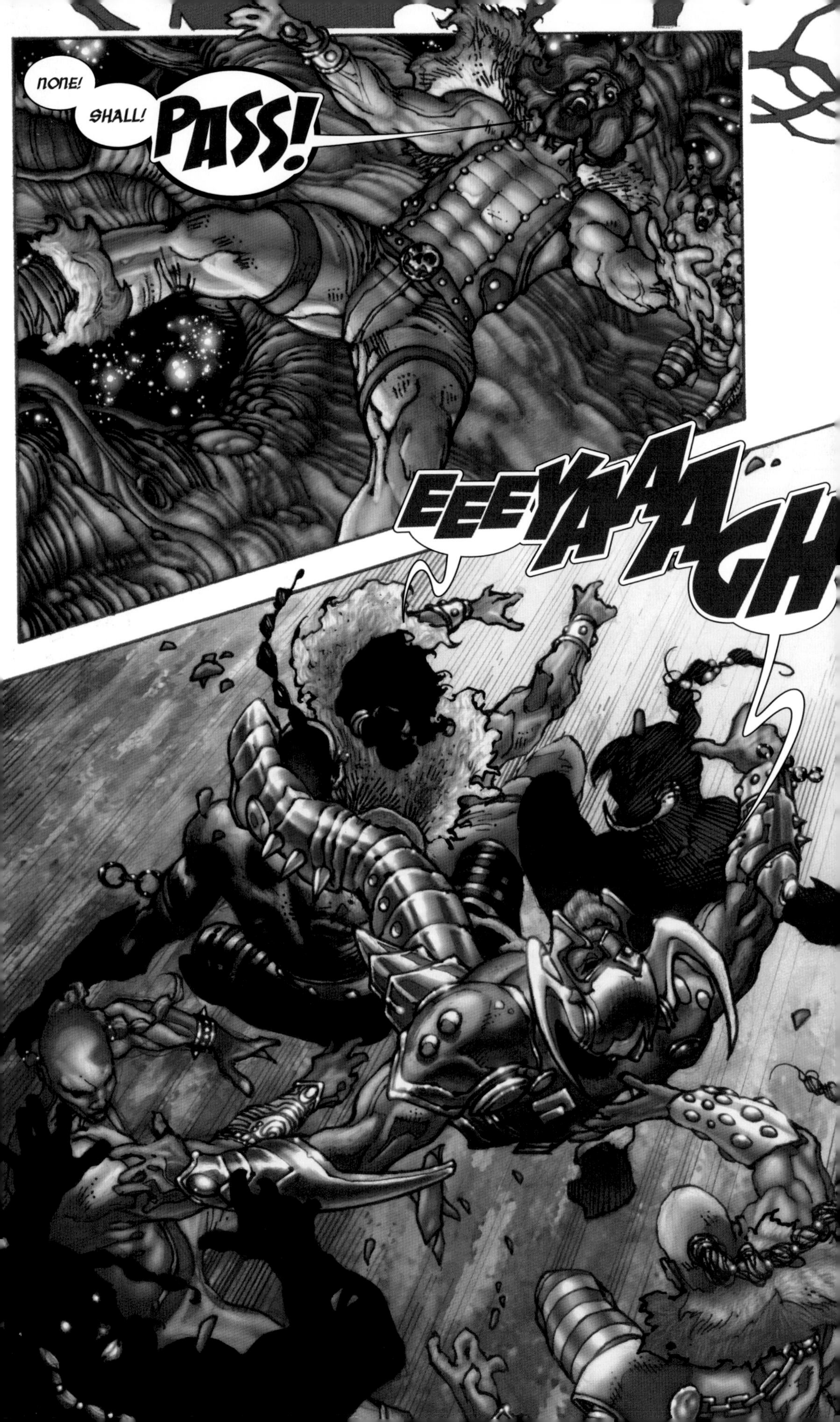
NONE!
SHALL!
PASS!
EEEYAAACH

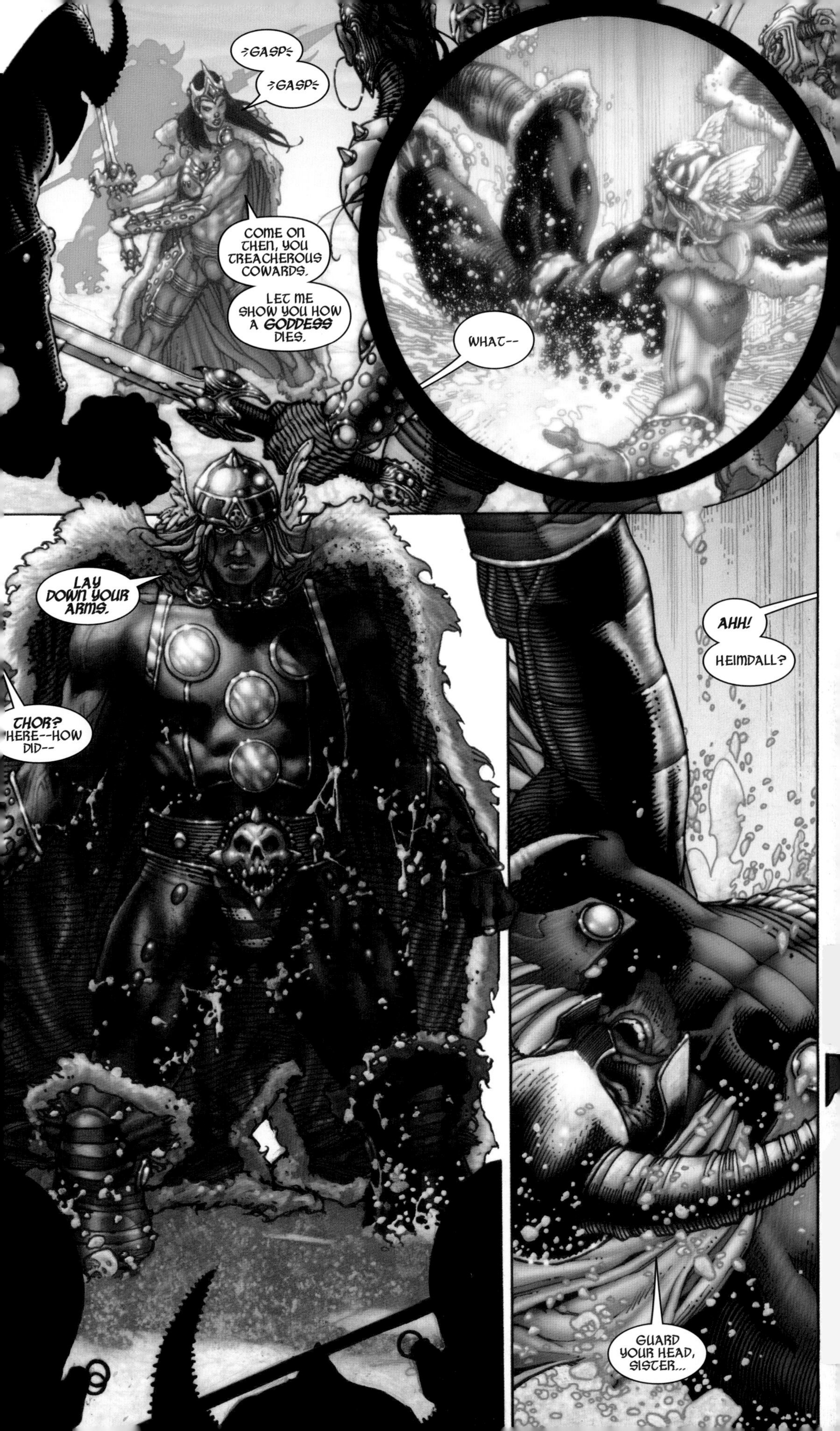

⇢GASP⇠
⇢GASP⇠
COME ON THEN, YOU TREACHEROUS COWARDS.
LET ME SHOW YOU HOW A GODDESS DIES.
WHAT--
LAY DOWN YOUR ARMS.
THOR? HERE--HOW DID--
AHH!
HEIMDALL?
GUARD YOUR HEAD, SISTER...

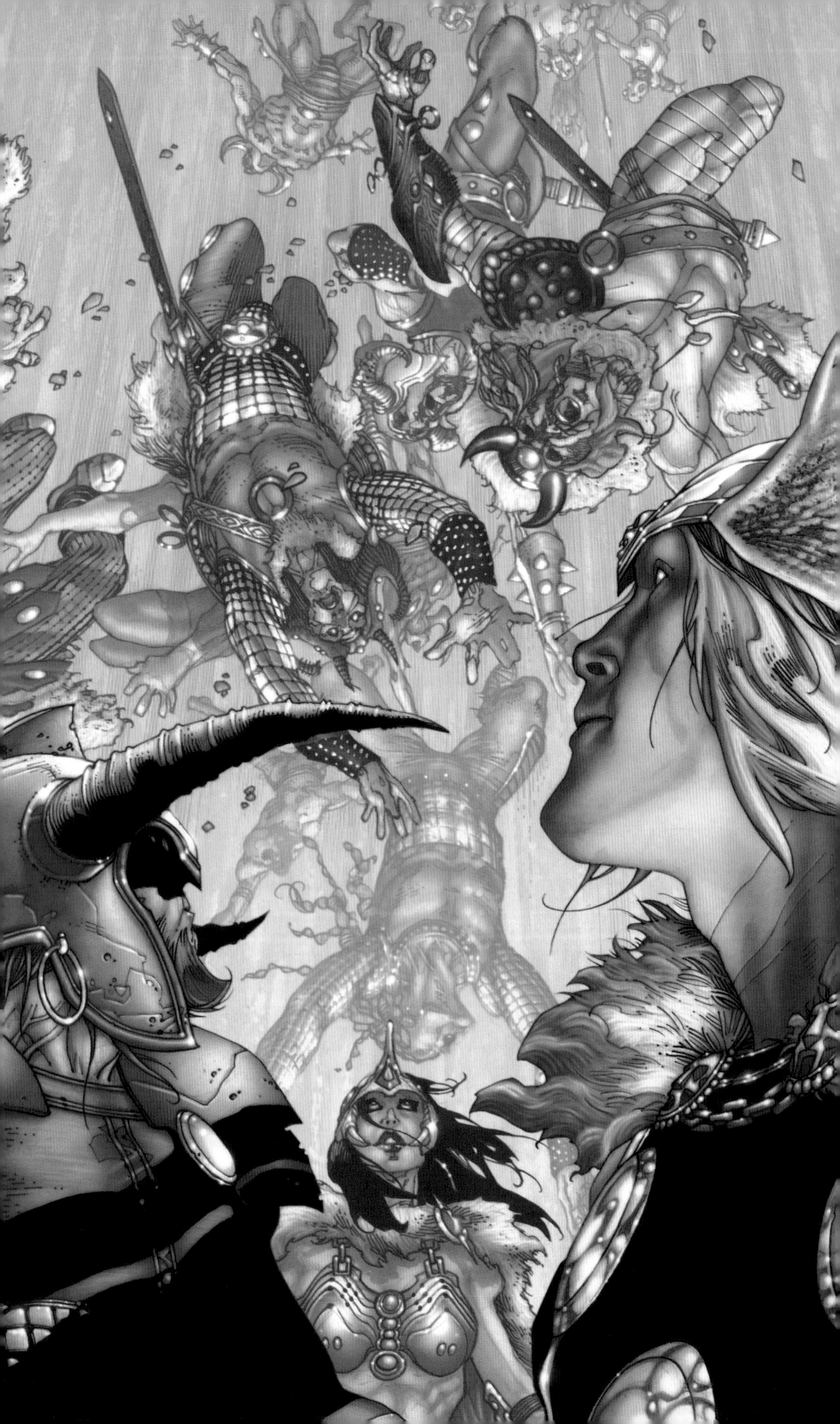

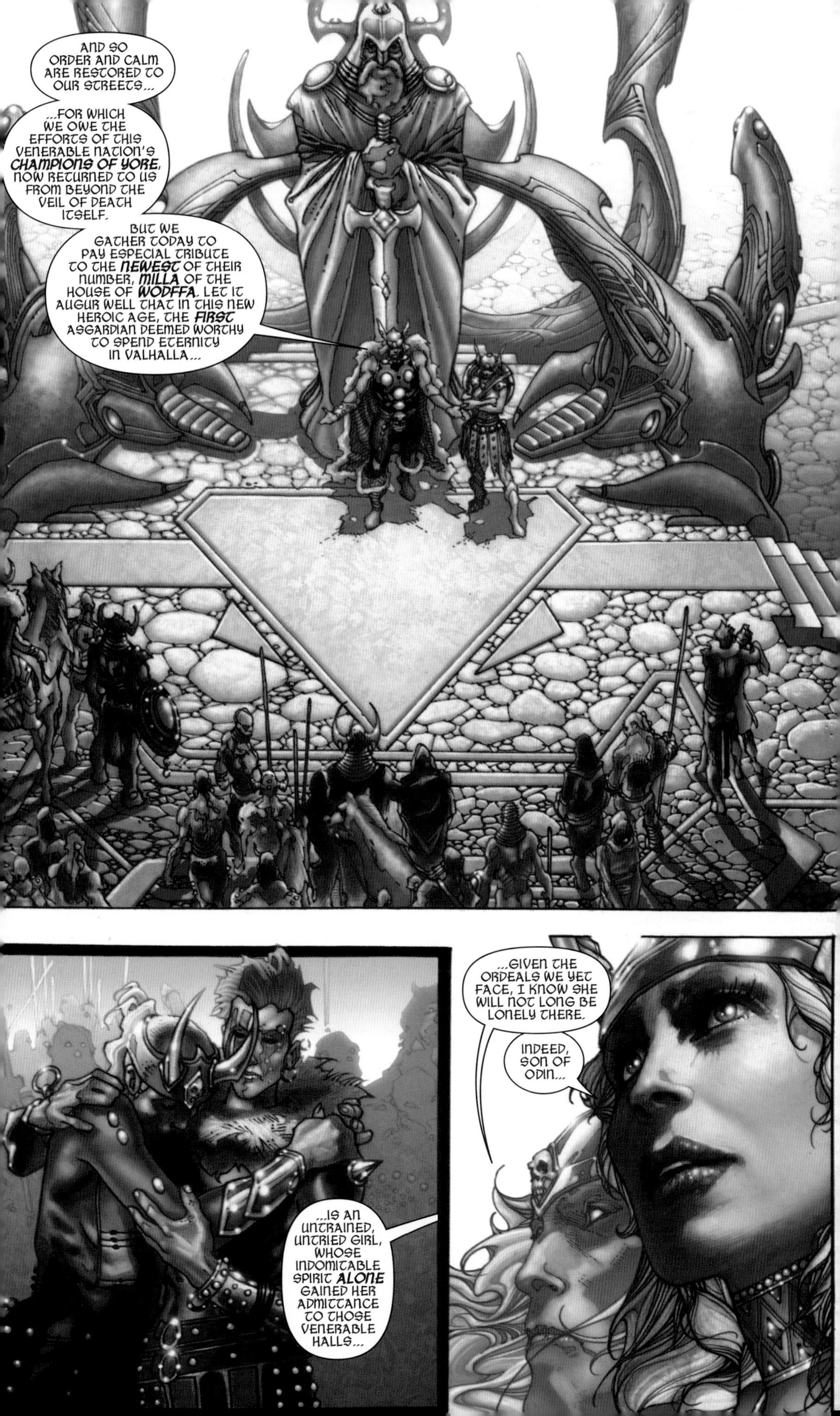
AND SO ORDER AND CALM ARE RESTORED TO OUR STREETS...
...FOR WHICH WE OWE THE EFFORTS OF THIS VENERABLE NATION'S **CHAMPIONS OF YORE**, NOW RETURNED TO US FROM BEYOND THE VEIL OF DEATH ITSELF.
BUT WE GATHER TODAY TO PAY ESPECIAL TRIBUTE TO THE **NEWEST** OF THEIR NUMBER, **MILLA** OF THE HOUSE OF **WODFFA**. LET IT AUGUR WELL THAT IN THIS NEW HEROIC AGE, THE **FIRST** ASGARDIAN DEEMED WORTHY TO SPEND ETERNITY IN VALHALLA...
...IS AN UNTRAINED, UNTRIED GIRL, WHOSE INDOMITABLE SPIRIT **ALONE** GAINED HER ADMITTANCE TO THOSE VENERABLE HALLS...
...GIVEN THE ORDEALS WE YET FACE, I KNOW SHE WILL NOT LONG BE LONELY THERE.
INDEED, SON OF ODIN...

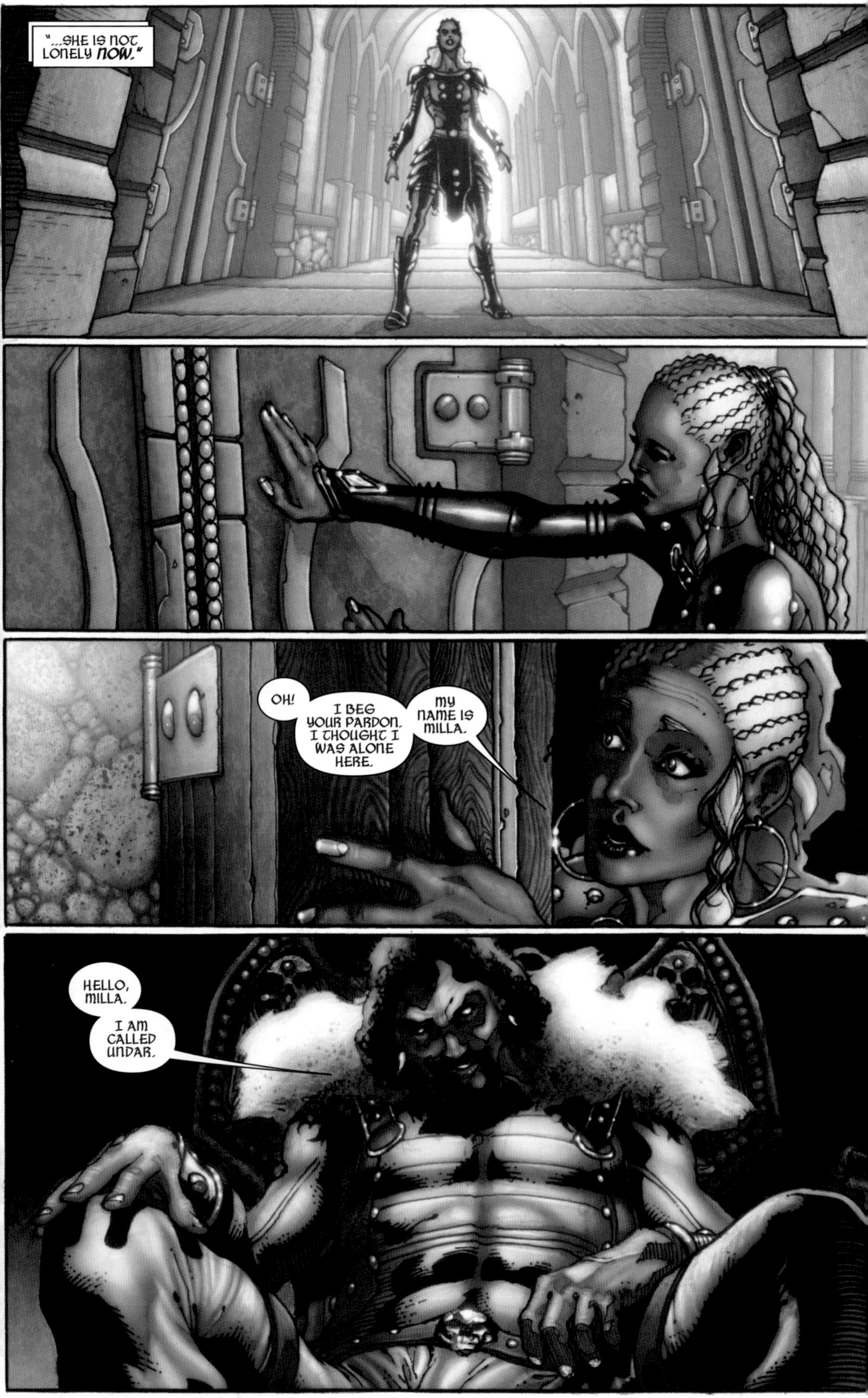
"...SHE IS NOT LONELY NOW."
OH!
I BEG YOUR PARDON. I THOUGHT I WAS ALONE HERE.
MY NAME IS MILLA.
HELLO, MILLA.
I AM CALLED UNDAR.

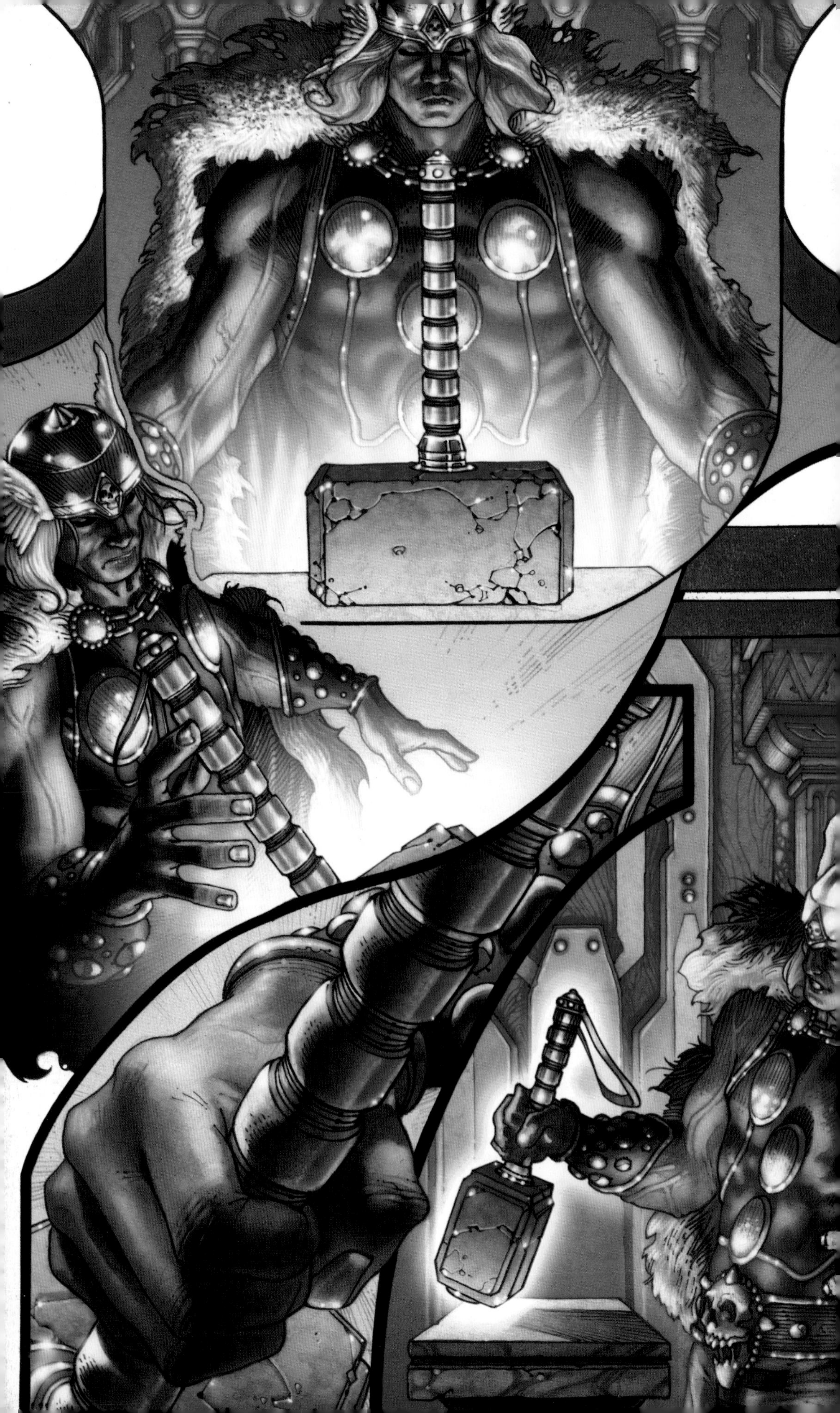

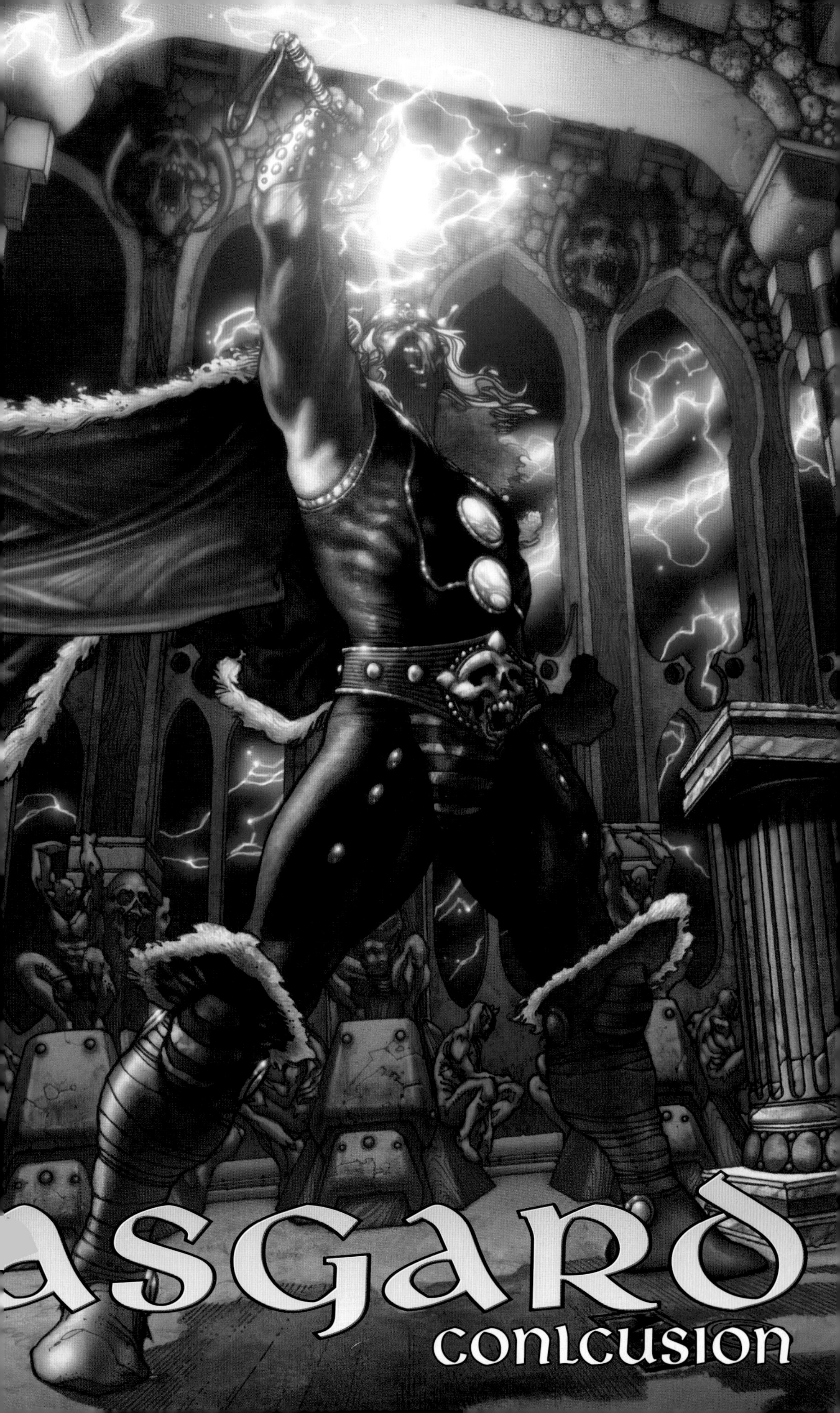
ASGARD
CONLCUSION

MAKE MINE
MARVEL®

THE VERY BEST FROM THE HOUSE OF IDEAS

MARVEL

SIEGE

BENDIS · COIPEL · LARK

ISBN: 978-1-84653-452-2 £12.99

MARVEL

FALL OF THE HULKS

LOEB · PAK · PARKER · ROMITA JR · McGUINNESS · PELLETIER

ISBN: 978-1-84653-462-1 £14.99

MARVEL

IRON MAN WHIPLASH

GUGGENHEIM · BRIONES · DJURDJEVIC

ISBN: 978-1-84653-450-8 £8.99

CAPTAIN AMERICA REBORN

BRUBAKER · HITCH

ISBN: 978-1-84653-440-9 £14.99

GREG PAK · CARLO PAGULAYAN · AARON LOPRESTI

MARVEL

PLANET HULK

ISBN: 978-1-905239-66-5 £14.99

MARVEL

SHADOWLAND

DIGGLE · TAN · CRESSIDY

ISBN: 978-1-84653-473-7 £12.99

MARVEL

SECRET INVASION

BENDIS · FRANCIS YU · DELL OTTO

ISBN: 978-1-84653-405-8 £14.99

MARVEL GRAPHIC NOVEL

WORLD WAR HULK

PAK · ROMITA JR

ISBN: 978-1-905239-77-1 £14.99

MARK MILLAR · STEVE McNIVEN

MARVEL

CIVIL WAR

ISBN: 978-1-905239-60-3 £10.99

BRIAN MICHAEL BENDIS · GABRIELLE DELL OTTO

MARVEL

SECRET WAR

ISBN: 978-1-905239-16-0 £14.99

NEIL GAIMAN · JOHN ROMITA JR

MARVEL

ETERNALS

ISBN: 978-1-905239-57-3 £14.99

ALAN MOORE · ALAN DAVIS · JAMIE DELANO

MARVEL

CAPTAIN BRITAIN

ISBN: 978-1-84653-459-1 £15.99

AVENGERS

THE NEXT GENERATION

MILLAR · PACHECO · HILL

ISBN: 978-1-84653-442-3 £12.99

SPIDER-MAN

THE WORLD ACCORDING TO PETER PARKER

BENDIS · LAFUENTE · PONSOR

ISBN: 978-1-84653-443-0 £12.99

AVAILABLE FROM ALL GOOD BOOKSTORES
AND ONLINE RETAILERS!